ED EMBERLEY'S DRAWING BOOK

MAKE A WORLD

LB
1837

THIS BOOK WILL SHOW YOU
HOW TO DRAW ENOUGH THINGS
TO MAKE A WORLD OF YOUR OWN.

I HOPE YOU WILL TRY THIS WAY,
CONTINUE TO DRAW YOUR OWN WAY,
AND KEEP LOOKING FOR NEW WAYS—
I DO.

Happy Drawing!

Ed Emberley

LIBRARY OF CONGRESS CATALOG CARD NO. 70-154962
20 19 18 17 16 15
PUBLISHED SIMULTANEOUSLY IN CANADA BY
LITTLE, BROWN AND COMPANY (CANADA) LTD.
PRINTED IN THE UNITED STATES OF AMERICA.

BP

IF YOU CAN DRAW THESE THINGS⟶
YOU CAN DRAW ALL THE OBJECTS
IN THIS BOOK. FOR, INSTANCE:
YOU USE THESE
TO MAKE THIS FISH
   THE DIAGRAMS ON THE
FOLLOWING PAGES WILL SHOW
      YOU HOW.

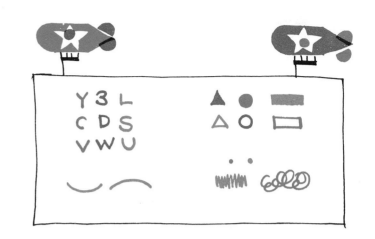

OTHER BOOKS BY ED EMBERLEY:
THE WING ON A FLEA
THE PARADE BOOK
ROSE BUD
PUNCH AND JUDY
LONDON BRIDGE IS FALLING DOWN
GREEN SAYS GO
ED EMBERLEY'S DRAWING BOOK OF ANIMALS

THE ARTWORK FOR THIS
BOOK WAS DRAWN ON
STRATHMORE PAPER
WITH FELT TIP AND
RAPIDOGRAPH PENS,
FOUR-COLOR, PRESEPARATED
AND HAND-LETTERED
BY THE AUTHOR.

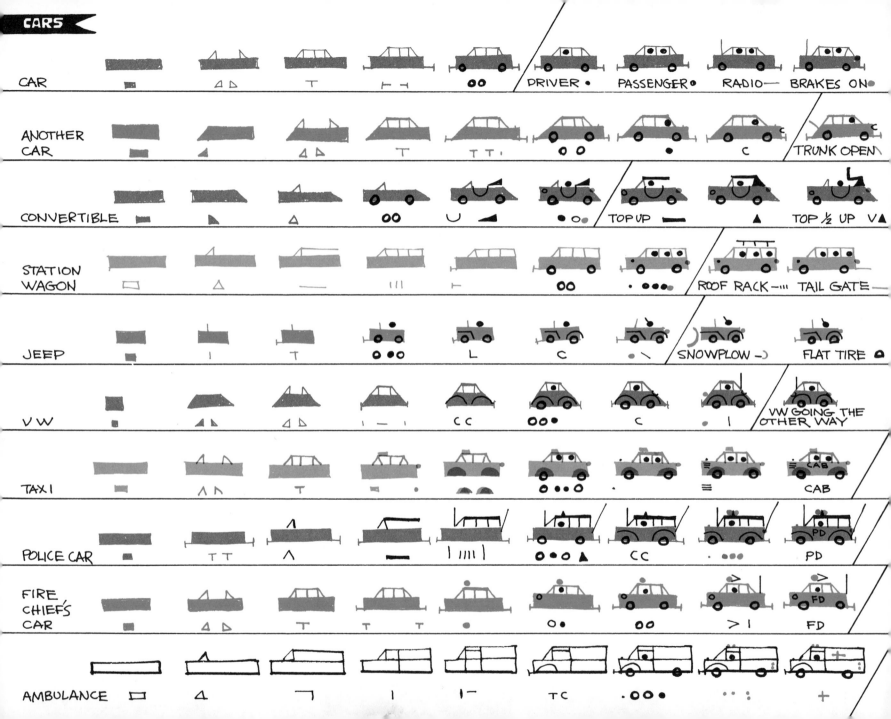

CARS

CAR						DRIVER •	PASSENGER •	RADIO —	BRAKES ON •
		△ △	T	⊢ ⊣	oo				

ANOTHER CAR									TRUNK OPEN
		◿	△ ▷	T	T T '	oo	•	C	

CONVERTIBLE						TOP UP ▬	▲	TOP ½ UP V ▲
	◹	△	oo	U ◢	• o•			

STATION WAGON						ROOF RACK —'''	TAIL GATE —
	▱	△	—	'''	⊢	oo	• •••

JEEP						SNOWPLOW ◡	FLAT TIRE ◖
			T	oo o	L	C	• ╲

V W								VW GOING THE OTHER WAY
	◿ ◢	△ ▷	ı — ı	C C	ooo•	C	• ı

TAXI								CAB
	∧ ⋀	T		◠ ◠	o o o o	•	≡	CAB

POLICE CAR								PD
	T T	∧	▬	ı ıııı ı	o•o ▲	C C	• •••	PD

FIRE CHIEF'S CAR								FD
	△ ▷	T	T T	•	o•	oo	> ı	FD

AMBULANCE ▱	△	⌐	ı	⊢	T C	• oo •	•• :	+

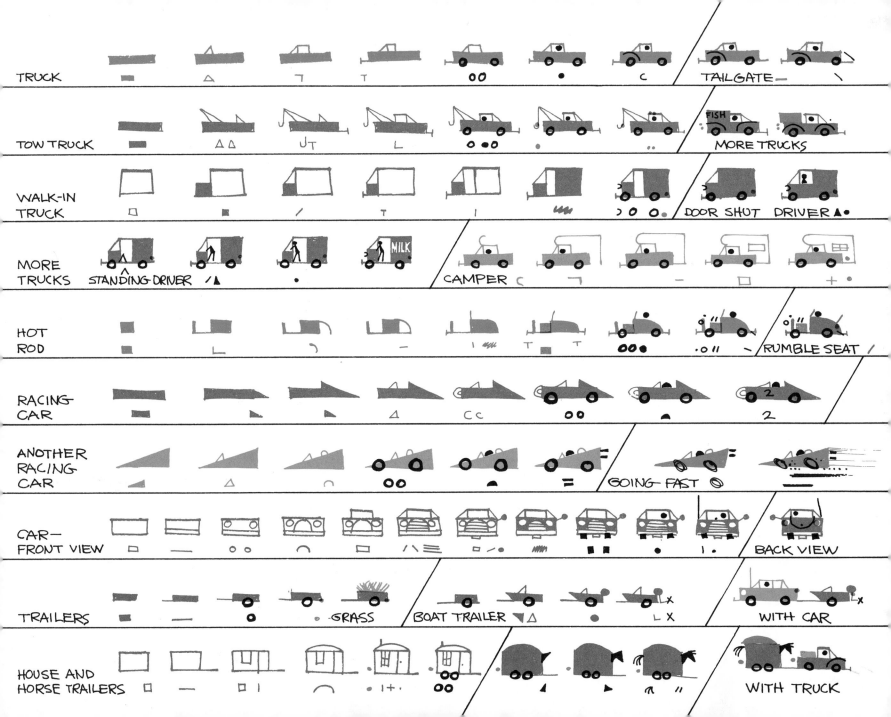

TRUCK

TAILGATE

TOW TRUCK

MORE TRUCKS

WALK-IN TRUCK

DOOR SHUT   DRIVER

MORE TRUCKS   STANDING DRIVER

CAMPER

HOT ROD

RUMBLE SEAT

RACING CAR

ANOTHER RACING CAR

GOING FAST

CAR—FRONT VIEW

BACK VIEW

TRAILERS   GRASS   BOAT TRAILER

WITH CAR

HOUSE AND HORSE TRAILERS

WITH TRUCK

MILK

FISH

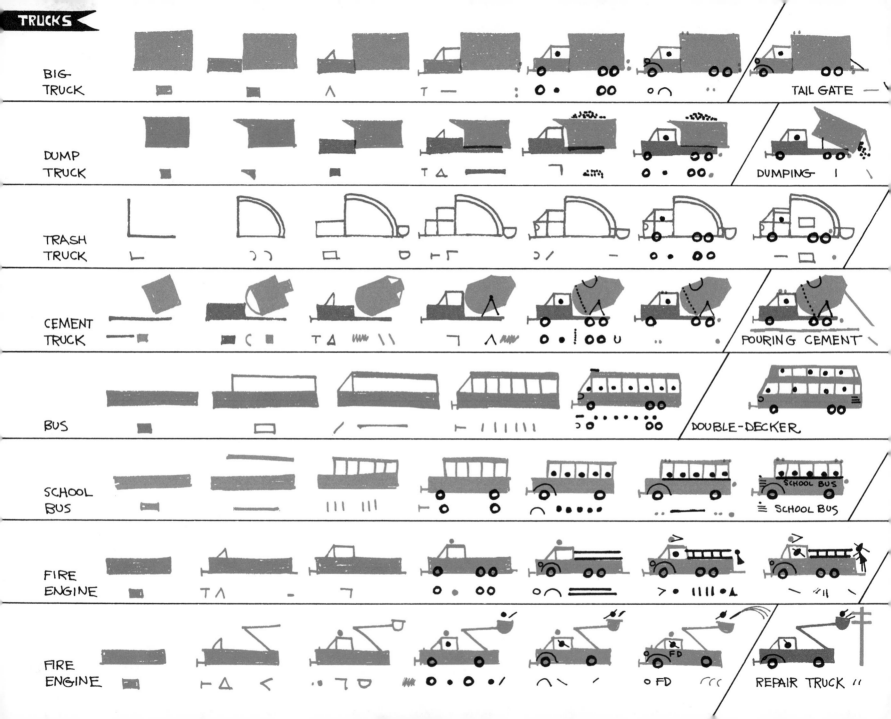

TRUCKS

BIG TRUCK — TAIL GATE

DUMP TRUCK — DUMPING

TRASH TRUCK

CEMENT TRUCK — POURING CEMENT

BUS — DOUBLE-DECKER

SCHOOL BUS — SCHOOL BUS

FIRE ENGINE

FIRE ENGINE — REPAIR TRUCK

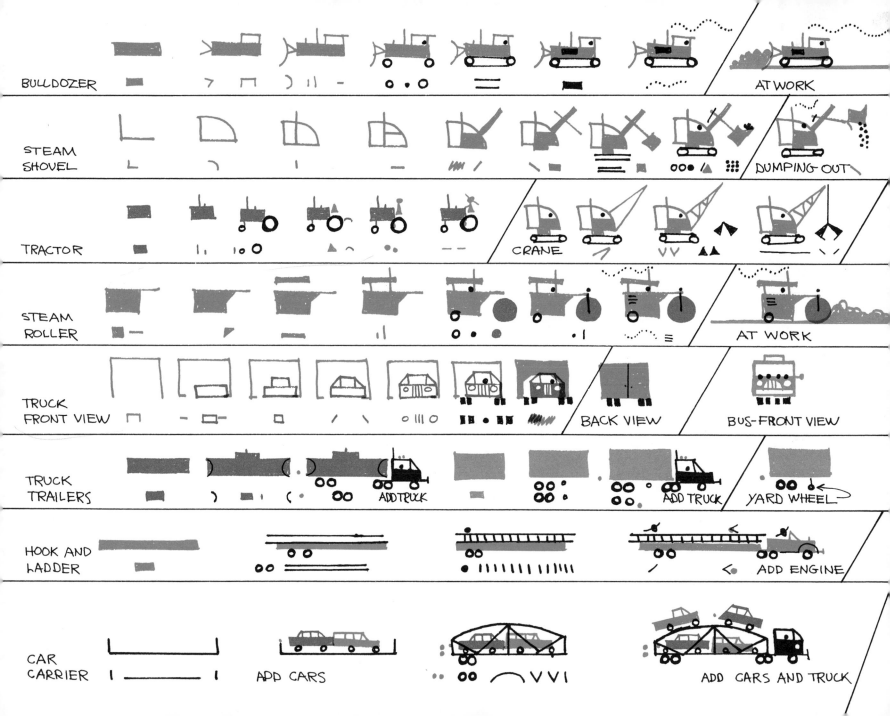

BULLDOZER — AT WORK

STEAM SHOVEL — DUMPING OUT

TRACTOR — CRANE

STEAM ROLLER — AT WORK

TRUCK FRONT VIEW — BACK VIEW — BUS-FRONT VIEW

TRUCK TRAILERS — ADD TRUCK — ADD TRUCK — YARD WHEEL

HOOK AND LADDER — ADD ENGINE

CAR CARRIER — ADD CARS — ADD CARS AND TRUCK

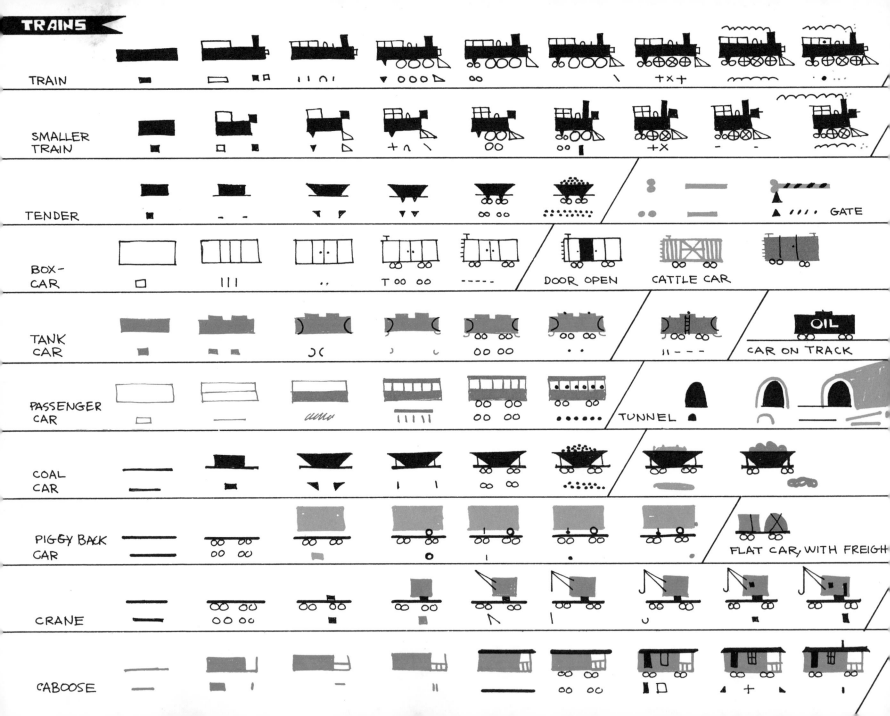

TRAINS

TRAIN

SMALLER TRAIN

TENDER — GATE

BOX-CAR — DOOR OPEN — CATTLE CAR

TANK CAR — CAR ON TRACK — OIL

PASSENGER CAR — TUNNEL

COAL CAR

PIGGY BACK CAR — FLAT CAR, WITH FREIGHT

CRANE

CABOOSE

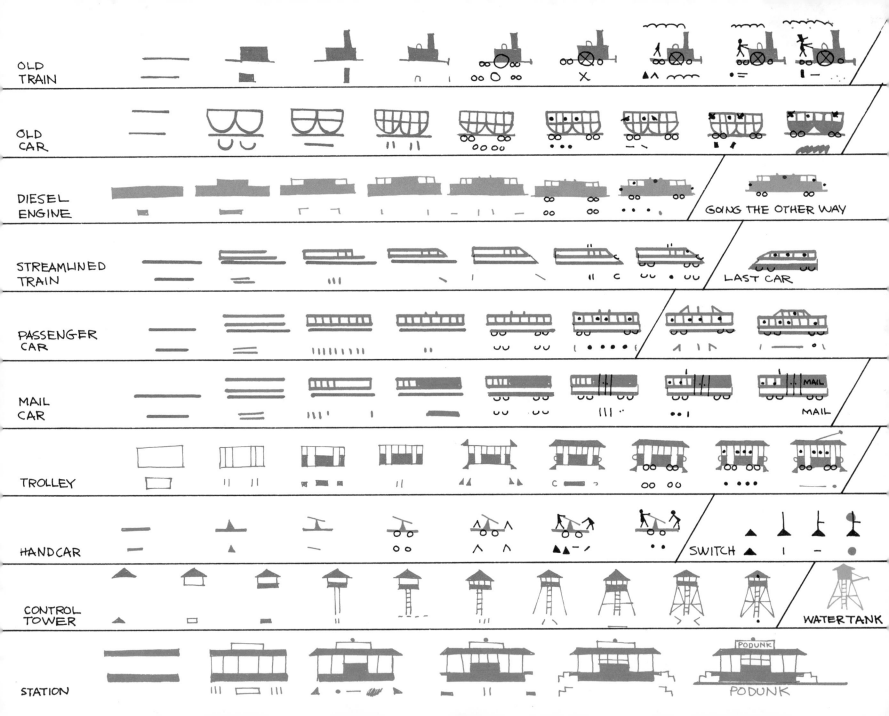

OLD TRAIN

OLD CAR

DIESEL ENGINE

GOING THE OTHER WAY

STREAMLINED TRAIN

LAST CAR

PASSENGER CAR

MAIL CAR

MAIL

TROLLEY

HANDCAR

SWITCH

CONTROL TOWER

WATERTANK

STATION

PODUNK

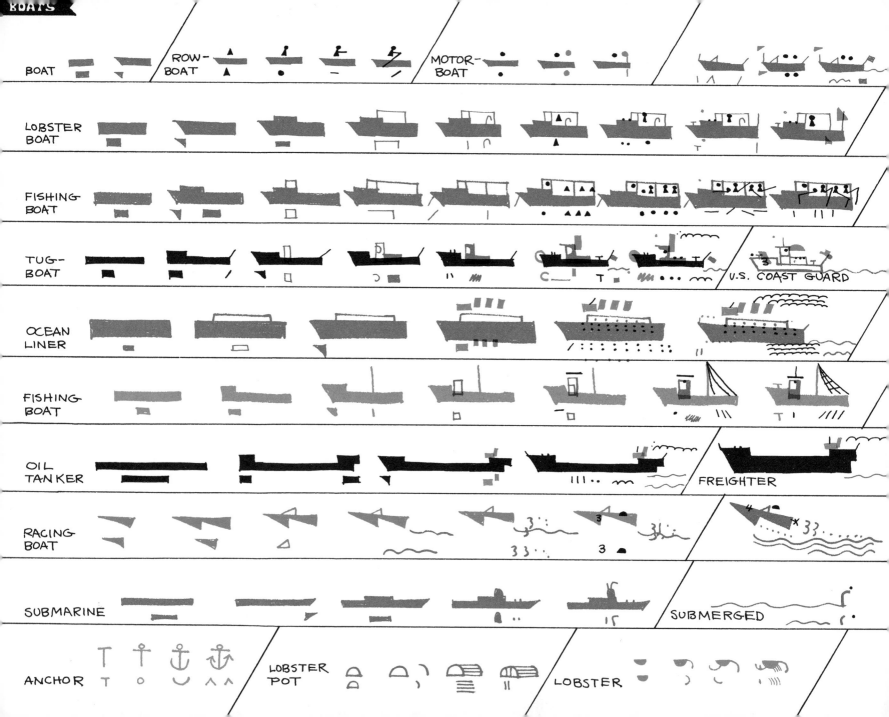

BOATS

BOAT   ROW-BOAT   MOTOR-BOAT

LOBSTER BOAT

FISHING BOAT

TUG-BOAT   U.S. COAST GUARD

OCEAN LINER

FISHING BOAT

OIL TANKER   FREIGHTER

RACING BOAT

SUBMARINE   SUBMERGED

ANCHOR   LOBSTER POT   LOBSTER

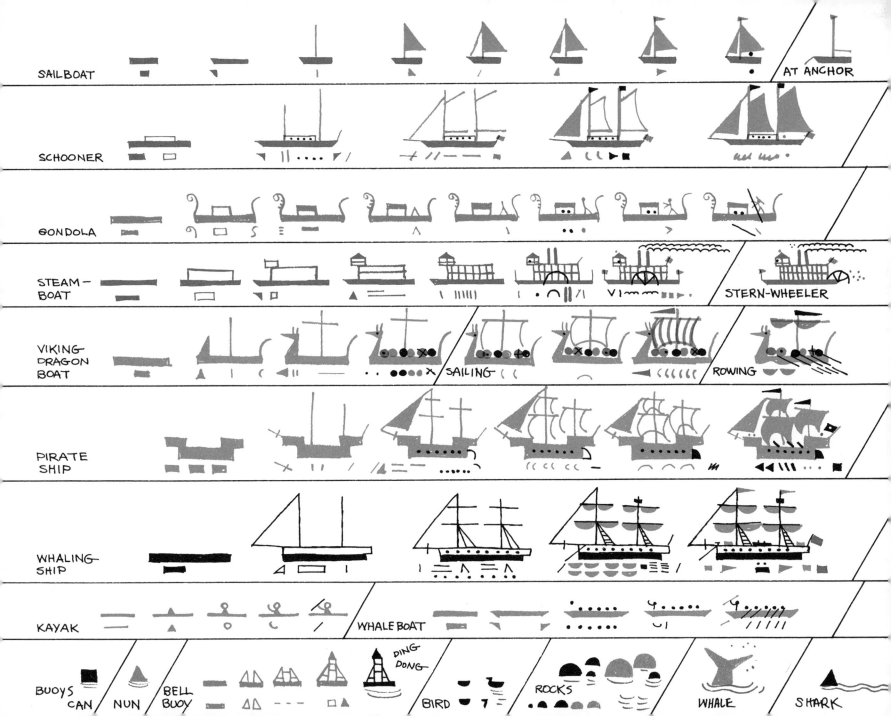

SAILBOAT

AT ANCHOR

SCHOONER

GONDOLA

STEAM-BOAT

STERN-WHEELER

VIKING DRAGON BOAT

SAILING

ROWING

PIRATE SHIP

WHALING SHIP

KAYAK

WHALE BOAT

BUOYS

CAN

NUN

BELL BUOY

DING DONG

BIRD

ROCKS

WHALE

SHARK

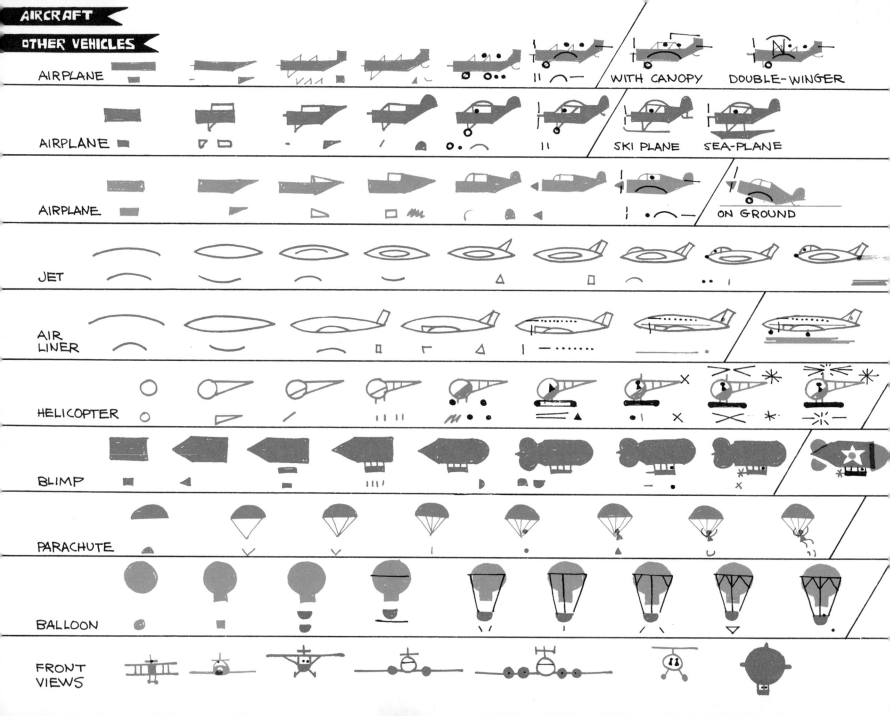

AIRCRAFT

OTHER VEHICLES

AIRPLANE — WITH CANOPY — DOUBLE-WINGER

AIRPLANE — SKI PLANE — SEA-PLANE

AIRPLANE — ON GROUND

JET

AIR LINER

HELICOPTER

BLIMP

PARACHUTE

BALLOON

FRONT VIEWS

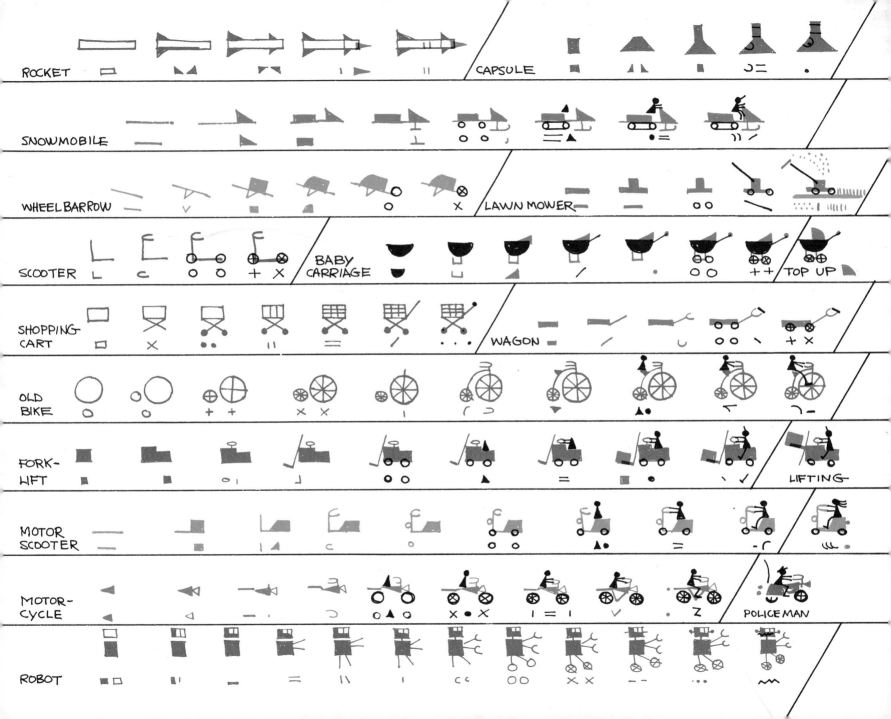

ROCKET   CAPSULE

SNOWMOBILE

WHEELBARROW   LAWN MOWER

SCOOTER   BABY CARRIAGE   TOP UP

SHOPPING CART   WAGON

OLD BIKE

FORK-LIFT   LIFTING

MOTOR SCOOTER

MOTOR-CYCLE   POLICEMAN

ROBOT

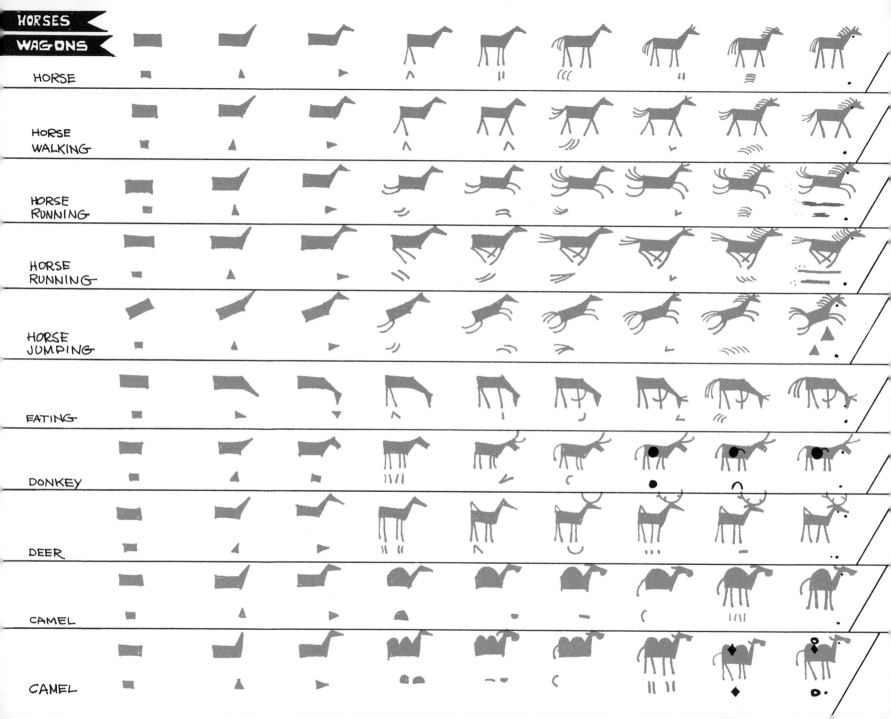

HORSES
WAGONS

HORSE

HORSE WALKING

HORSE RUNNING

HORSE RUNNING

HORSE JUMPING

EATING

DONKEY

DEER

CAMEL

CAMEL

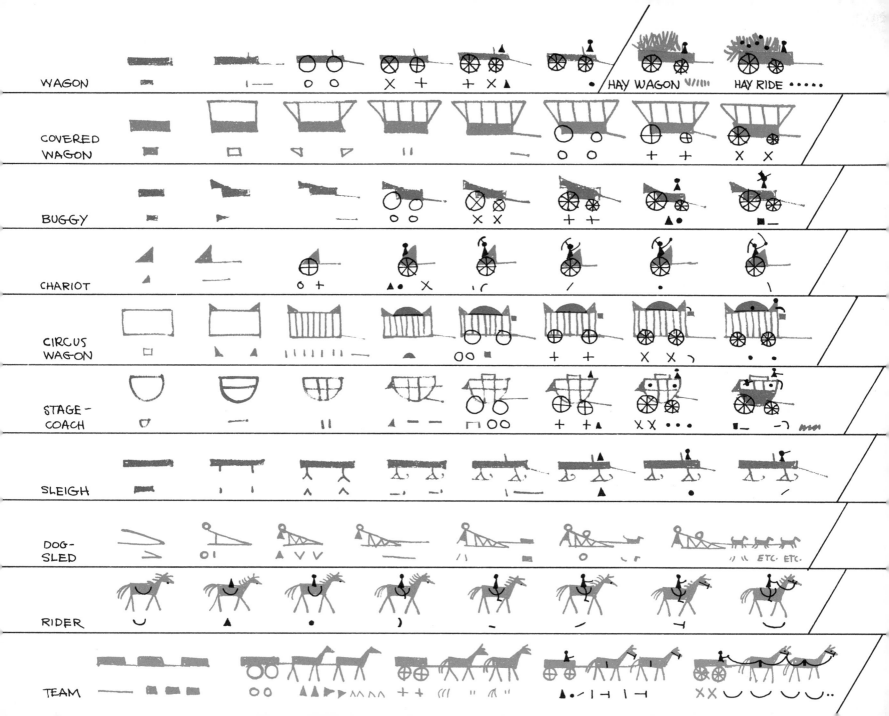

WAGON   HAY WAGON   HAY RIDE

COVERED WAGON

BUGGY

CHARIOT

CIRCUS WAGON

STAGE-COACH

SLEIGH

DOG-SLED   ETC. ETC.

RIDER

TEAM

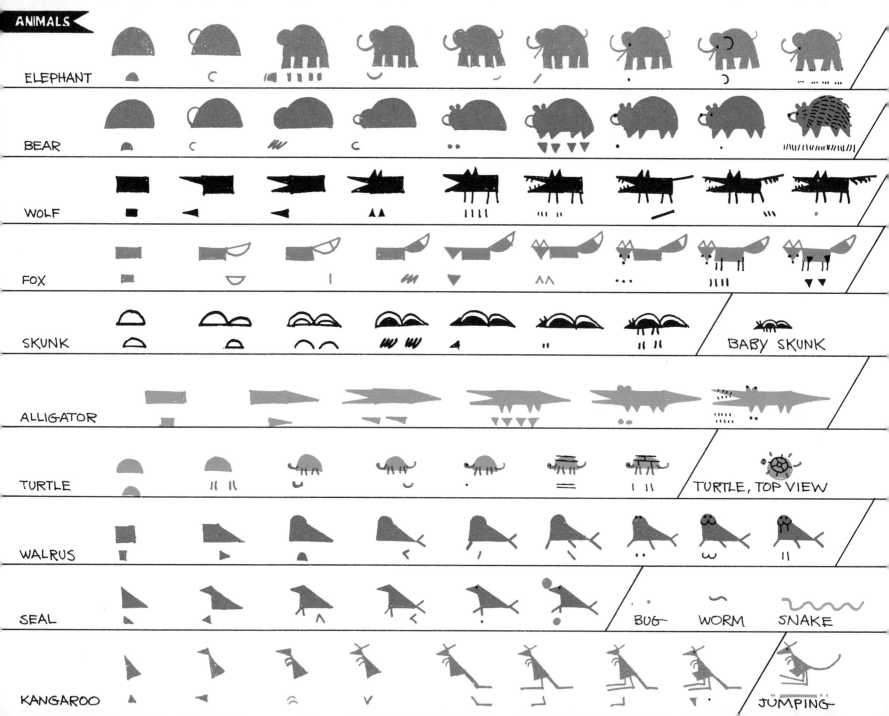

ANIMALS

ELEPHANT

BEAR

WOLF

FOX

SKUNK — BABY SKUNK

ALLIGATOR

TURTLE — TURTLE, TOP VIEW

WALRUS

SEAL — BUG   WORM   SNAKE

KANGAROO — JUMPING

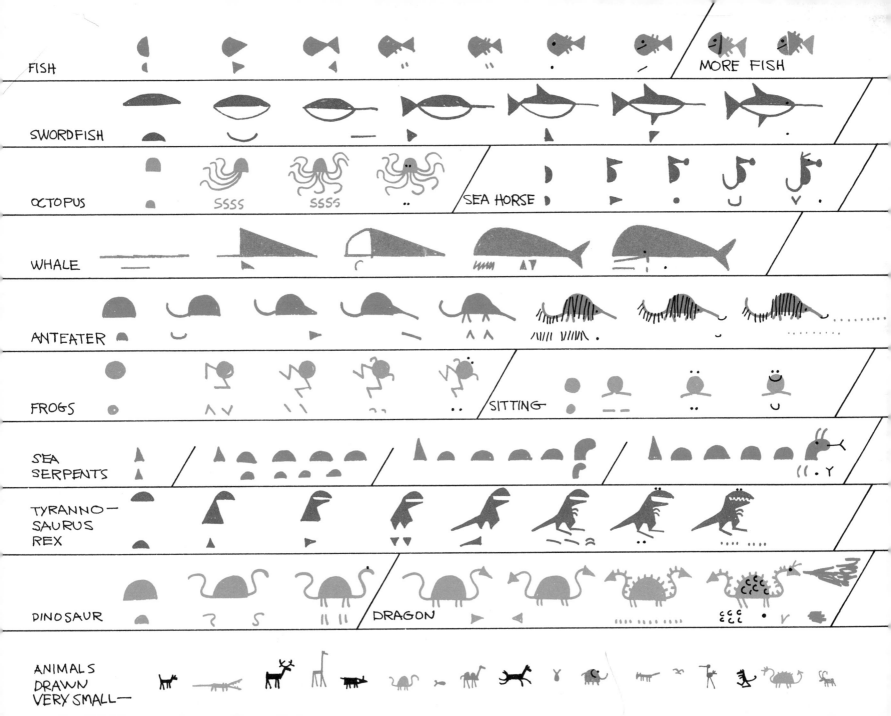

FISH

MORE FISH

SWORDFISH

OCTOPUS

SSSS

SSSS

SEA HORSE

WHALE

ANTEATER

FROGS

SITTING

SEA
SERPENTS

TYRANNO-
SAURUS
REX

DINOSAUR

DRAGON

ANIMALS
DRAWN
VERY SMALL—

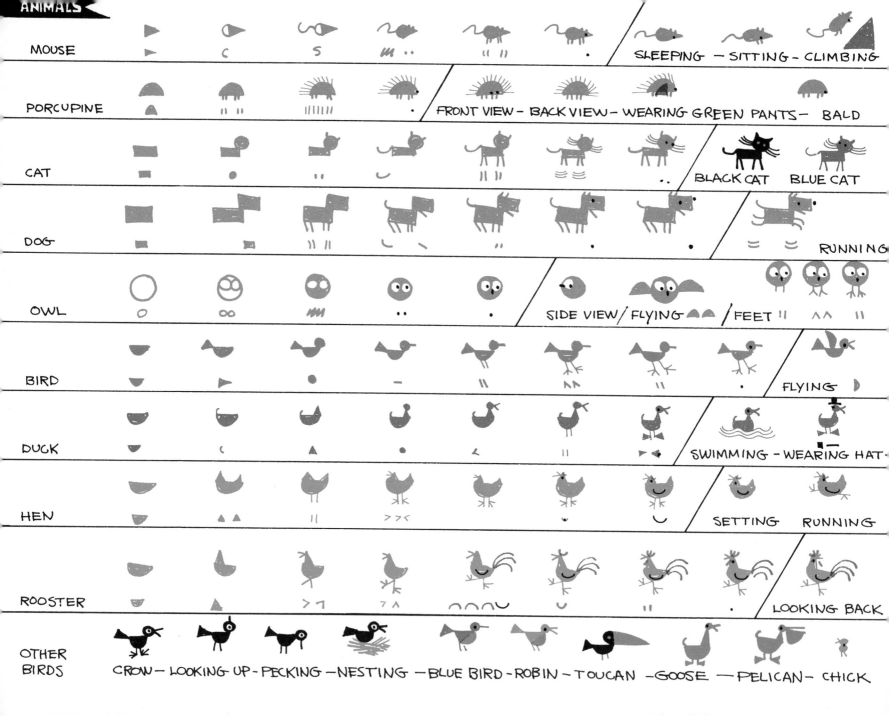

ANIMALS

MOUSE   SLEEPING — SITTING — CLIMBING

PORCUPINE   FRONT VIEW — BACK VIEW — WEARING GREEN PANTS — BALD

CAT   BLACK CAT   BLUE CAT

DOG   RUNNING

OWL   SIDE VIEW / FLYING / FEET

BIRD   FLYING

DUCK   SWIMMING — WEARING HAT

HEN   SETTING   RUNNING

ROOSTER   LOOKING BACK

OTHER BIRDS   CROW — LOOKING UP — PECKING — NESTING — BLUE BIRD — ROBIN — TOUCAN — GOOSE — PELICAN — CHICK

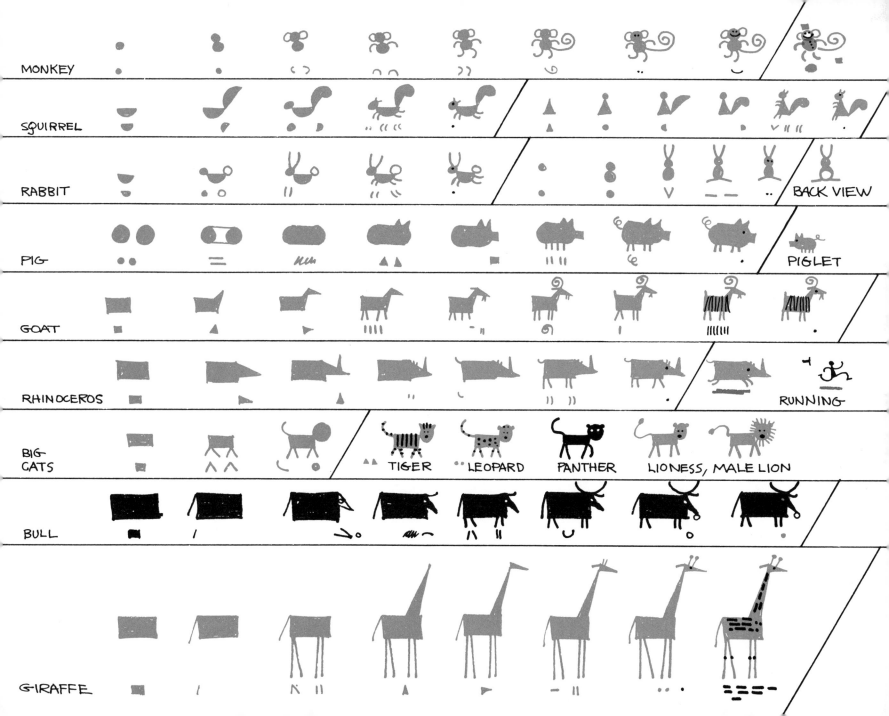

MONKEY

SQUIRREL

RABBIT   BACK VIEW

PIG   PIGLET

GOAT

RHINOCEROS   RUNNING

BIG CATS   TIGER   LEOPARD   PANTHER   LIONESS, MALE LION

BULL

GIRAFFE

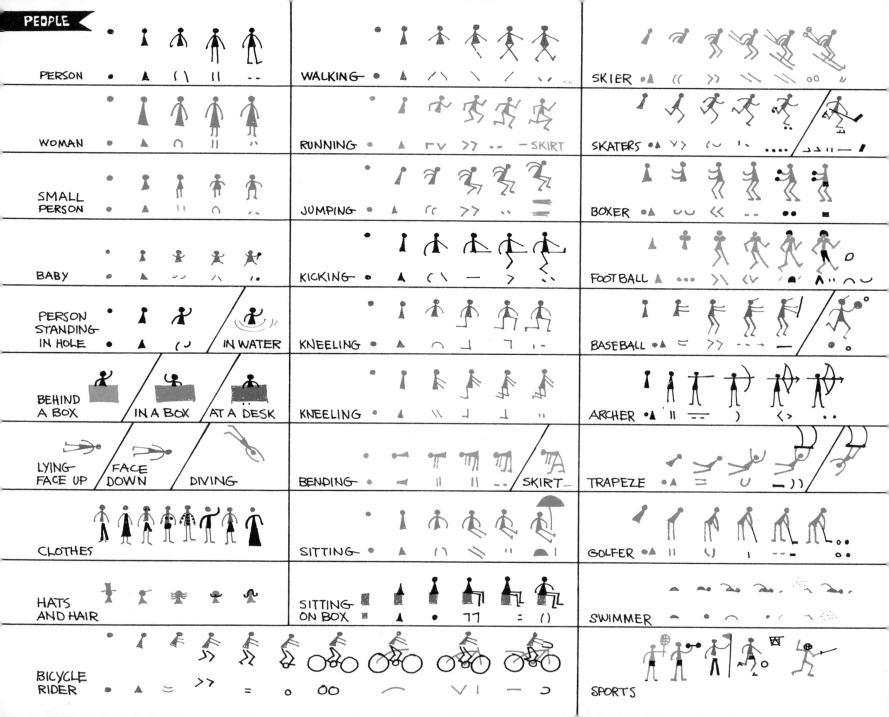

PEOPLE

PERSON

WOMAN

SMALL PERSON

BABY

PERSON STANDING IN HOLE · · · IN WATER

BEHIND A BOX · IN A BOX · AT A DESK

LYING FACE UP · FACE DOWN · DIVING

CLOTHES

HATS AND HAIR

BICYCLE RIDER

WALKING

RUNNING · · · · · · — SKIRT

JUMPING

KICKING

KNEELING

KNEELING

BENDING · · · · · · SKIRT

SITTING

SITTING ON BOX

SKIER

SKATERS

BOXER

FOOTBALL

BASEBALL

ARCHER

TRAPEZE

GOLFER

SWIMMER

SPORTS

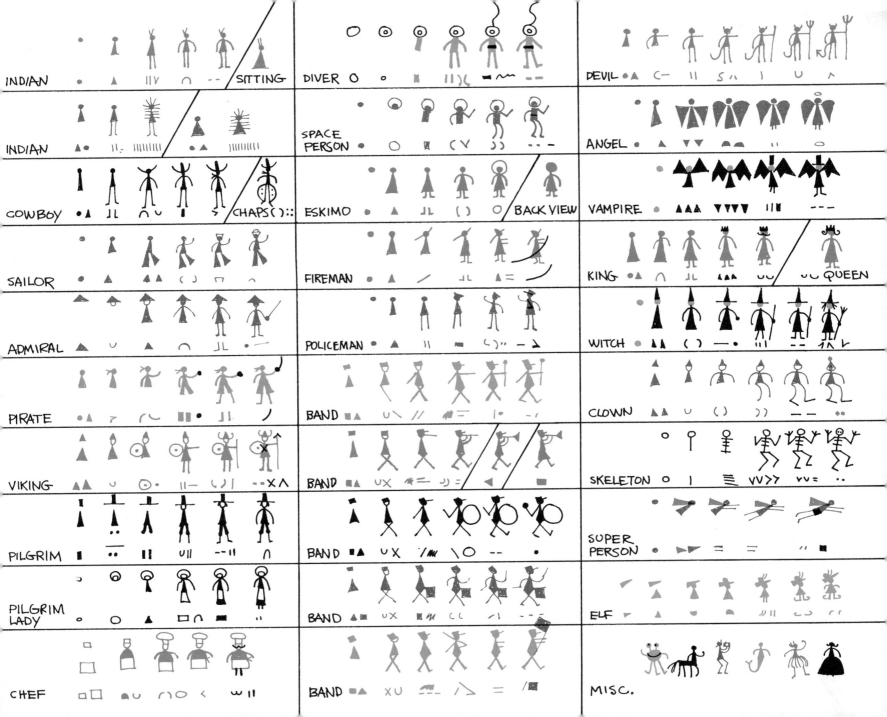

INDIAN | SITTING

INDIAN

COWBOY | CHAPS

SAILOR

ADMIRAL

PIRATE

VIKING

PILGRIM

PILGRIM LADY

CHEF

DIVER

SPACE PERSON

ESKIMO | BACK VIEW

FIREMAN

POLICEMAN

BAND

BAND

BAND

BAND

BAND

DEVIL

ANGEL

VAMPIRE

KING | QUEEN

WITCH

CLOWN

SKELETON

SUPER PERSON

ELF

MISC.

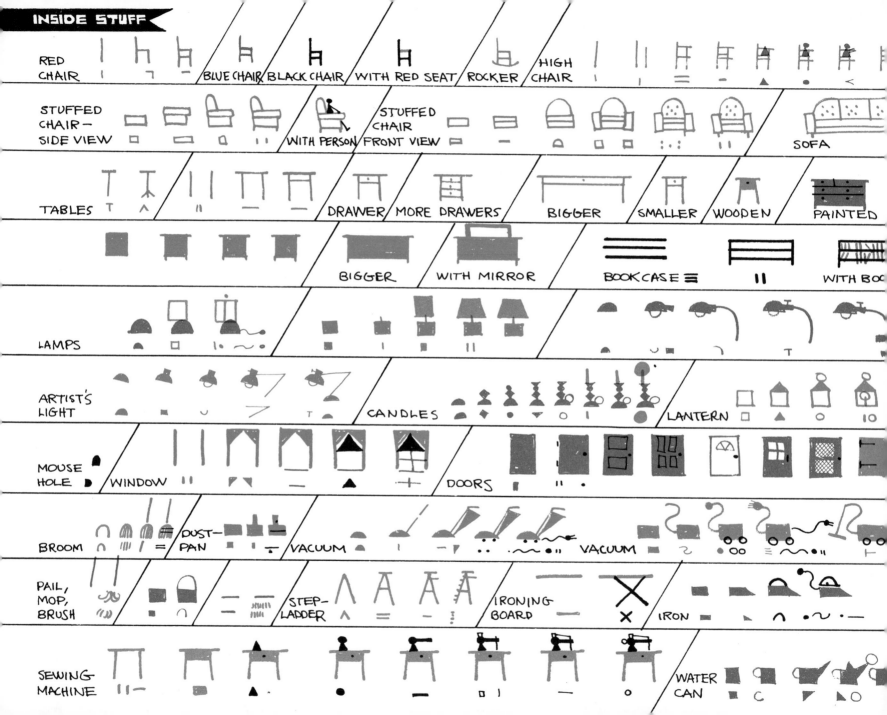

INSIDE STUFF

RED CHAIR · BLUE CHAIR · BLACK CHAIR · WITH RED SEAT · ROCKER · HIGH CHAIR

STUFFED CHAIR — SIDE VIEW · WITH PERSON · STUFFED CHAIR FRONT VIEW · SOFA

TABLES · DRAWER · MORE DRAWERS · BIGGER · SMALLER · WOODEN · PAINTED

BIGGER · WITH MIRROR · BOOKCASE · WITH BOO

LAMPS

ARTIST'S LIGHT · CANDLES · LANTERN

MOUSE HOLE · WINDOW · DOORS

BROOM · DUST-PAN · VACUUM · VACUUM

PAIL, MOP, BRUSH · STEP-LADDER · IRONING BOARD · IRON

SEWING MACHINE · WATER CAN

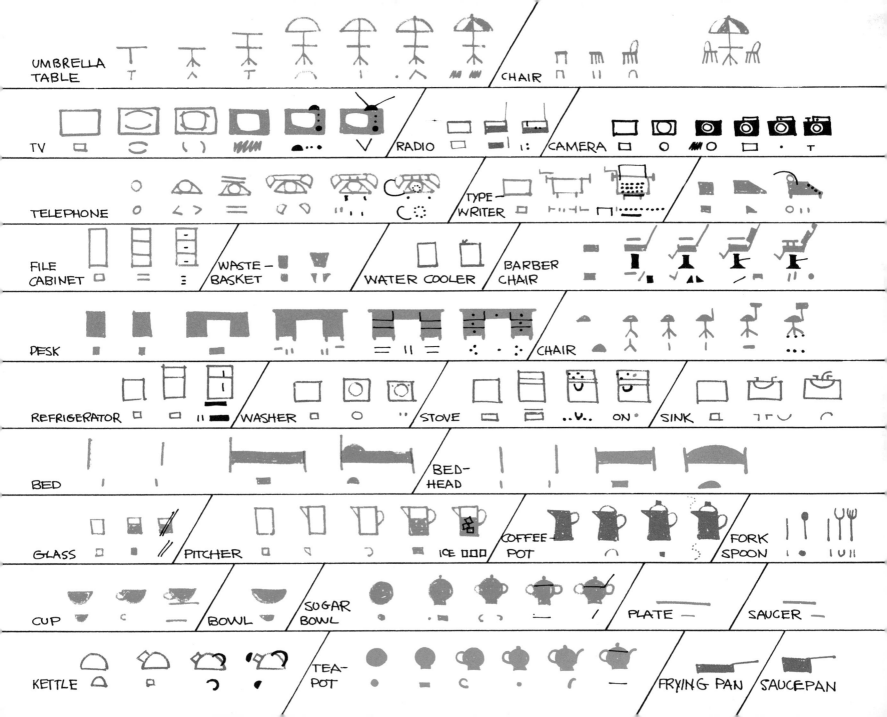

UMBRELLA TABLE

CHAIR

TV

RADIO

CAMERA

TELEPHONE

TYPE WRITER

FILE CABINET

WASTE-BASKET

WATER COOLER

BARBER CHAIR

DESK

CHAIR

REFRIGERATOR

WASHER

STOVE

SINK

BED

BED-HEAD

GLASS

PITCHER

ICE

COFFEE-POT

FORK SPOON

CUP

BOWL

SUGAR BOWL

PLATE

SAUCER

KETTLE

TEA-POT

FRYING PAN

SAUCEPAN

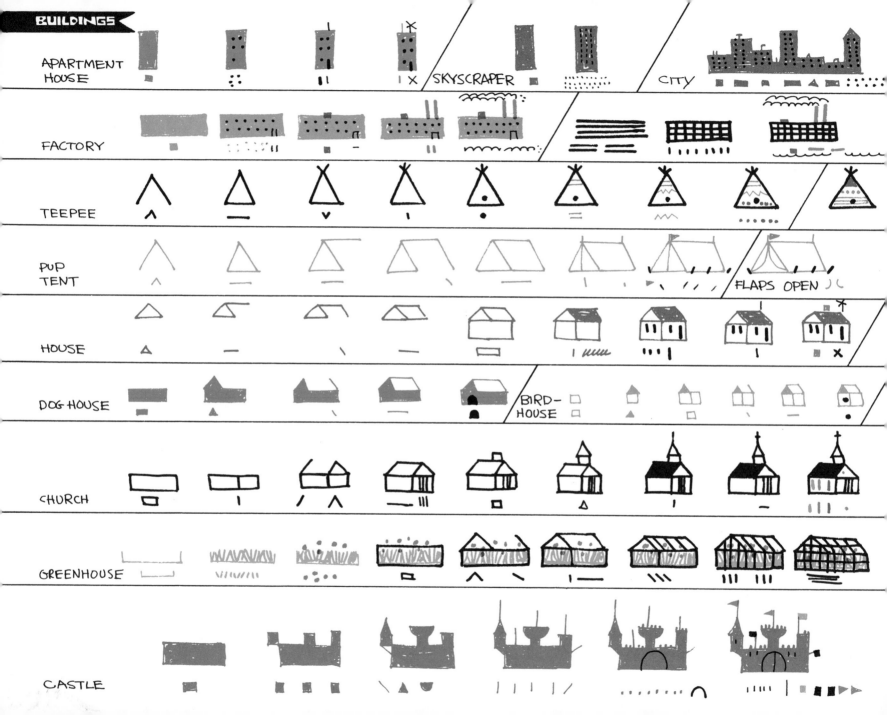

BUILDINGS

APARTMENT HOUSE

SKYSCRAPER

CITY

FACTORY

TEEPEE

PUP TENT

FLAPS OPEN

HOUSE

DOG HOUSE

BIRD-HOUSE

CHURCH

GREENHOUSE

CASTLE

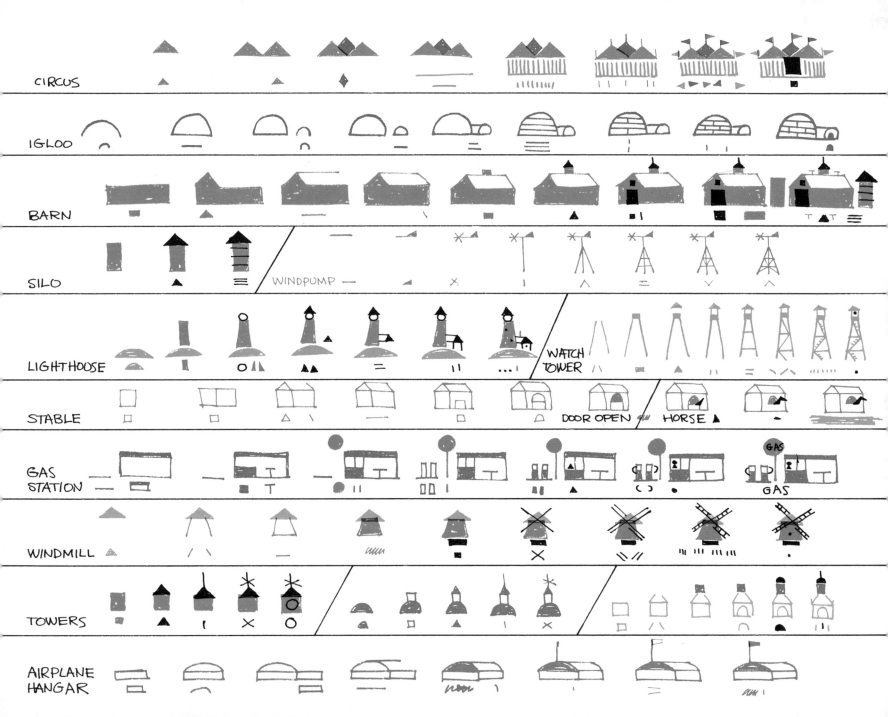

CIRCUS

IGLOO

BARN

SILO　WINDPUMP

LIGHTHOUSE　WATCH TOWER

STABLE　DOOR OPEN　HORSE

GAS STATION　GAS

WINDMILL

TOWERS

AIRPLANE HANGAR

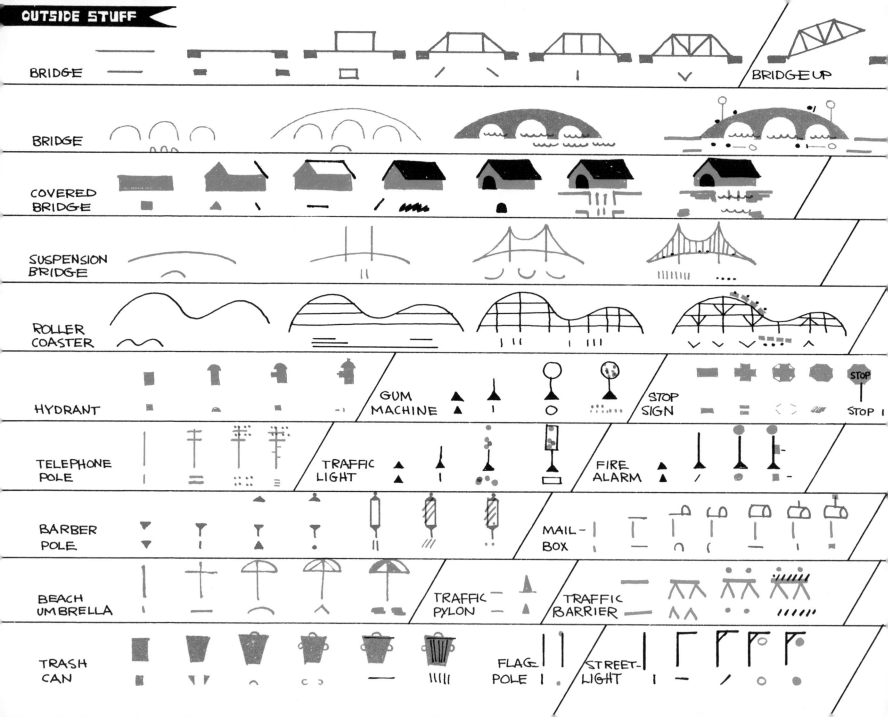

OUTSIDE STUFF

BRIDGE

BRIDGE UP

BRIDGE

COVERED BRIDGE

SUSPENSION BRIDGE

ROLLER COASTER

HYDRANT

GUM MACHINE

STOP SIGN

STOP

TELEPHONE POLE

TRAFFIC LIGHT

FIRE ALARM

BARBER POLE

MAIL-BOX

BEACH UMBRELLA

TRAFFIC PYLON

TRAFFIC BARRIER

TRASH CAN

FLAG POLE

STREET-LIGHT

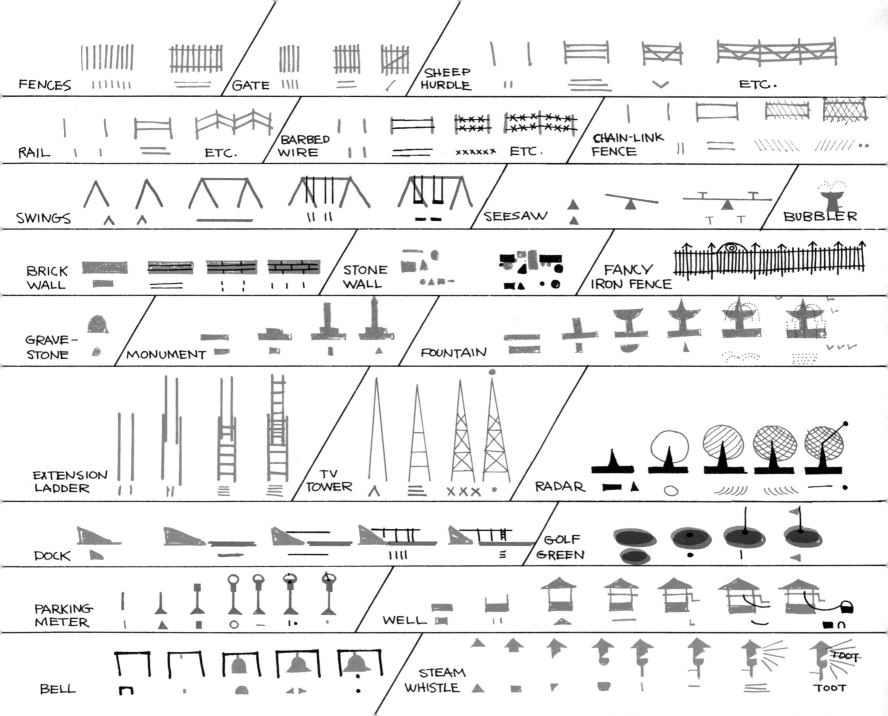

FENCES   IIIIII   GATE IIII   SHEEP HURDLE   ETC.

RAIL   ETC.   BARBED WIRE   xxxxx   ETC.   CHAIN-LINK FENCE

SWINGS   II II   SEESAW   T   T   BUBBLER

BRICK WALL   STONE WALL   FANCY IRON FENCE

GRAVE-STONE   MONUMENT   FOUNTAIN

EXTENSION LADDER   II II   TV TOWER   xxx   RADAR

DOCK   IIII   GOLF GREEN

PARKING METER   WELL

BELL   STEAM WHISTLE   TOOT   TOOT

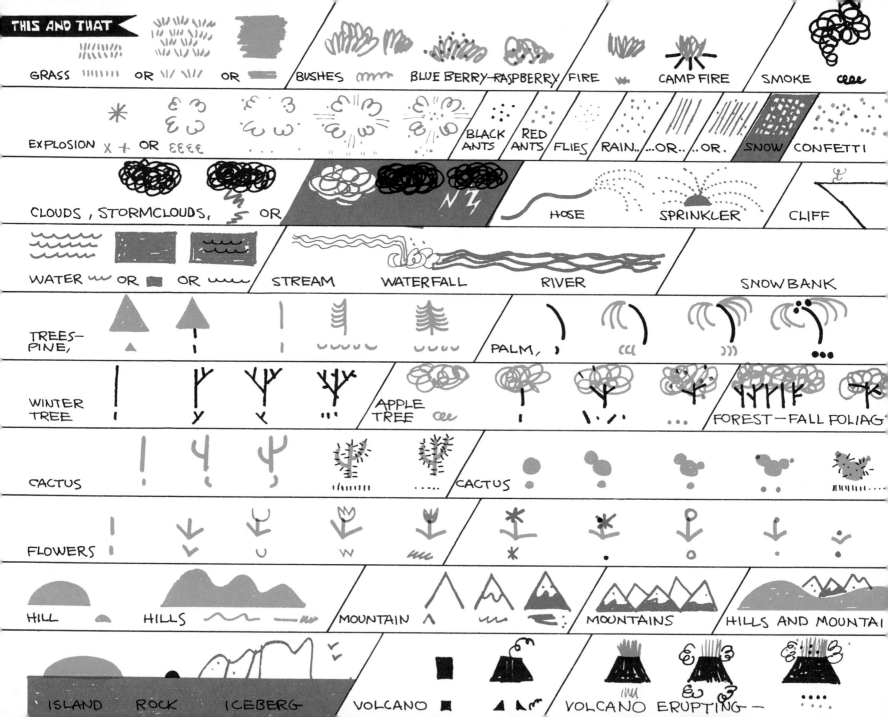

THIS AND THAT

GRASS ||||| OR \|/ \|/ OR ▬ BUSHES ᴍᴍᴍ BLUE BERRY—RASPBERRY FIRE CAMP FIRE SMOKE ᴄᴇᴇ

EXPLOSION X + OR ƐƐƐƐ BLACK ANTS RED ANTS FLIES RAIN... ...OR... ...OR. SNOW CONFETTI

CLOUDS, STORMCLOUDS, OR HOSE SPRINKLER CLIFF

WATER ᴡᴡ OR ▪ OR ᴡᴡᴡ STREAM WATERFALL RIVER SNOWBANK

TREES— PINE, PALM,

WINTER TREE APPLE TREE ᴄᴇᴇ FOREST—FALL FOLIAGE

CACTUS CACTUS

FLOWERS

HILL HILLS MOUNTAIN ʌ MOUNTAINS HILLS AND MOUNTAINS

ISLAND ROCK ICEBERG VOLCANO ▪ ▲ ᴀᴍ VOLCANO ERUPTING —

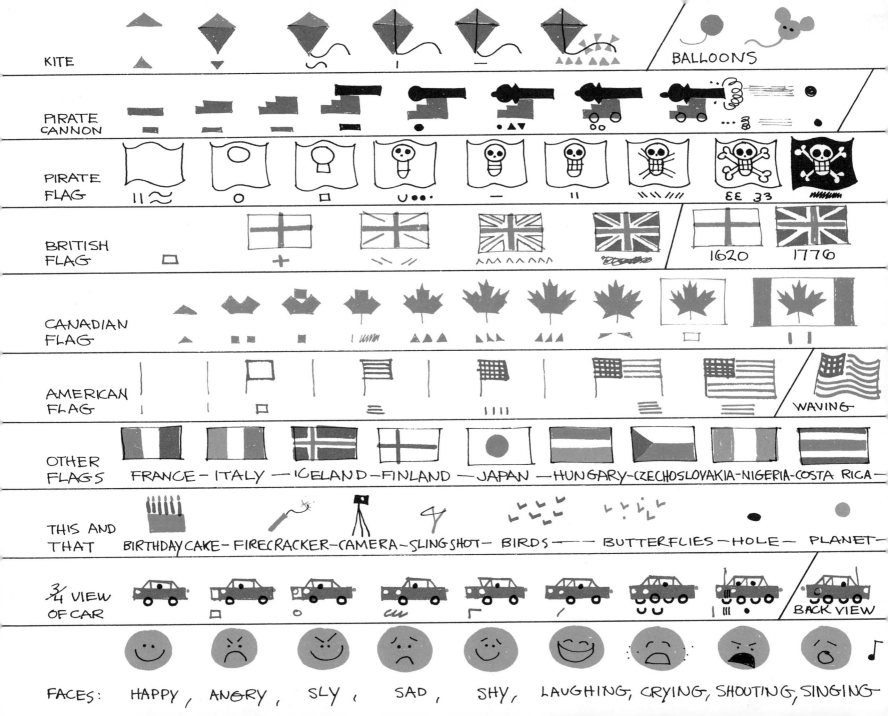

KITE

BALLOONS

PIRATE CANNON

PIRATE FLAG

II ≈   O   □   U •••   —   II   \\\ ///   ЄЄ ₃₃

BRITISH FLAG

□   +   \\   ∧∧∧∧∧   1620   1776

CANADIAN FLAG

AMERICAN FLAG

WAVING

OTHER FLAGS

FRANCE — ITALY — ICELAND — FINLAND — JAPAN — HUNGARY — CZECHOSLOVAKIA — NIGERIA — COSTA RICA —

THIS AND THAT

BIRTHDAY CAKE — FIRECRACKER — CAMERA — SLINGSHOT — BIRDS — — — BUTTERFLIES — HOLE — PLANET —

¾ VIEW OF CAR

BACK VIEW

FACES: HAPPY ,   ANGRY ,   SLY ,   SAD ,   SHY,   LAUGHING, CRYING, SHOUTING, SINGING

✳ HERE ARE SOME OF THE THINGS
YOU CAN DO WITH YOUR PICTURES...

COMIC STRIPS...

POSTERS...   PATTERNS...   BORDERS...

  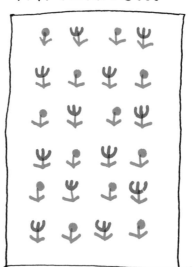 

BOOKS....

GOOD KNIGHT

ONCE UPON A TIME...

THERE WAS A GOOD KNIGHT.

HE FOUGHT THE DRAGON

AND THEY LIVED HAPPILY EVER AFTER.

MOBILES...

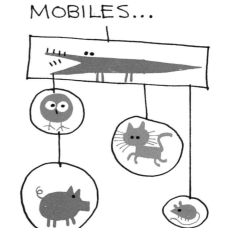

SIGNS...

KEEP OUT

WELCOME

CARDS...

BON VOYAGE

GREETINGS

LETTERS...

DEER ANNE:

HAVING FUN AT CAMP— WISH YOU WERE HERE.

SUE

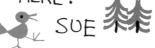

GAMES, ETC...

PIN THE TAIL ON THE DRAGON

THERE ARE MANY WAYS
THE DRAWINGS IN THIS BOOK AND YOUR OWN DRAWINGS
CAN BE PUT TOGETHER, ADDED TO OR CHANGED
TO MAKE SOME WORLDS OF YOUR OWN.
FOR INSTANCE...

IRISH ART

during the Viking Invasions (800-1020 A.D.)

FRANÇOISE HENRY

Cornell University Press
ITHACA, NEW YORK

CORNELL UNIVERSITY PRESS

Library of Congress Catalog Card Number: 67–15300

Text printed in Great Britain by Robert MacLehose & Co Ltd, The University Press, Glasgow
Colour and monochrome plates printed by Les Presses Monastique and L'Imprimerie Darantière, Dijon, France
Monochrome gravure plates printed by L'Imprimerie Braun, Mulhouse, France

Contents

v

ABBREVIATIONS USED IN THE TEXT

Bel. M.	*Ulster Museum, Belfast*
Br. M.	*British Museum, London*
N.M.D.	*National Museum of Ireland, Dublin*
R.I.A.	*Royal Irish Academy*
T.C.D.	*Trinity College, Dublin*
Ashm. M.	*Ashmolean Museum, Oxford*
Bodl. Libr.	*Bodleian Library, Oxford*
Lambeth P.L.	*Lambeth Palace Library*

List of Maps and Drawings

List of Colour Plates

The colour photographs are by P. Belzeaux-Zodiaque

- ● VIKING TOWN
- ○ Other site

Cloncagh

Derry
Raphoe ○   Banagher ○
ULSTER
Ahoghill

Lough
Neagh
Bangor
Lissue
Movi
Nendrum

White Island
Killadeas ○
Inismurray ○   Devenish ○
Lough Erne
Armagh

ANAGASSAN
Monasterboice ○

MEATH

Ardagh   Kells   Slane
Lough Lene
Clonmacnois ○
Lough Ree   Ballinderry ○   Clonard   Boyne   Tara
Durrow ○   Liffey
Clonfert ○   DUBLIN
CONNACHT

Kildare
Lorrha ○
Terryglass ○   LEINSTER
Lough Derg   Glendalough ○
Inis Cealtra ○   Barrow   Castledermot ○
Tuamgreiney ○
Killaloe ○   Aghowle ○
Scattery ○   Shannon
LIMERICK ●
Cashel ○
MUNSTER
Suir
WEXFORD ●
Blackwater   WATERFORD ●
Lismore ○

CORK ●

Skellig ○

0 ———— 50 miles
0 —— 50 —— 100 km

PRINCIPAL SITES

Preface

THOUGH IT embodies here and there some *membra disjecta* of the 1940 edition of *Irish Art in the Early Christian Period*, this book cannot in any way be described, as can its predecessor[1] as a revised edition of the earlier work. Whilst the Viking period and the art of the High Crosses were only examined in general terms at the end of the volume, and metalwork of the Viking time was hardly touched upon, the present book tries to cover the whole field of Irish art during this troubled period. 'Tries' is indeed the right word, as our knowledge of what was destroyed and what was made at that time is very hazy on many points.

It is essential to remember that no strict division can be made between the art of the eighth century and what comes immediately afterwards. Practically all the illumination of the eighth century constitutes the background from which emerge the Book of Kells and the Book of Armagh, and there is no violent antinomy between the eighth century crosses and those of the ninth century. In fact opinions vary as to which of these two centuries saw the carving of the Moone cross. Even so, allowances being made for a relatively extensive transition period, new features appear fairly soon. Figure sculpture, possibly owing to Continental impulses, takes an unexpected prominence, and soon develops into a sort of prefiguration of Romanesque art. At the same time, the upheavals caused by the raids of the Vikings and their eventual settlements in various parts of Ireland, caused an exodus towards the Continent which spread Irish decorative schemes whilst at the same time depleting the Irish scriptoria.

Eighth century Irish art was based on a perpetual paradox, that of the survival of a prehistoric art right into early Medieval times. It sometimes gives the impression that one is watching the improbable progress

[1] F. Henry, *Irish Art in the Early Christian Period to 800 A.D.*, London (Methuen), 1965.

xiii

of a dancer, wondering how long he will be able to pursue his acrobatics on that rope tightened so high up—it seems outside the realm of Time. With the ninth century we come out of that atmosphere of unreality, though some aspects of the Book of Kells still give an exacerbated form of it, and we find ourselves back to the level of the uncertainties, of the panics which had been for centuries the common lot of the average European. The detached outlook of the Irish artist gets a strong jolt and he finds himself emerging from the rarefied atmosphere of abstract speculation and having to stand up squarely to the task of carving the massive and stolidly real figures of the Monasterboice cross. So all this period appears in many ways as a transition between Celtic art still alive in eighth century decoration and Romanesque art which is already fore-shadowed in many a high cross panel and even in some ninth and tenth century illuminations. That it is in fact more than this transition is a point on which we shall have to dwell later.

Our guides in the search for the historical background are nearly the same as for the earlier period. First the Irish Annals: Annals of Inisfallen, Annals of Tigernach, Annals of Ulster, Annals of the Four Masters, Chronicon Scotorum, and English translation of the Annals of Clonmacnois, to which must be added the Chronicle of Marianus Scottus of Mainz. Then we shall have to use often a strange work, the *War of the Gaedhil with the Gaill*, which pretends to be written by Mag Liag, Brian Boru's bard, but is probably slightly later. It is written in a style so high in colour as to be occasionally preposterous, stuffed with bold images and contrasting violently with the dryness of the annalistic texts. It can hardly be described as a reliable document, as it is full of interpolations and biased views. Even so, it remains invaluable, if only for the fact that it puts us in contact with an atmosphere very little removed in time from the events themselves. Its outbursts are those of a man of the late eleventh or twelfth century casting a long look back on two centuries of foreign intrusion. This, in any case, deserves attention, even if the accuracy of some facts has to be checked. Another text of importance is a fragment of annals which takes at times the form of a vivid and very detailed chronicle; it is included[1] in the *Three Fragments of Irish Annals*

---

[1] Third fragment, pp. 114–247. (See list of Bibliographical abbreviations.)

xiv

copied in the seventeenth century by Mac Firbis and published in 1860 by John O'Donovan. Beside these documents of Irish origin we shall mention some Scandinavian texts and the Anglo-Saxon Chronicle which enables us to make useful comparisons between the state of Ireland in the Viking period and that of England.

I am glad to acknowledge for this volume the same understanding on the part of the authorities of University College, Dublin, and help from the Department of Archaeology as made the making of the first volume possible. Amongst the friends who gave me assistance in the revision of the text, I want to mention especially Willam and Aíne O'Sullivan, and Maureen Murphy, who, in addition undertook the thankless task of making the index; as usual I am greatly indebted to Geneviève Marsh-Micheli for much information on manuscripts and many useful suggestions.

I am very grateful for the way in which my work has always been facilitated by all the staff of the National Museum of Ireland and especially by the Director, Dr Lucas and the Keeper of Antiquities, Dr Raftery; by Dr Parke and all the staff of the Library of Trinity College, Dublin; by Mr Percy Le Clerc, Inspector of National Monuments and his staff; by Dr R. Hayes, Director of the National Library of Ireland; by Professor O'Kelly in Cork and Mr L. Flanagan in Belfast; by several members of the staff of the British Museum, especially by Mr R. Bruce-Mitford, Keeper of British Antiquities. I have been greatly helped in my work in the Vatican Library by Père Hyacinthe Laurent O.P., and in research in the Victoria and Albert Museum by Mr Beckwith, Keeper of Ivories. I am also grateful for the facilities granted me in Cambridge in the Libraries of Corpus Christi College and St John's College and in the University Library; in London in the Library of Lambeth Palace; in Turin in the University Library. As for the first volume, the photographic illustration is due for a great part to the untiring efforts of Dom Angelico Surchamp, O.S.B., and Mr Belzeaux. All the other photographs come from the photographic Archives of the Department of Archaeology of University College, Dublin. I am glad to thank for the authorizations to take or use some of these photographs : the National Museum of Ireland, the Commissioners of Public Works

PREFACE

in Ireland, Trinity College Dublin, the Director of the Ulster Museum, Belfast, the President and Council of the Royal Irish Academy, the Royal Society of Antiquaries of Ireland, the Trustees of the British Museum, the Society of Antiquaries of London, the Vatican Library, the Bibliothèque nationale, the Institut pour l'Histoire des Textes, the Municipal Libraries of Amiens and Rouen, the Archaeological Museum, Cambridge, Mrs Marsh-Micheli and Liam and Máire de Paor (Máire Mac Dermott).

The maps and plans on pp. XI, XII, 44, 153 and facing p. 41 are based on maps of the Ordnance Survey of Ireland.

Biblical quotations are from the Douay Version as is the numbering of the psalms.

The French edition of this book, published by the Editions Zodiaque, appeared in June 1964.

xvi

1. Historical Data

IRISH SOCIETY at the end of the eighth century was not very different from what it had been in the fifth century at the time of the coming of St Patrick.[1] The country was still divided into a great number of petty kingdoms each owing allegiance to an over-king. We have seen that the courts of these kings had lost something of the lustre they had had in prehistoric times. The kings were still living in houses surrounded by a circular rampart (rath) or built on an artificial island in a lake (crannog). There were no towns or villages, and all through the country, scattered dwellings remained the standard type of habitation, partly no doubt because of the dampness of the climate which does not require the concentration of houses near supplies of water. At certain times the people gathered at traditional meeting places in vast assemblies (oenach) which were not only fairs, but the occasion of all sorts of political and religious transactions. However, as these were only temporary gatherings they did not imply the existence of permanent buildings.

Meanwhile the monasteries had developed during the seventh and eighth centuries.[2] Foundations which had originated in the cells of a few hermits had gradually become, partly as a consequence of the missionary activities of the Irish monks, busy cities full of students, professors, craftsmen and farm labourers. In these one finds the beginnings of something resembling town life in a country which had never known the urban development of Romanized lands. But these monastic cities were primarily intellectual centres and not merchant towns like those – Hedeby, Birka, etc. – which were to appear in other non Romanized countries. Trade did not play an essential role in Irish life. The Irish did

[1] *Vol. I*, pp. 17 sqq.

[2] For all ecclesiastical problems connected with this chapter, see : J. Kenney, *The Sources for the Early History of Ireland, I, Ecclesiastical* (New York, 1929); vol. II has not been published.

not mint coins; barter and compensation in kind were the basis of economy and law.

For centuries the political balance of the country depended on the rivalries or alliances of a few ruling families.[1] Prior to the introduction of Christianity, the mainspring of Irish political history seems to have been the antagonism of the kingdoms of Connacht and Ulster. Later, Connacht lost its importance; the south (Munster) was partly at least under the sway of the kings of Cashel; whilst the two families of the Northern Uí Néill and the Southern Uí Néill shared control of the country farther north and in turn supplied candidates for the high kingship. The árd-rí (high king) was still called 'king of Tara', though the old sanctuary and royal residence on the Hill of Tara (Meath) had become almost completely deserted.

In the ninth century, a new situation arose as the kings of Munster began to nurse the ambition of attaining to the high kingship. In fact, one of them, Felim (Feidhlimidh mac Crimhtainn) seems to have succeeded in doing so for a short while around 840. The Annals tell us that he received the submission of Niall, the reigning high king in the monastery of Clonfert (Galway), when, in order it seems to confirm his right to the high kingship, he sat in the chair of the abbot of Clonfert.[2] Soon afterwards, perhaps as a further confirmation of his sovereignty, he went to Tara.[3] This was in fact only a passing episode and Niall was restored to his rights after a short time. Felim, however, went on intriguing and among his efforts to gain power seem to have been his repeated attempts to impose his candidate for the abbacy of Armagh.

The monastery of Armagh, at least from the end of the seventh century, had claimed with increasingly marked insistence the honour and privilege of having been founded by St Patrick himself and to be, because

---

[1] *See:* E. Mac Neill, *Phases of Irish History* (Dublin, 1920).

[2] 'A great assembly of the men of Ireland in Cluain Ferta Brénainn, and Niall son of Aed, king of Temuir (Tara; i.e. high king), submitted to Feidlimid, son of Crimthann, so that Feidlimid became full king of Ireland that day, and he occupied the abbot's chair of Cluain Ferta (Clonfert)' (*A.I.*, 838). Similar examples of investiture conferred by sitting in an abbot's chair (generally that of the successor of an important saint) could be quoted from Medieval French sources.

[3] *A.U.*, 839; *A.F.M.*, 839; *A.I.*, 840 (see footnote); *War*, p. XLV, note 1.

2

of this, the first of all Irish monasteries in date and importance. In the early years of the ninth century a series of texts relating to St Patrick were copied into a volume which included a New Testament and which is now known as the Book of Armagh.[1] In a country where the clergy had taken such an essential role, it was not surprising that the great monastery which aspired to the primacy and the candidates for the high kingship should join forces. Felim began his quest for sovereignty with a public acknowledgment of the rights of Armagh to proclaim the Law of Patrick (Lex Patricii) – most probably the right of the monastery to levy a tribute by carrying the revered shrines of Armagh through various parts of Ireland. His temporary occupation of the chair of the abbot of Clonfert as a means of asserting his kingly rights was in fact only a poor substitute, brought about by necessity, for sitting in the abbatial throne of Armagh which seems to have conferred a sort of investiture to the king who occupied it. Hence the need for a candidate high king to have 'his' abbot of Armagh. And this is probably why there were nearly always two abbots of Armagh during the ninth century, each being expelled in turn by a rival faction, led perhaps by a chieftain of one of the northern tribes or the king of Tara or Cashel.

A mysterious aspect of the kings of Cashel is the fact that they seem to have had, up to a point, an ecclesiastical character. Felim, later the scholarly king Cormac mac Cuileannáin and finally in the twelfth century Cormac mac Carthy seem to have had the title of bishop. Felim, one of the fiercest plunderers of monasteries in Irish history, went about crozier in hand and is supposed to have left it in the course of a battle hanging on the bushes.[2] One might wonder if his plundering expeditions were not merely attempts to assert his authority and to call to order rebellious vassal monasteries.

Two centuries after his time the ambition of the Munster kings found its fulfilment for a short spell of twelve years. In 1002 Brian Boru used his immense prestige to take the place of Máelsechlainn, the high king, apparently without antagonizing him. Shortly afterwards he spent a

---

[1] See p. 100.
[2] 'The crozier of the devout Feidhlimidh was left in the shrubbery' (*A.F.M.*, 840; *A.U.*, 840).

week in Armagh where he proclaimed again the rights of Armagh to the 'Law of Patrick' by a note which he caused to be inserted in the Book of Armagh. In this he is proudly described as 'Imperator Scottorum'.[1] It would be difficult not to conclude that his stay in Armagh had conferred on him the kingly status in exchange for which he ratified the rights granted two centuries earlier by one of his predecessors.

It is a strange thing that all these intrigues could have taken place in a country which was faced with the worst catastrophe in its history for centuries, the invasion of the Vikings.[2] Since the last Celtic groups had reached Ireland, at the time of the conquest of Gaul by Caesar (in the middle of the first century B.C.), Ireland had been spared all the conquests and catastrophes which had swept over western Europe. The Romans settled in England but did not cross the Irish Sea. In the fifth century the Germanic invasions had taken place on the Continent and the Angles, Jutes and Saxons had landed in England. Of these perturbations Ireland had felt only indirect repercussions. Not that she enjoyed idyllic peace. The Annals of the seventh and eighth centuries are full of records of the internecine strife of the petty Irish dynasties, of tales of plundered monasteries and even of battles between rival abbeys. But, reading between the lines, one can guess that all that was not very serious. The 'battles' mentioned had probably a good deal in common with the fights between the Italian cities of the Middle Ages, where the dead and wounded were counted in a few units. They were in fact hardly more than epic tournaments rich in words and boasts, from which the victor came back with the heads of a few enemies hanging from his belt and driving before him the cattle seized from his opponent. All this was in the nature of family discord and was taking place in a world where

[1] Gwynn, *Lib. Ardm.*, p. CIII.

[2] J. Steenstrup, *Normannerne* (Copenhagen, 4 vols., 1876–80); T. D. Kendrick, *A History of the Vikings* (London, 1930); H. Shetelig, *An Introduction to the Viking History of Western Europe*, vol. I of: *Viking Antiquities in Great Britain and Ireland* (Oslo, 1940); J. Brøndsted, *The Vikings* (Harmondsworth, 1960); H. Arbman, *The Vikings* (London, 1961); for the Vikings in Ireland, beside the relevant chapters of the books listed above, see: J. Ryan, S.J., 'Pre-Norman Dublin', *J.R.S.A.I.*, 1949, pp. 64 sqq.

war had its rules and its limits. Sacrilege was not excluded – whether plunder of churches of stealing or relics. But the offended saint, with the help of the families whose patron he was, took his revenge, the beaten culprits submitting meekly enough, making restitution and giving compensation, so that everything was all right again.

Not so with the Vikings. They belonged to a different world that knew nothing of all these unwritten laws. They brought havoc, cutting mercilessly through the network of family relations and established loyalties. Pagans, they violently shocked a society which had become essentially Christian. They plundered without restitution, destroyed without redress. Yet their presence did not stop the Irish petty wars. It remains one of the strangest aspects of the Annals of the ninth and tenth centuries that they record with complete impartiality the bickerings of the local chieftains and the destructions by the 'Strangers'. This short-sighted presentation of events does not make it easy to gauge their real importance which one is forced to estimate chiefly from the consequences.

Whatever the real cause – change of climate, over-population, political events – from the end of the eighth century expedition after expedition, aiming at plunder or colonization, poured out of Scandinavia onto the western coasts of Europe. Most probably landings on the sparsely populated Northern isles, Orkneys, Shetlands, served as a preparation for the first recorded attacks and established bases for the raids farther south.[1] However, shortly after 790, these obscure movements on the fringes of the inhabited world suddenly emerged into the light. The Scandinavian longboats with their red-striped sails made their appearance before Lindisfarne, the monastery and bishop's see established a hundred and sixty years earlier by the Irish missionaries from Iona and from which all Northumbria had been converted.[2] In the Anglo-Saxon Chronicle,[3] a whole array of signs fortells the event, 'immense whirl-winds and flashes of lightning, and fiery dragons . . . flying in the air', showing the hold it had taken on the imagination of contemporary

[1] F. T. Wainwright, 'The Scandinavian Settlements', in: *The Northern Isles* (ed. by F. T. Wainwright; Edinburgh, etc., 1962), pp. 117 sqq.

[2] *A.Clon*, 791; *A.U.*, 793: 'Vastatio omnium insolarum Britanniae a Gentilibus'.

[3] *Anglo-Saxon Chr.*, 793.

people. Then at the date of the 8th of June 793 it announces that 'the ravages of the heathen men miserably destroyed God's church on Lindisfarne, with plunder and slaughter'. We have a pathetic letter from Alcuin, who by that time had left York for the imperial court and who writes to king Ethelred of Northumbria that since the landing of the Saxons, some three hundred and fifty years earlier, England had not known such a calamity : 'Behold this church of St Cuthbert besprinkled with the blood of God's priests, despoiled of all its ornaments, this holiest of all holy places in Britain abandoned to the ransackings of the pagans.' Only the lamentation of Isaiah 'Vineam electam vulpes depredarunt' seems to him a fit commentary on such a catastrophe.[1]

It was not long before Iona in its turn felt the brunt of the attack. The island metropolis of all the monasteries of St Columba was burnt down in 801 or 802;[2] again, three or four years later, the 'Foreigners', the 'Gentiles' reappeared and sixty-eight members of the 'familia' of the monastery – layfolk and ecclesiastics – were massacred.

The disaster appeared so complete that it was decided to abandon the too exposed island or at least to transfer the metropolis of the Columban order to Ireland. This assumption that the threat was permanent enough to justify radical solutions seems to imply that, by that time, the Vikings were firmly established in the Hebrides and had bases there from which they could conveniently raid the neighbourhood. It helps us also to understand the terror created by these first attacks. There is no record that the plunderings of an Irish chieftain ever caused the removal of a monastery. There is only one parallel exodus in the earlier history of Irish monasteries, the wholesale migration of the monastery of St Fursa at Burgh Castle, on the coast of East Anglia, in the face of attacks by Penda of Mercia.[3] The two episodes follow a similar pattern though

---

[1] *Mon. Alcuiniana*, p. 180.

[2] *A.I.*, 795 : 'The plundering of Í Choluim Chille (Iona), and of Inis Muiredaig (Inismurray), and of Inis Bó Finne (Inishbofin).' *A.F.M.*, 797 (*recte* 802) : 'Hi-Coluim-Cille was burned by foreigners, i.e. by Norsemen.' *A.U.*, 801 : 'I-Coluim-Cille was burned by Gentiles.' *A.F.M.*, 801 (*recte* 806) : 'Hi-Coluim-Cille was plundered by foreigners, and great numbers of the laity and clergy were killed by them, namely sixty-eight.' *A.U.*, 805 : 'The "family" of Ia (Iona) slain by Gentiles, that is (to the number of) sixty-eight.'

[3] *Vol. I*, p. 40.

separated by a century and a half. Penda was a pagan king; but while the flight of the monks of St Fursa marks one of the last outbursts of paganism in Saxon England, the transfer of Iona, one of the most celebrated of the Irish foundations, is but the preface to two centuries of upheaval.[1] The scribe of the Book of Armagh leaves us in no doubt as to the magnitude of the catastrophe. When a year or two later (in 807) he copied the passage of St Mark where Christ announces the destruction of the Temple : 'Seest thou all these great buildings? There shall not be left a stone upon a stone that shall not be thrown down . . .', he entered in the margin of the following verse 'but for the sake of the elect which he hath chosen, he hath shortened the days' the name of Cellach, the abbot of Iona who had just taken refuge in Kells,[2] thus implicitly likening the destruction of Iona to that of Jerusalem and casting on the tragedy a shadow of the final Tribulation.

About the same time, according to the Irish Annals, the long boats began to explore the coasts of Ireland. The Annals of Inisfallen tell of the destruction of the monasteries on Inismurray and Inisboffin, on the west coast. Other Annals mention raids in the Irish Sea, perhaps as far as Dublin Bay. After that, from year to year, the plunderings are listed in increasing numbers and one can feel the growing anxiety of the chroniclers. Other large monasteries were attacked. In 821 or 824 it was the turn of Bangor, on Belfast Lough, the great foundation of St Comgall from which had started in the late sixth century the mission of St Columbanus. The Annals describe the wooden church reduced to ashes and the monastery plundered.[3]

---

[1] *A.U.*, 803 : 'The giving of Cenannas (Kells) in this year, without battle, to Colum-Cille the musical.' *A.U.*, 806 : 'Constructio civitatis Columbae Cille hi (in) Ceninnus' (and not 'of the new church' as the translation says). *A. Clon.*, 804 : 'There was a new church founded in Kells in honour of St Colume.' *A.F.M.*, 802 (*recte* 807) : 'The church of Coluim-Cille at Cenannus was destroyed (the text has "do díothláithriucchadh, was destroyed", which is probably a mistake for "do do laithriucchadh, was built". See Reeves, *St Columba*, p. 388, note.

[2] Fol. 65v; Gwynn, *Lib. Ardm.*, p. 121.

[3] *A.F.M.*, 822 : 'The plundering of Beannchair (Bangor) by the foreigners; the oratory (dertach) was broken, the relics of Comhgall were shaken from the shrine in which they were'; *A.U.*, 823 : 'The plundering of Bennchair in the Ards, by Foreigners, and the spoiling of its oratory (dertach); and the relics of Comgall

The most austere establishments were not immune from the pirates who were aware, by that time, that there were treasuries of gold and silver even on the most desolate rocks, and we are left to guess at a tragedy of desolation and hunger on the Skellig. About the same time the Irish Church had its first martyr. The Four Masters record that 'Blathmac, son of Flann, received the crown of martyrdom, for he was killed by the Foreigners at Hi-Coluim-Cille (Iona)'.[1] His daring return to the exposed monastery and his death for refusing to tell where he had buried the reliquary of St Columba made such an impression that the story reached the monastery of Reichenau, on Lake Constance, where Walafrid Strabo celebrated it in verse.

All this amounted to no more than haphazard attacks along the coasts, summer raids in quest of plunder and adventure. Other flotillas had ventured farther south : in 799 the presence of the Vikings is recorded on the western coast of France and in 820 on the lower Seine. About the middle of the century, however, the attacks took on a new aspect everywhere. In 851 the Vikings wintered in France for the first time after ten years of summer raids. They had already wintered on Thanet, at the mouth of the Thames in the preceding year.[2] Ireland having been explored first, was also the first to be subjected to a massive attack. Norwegian fleets started sailing up the rivers and into the lakes. In 836, a fleet of sixty sail is mentioned on the Boyne, another entered the Liffey.[3] The Norwegians established a camp at Ath Cliath (the Ford of the Wattles) or Dubh Linn (the Black Pool), on the site of what will become the first city of Dublin. They entrenched themselves here and there. From Dubh Linn, from Linn Duchaill a little farther north, from

---

were shaken out of their shrine'; *A.I.*, 823 : 'The invasion of Bennchor by the heathens (a gentib) and the shrine of Comgall was broken by them and its learned men and its bishops were put to the sword.' See also shorter notices in *A. Clon.*, *Chr. Sc.* Also *War*, pp. 6–7, and p. 223 (fragment in the Book of Leinster) : 'There came another fleet in the North of Ireland, i.e. in the fourth year after the death of Aedh (Aedh Oridnidhe), king of Ireland, and they plundered Bendchuir of Uladh and they broke the shrine of Comhgall. They killed the bishop of the place and his wise men and his clergy.'

[1] *A.F.M.*, 823.   [2] H. Shetelig, *V. Ant.*, I, p. 15.
[3] *A.U.*, 836, *A.F.M.*, 836.

bases which were sometimes no more than a cluster of anchored boats, but which could be also a fortified camp, they went raiding through the countryside, sometimes far away, probably using stolen horses as they did on the Continent. Their swords, which sometimes came from Frankish workshops, were longer and stronger than the short blades of the Irish. All their weapons were on a different scale. Their notion of war and massacre was merciless. One of the fragments of chronicle copied by Mac Firbis shows the envoys of the Irish high king arriving at the camp of a Danish army which had just defeated the Norwegians.[1] The envoys see with dismay that the Danes have lighted their camp fires on heaps of corpses, planting the supporting posts of the roasting-spits through the bodies. To their indignant reproaches, the Danes answer cynically: 'They would have done the same with us.' Adding to this the constant dissentions of the Irish, one can understand the overwhelming success of the Vikings as soon as they arrived in strength. The same chronicler remarks bitterly: 'Alas for the fact which I shall often mention: it is pitiful for the Irish to continue the evil habit of fighting amongst themselves and that they do not rise together against the Lochlanns (Norwegians).'[2]

A powerful attack came around 839. The Four Masters and the Annals of Ulster, with their usual dryness, mention only that Armagh was burned by the Foreigners with its stone church and its wooden oratories. But the more emphatic author of *The War of the Gaedhil with the Gaill* leaves us in no doubt as to the magnitude of the catastrophe: 'There came a great royal fleet into the north of Erinn, with Turgeis, who assumed the sovereignty of the foreigners of Erinn; and the north of Erin was plundered by them and they spread themselves over Leth Cuinn (Conn's half: the northern part of Ireland). A fleet of them also entered Loch Eathach, and another fleet entered Lughbudh (Louth) and another fleet entered Loch Rai (Lough Ree). Moreover Armagh was plundered three times in the same month by them; and Turgeis himself usurped the abbacy of Armagh and Farannan, abbot of Armagh and chief successor (comharba) of Patrick was driven out and went to Munster, while Turgeis was in Armagh and in the sovereignty of the

---

[1] *Fragm.*, pp. 122–3 and 124–5.   [2] Id., pp. 140–1.

9

north of Erinn.' Clonfert, Lorrha, Terryglass, Inis Cealtra and the churches of Lough Derg were plundered, 'and the place where Ota, the wife of Turgeis, used to give her audience was upon the altar of Clonmacnois'. And the historian, carried away by his subject, goes on, quoting prophetic poems:

'Gentiles shall come over the soft sea;
    They shall confound the men of Erinn;
. . . .

Seven years shall they be; not weak their power,
    In the high sovereignty of Erinn
    In the abbacy of every church
    The black Gentiles of Dubhlinn.

There shall be of them an abbot over this my church,
    Who will not attend matins;
    Without Pater and without Credo;
    Without Irish, but only foreign language.'[1]

A Norse king established in Armagh, holding in mock power the place of the abbot, successor of St Patrick, his queen keeping her court in the churches of the most hallowed of all Irish monasteries, destruction by the invader with 'only foreign language', desecration by the pagan 'without Pater, without Credo', the calamity had reached its most dramatic point.

And this was to be no mere passing storm. It is true that Turgeis was made prisoner in 845 and incurred the usual punishment for sacrilege: drowning. But in 840 the Norwegians had already established a fort in Dublin, which was soon to become one of their wealthiest trading posts in the Western World. The invaders became a permanent

[1] *War*, pp. 9–10. It is remarkable that the memory of Turgeis' invasion was still alive at the time of the coming of the Normans. See: O'Meara, *Giraldus Cambrensis*, p. 173: 'In the time of king Fedlimid the Norwegians invaded the coasts of Ireland in a great fleet. They held the land with a strong hand . . . and destroyed nearly all the churches. Their leader called Turgeis, subjugated the island in a short time after several violent battles.'

plague rooted in the midst of the land and laid the foundations of a colony soon to be linked to the much more widespread hegemony taking shape about the same time in England.

Towards the middle of the century, the Norwegians whom the Annalists are wont to describe as the 'White (or fair-haired) Foreigners', were joined by the 'Black Foreigners', the Danes, who in fact pounced on the first invaders and tried to wrench Dublin from them. The outcome was a series of confused struggles, in which the Irish seem to have made use of the antagonism of the two groups of Vikings, occasionally using the Danes to beat the Norwegians. But as soon as the news of the Danish attack reached Scandinavia, the Norwegian colony was reinforced. In 853 a new 'royal fleet' appeared, commanded by Olav Huite (the 'white' or the 'fair-haired'), who is described in the Irish Annals as the son of a Norwegian king sent to lead the Vikings of Ireland and to extract 'taxes' from the Irish. He seems to have got rid of the Danes. Firmly entrenched in Dublin for twenty years, he used the city as a base from which he waged war in England and Scotland. Shetelig considers him, probably rightly, as a kind of viceroy in charge of overseas territories,[1] governing for his father who, shortly after 870, called him back to Norway to deal with an unsettled political situation. He was succeeded in Dublin by his brother Ivar, who is described in the Annals of Ulster as 'rex nordmannorum totius Hiberniae et Britanniae – king of the Northmen of all Ireland and Britain'.[2] He died in 874, probably a Christian, but a century and a half elapsed before the official conversion of Dublin.

His death marks the beginning of that period of forty years, the 'Forty year Recess', from about 874 to 917, which Irish chroniclers consider as a time of restored peace.[3] It was only a relative peace, of course, as the local quarrels ran their usual nefarious course and from time to time the Scandinavians made a show of activity. Nevertheless

---

[1] H. Shetelig, *V. Ant.*, I, pp. 54–5.   [2] *A.F.M.*, 872; *A.U.*, 879.

[3] *War*, p. 27: 'There was some rest to the men of Erinn for a period of forty years without ravage of the foreigners: viz., from the reign of Maelseachlainn, son of Maelruanaidh (862 or 863) to the year before the death of Flann, son of Maelseachlainn and the accession to the throne of Niall Glundubh (915)' (which of course is more than forty years).

there is no doubt that a great change had come and life seems almost to have returned to normal. This period corresponds fairly exactly with the reign of the high king Flann Sinna (877–915),[1] a builder of churches, and partly with that of the celebrated king-bishop of Cashel, Cormac mac Cuilleannáin, a poet and a scholar (900–7).[2] Armagh regained a measure of stability under the government of two great ecclesiastics. The abbot, Maelbrigte mac Durnan (888–927), who in 891 added to his charge that of head of the Columban monasteries, belonged to a royal sept of the north of Ireland and seems to have shown great firmness and decision.[3] The Annals show us his appointed successor beside him, Muiredach mac Domhnall, abbot of Monasterboice, counsellor of the Southern Uí Néill and administrator of the possessions of Armagh in the south, which corresponded more or less to part of the present County of Louth.[4] Clonmacnois also seems to have had in Colman a great abbot who built a church in the monastery with the help of Flann Sinna.[5]

As this time no reinforcements came from Scandinavia, the power of the Dublin Vikings waned quickly; besides, the colony was losing much of its population through large-scale migrations to Iceland, and Dublin's strategic importance was declining in face of the wholesale Viking invasion of England which was occupied from the Scottish border to the Thames. King Edmund met a martyr's death in 870; the following years saw the desperate struggle of Alfred in the south, gradually enlarging his kingdom towards the north as he drew back the Vikings. In 892 a powerful joint attack was launched against him by two hundred and fifty Viking ships from the Seine, eighty longships which Hastings brought from the mouth of the Somme and one hundred and forty others arriving from Scandinavia. The king of Dublin joined the affray and landed in the north of England. However, Alfred's policy of perpetually

---

[1] *A.U.*, 914 (*recte* 915).   [2] *A.U.*, 900, 907.
[3] See *A.F.M.*, 889, and the same episode in *Chr. Sc.*, 893.
[4] See p. 19.
[5] 'The Daimhliag (stone church) of Cluain-mic-Nois was erected by the king, Flann Sinna, and by Colman Conailleach,' *A.F.M.*, 904; see also: *Chr. Sc.* and *A. Tig.*, 908, *A. Clon.*, 901 (*recte* 908).

harrying the Vikings bore fruit in the end and their armada was disbanded in 896.[1] By that time the king of Dublin had been killed and the city had lost its best warriors. The Irish under the king of Leinster took and occupied it in 901 and the Norwegian colonists fled.[2] The situation had so far altered that in 912 an Irish fleet was sent to England to help the Anglo-Saxons in the fight against the Vikings.

This adventurous spirit may have called for an answer. Still, if the position was reversed again, there was also another factor involved. In 911, Normandy had been granted to the Viking chief Rollo at the treaty of St Clair-sur-Epte. As a consequence, access to that part of the French coast was denied to all Scandinavians except his immediate followers. All possible rivals were kept at bay and fleets of Vikings looking for territories to conquer were roaming the sea anew. As was to be expected, they took to old, well-known sea-routes. Once again, the Annalists list the foreboding portents of great upheavals; there were 'horrid signs . . . the heavens seemed to glow with comets. A mass of fire was observed, with thunder, passing over Ireland from the West, which went over the sea eastwards.'[3] The fleets of the Norsemen reappeared and after fierce fighting Dublin again fell to them.[4]

For half a century it was governed by the dynasty of Ivar, which was closely allied to the Scandinavian dynasty of Northumbria, and fought relentlessly to assert its authority in Ireland. According to the *War of the Gaedhil with the Gaill*,[5] it succeeded only too well and towards the middle of the tenth century there was not a place in Ireland which did not pay tribute to the 'Foreigners', who were now settled in several cities, Dublin, Limerick, Wexford, Waterford and Cork and who seem to have had representatives in every part of the country. As a consequence the monasteries were subjected to new attacks and plundered again. In 922 the fleet of Tomrar, son of Elge, sailed up the Shannon laying waste the abbeys of Lough Derg, then on to Clonmacnois, and

---

[1] Shetelig, *V. Ant.*, I, p. 86; Kendrick, *Vikings*, p. 245.
[2] The *A. U.* proclaim : 'The expulsion from Ireland of the heathen.'
[3] *A.U.*, 916 (*recte* 917).
[4] The 17th of October 917, according to *A.F.M.*
[5] *War*, pp. 48–51.

farther to the islands of Lough Ree.[1] In the north, final disaster overtook communities which had managed to survive so far, Nendrum,[2] and perhaps Bangor.[3]

To make the picture more complex, one has to remember that Christianity was beginning to penetrate amongst the Scandinavians, and that they were by that time intermarrying with the Irish. Already around the year 920 Gotfried, king of Dublin, when plundering Armagh, respected 'the churches, the monastery of the Céli Dé, and the Hospital'.[4] One of the most striking personalities of the Scandinavian colonial world in the tenth century, Olav Cuaran, who governed Northumbria for almost ten years (from 941 to 944 and from 949 to 952) and Dublin for thirty years, had been baptized in England in 943, and when at seventy he was defeated by the high king, he went to spend the end of his life, piously at Iona.[5] Shortly afterwards the kingdom of Dublin passed to Sitric Silkenbeard, who was only half Scandinavian, being the son of a Leinster princess. In the eleventh century, he was to build the first cathedral of Dublin, the church of the Holy Trinity (or Christ Church).

Meanwhile a new power was growing in Ireland. An obscure Munster family occuping a small territory in the south of present-day County Clare, the Dál Cais, suddenly came to the front through the prowess of two of its members, Mahon and his younger brother Brian, in the fight against the oppression of the Northmen.[6] Brian, who was probably

---

[1] *A.I.*, 922: 'Tomrair, son of Elgi, a Jarl of the Foreigners on Luimnech (the lower Shannon) and he proceeded and plundered Inis Celtra and Muicinis and burned Cluain Moccu Nóis; and he went on Loch Rí and plundered all its islands, and he ravaged Mide (Meath).'

[2] See: Lawlor, *Nendrum*, p. 68; *Vol. I*, p. 79.

[3] See pp. 21–2.   [4] *A.U.*, 920.

[5] *A.F.M.*, 979 (*recte* 980); *A. Tig.*, 980; *War*, p. 47.

[6] In the flamboyant words of the author of the *War*: 'There were then growing and ruling this tribe (the Dál Cais) two stout, able, valiant pillars, two fierce, lacerating, magnificent heroes, two gates of battle, two poles of combat, two spreading trees of shelter, two spears of victory and readiness, of hospitality and munificence, of heart and strength, of friendship and liveliness, the most eminent of the west of Europe, viz., Mathgamhain (Mahon) and Brian, the two sons of Cennedigh' (*War*, pp. 56–7 and 58–9).

born in 941,[1] appears first in history as the leader of guerilla fighters who were mercilessly harassing the Limerick Vikings by methods rather similar to those used a century earlier by Alfred in England.[2] Mahon, who had become king of Cashel, inflicted a crushing defeat on the Norwegian king of Limerick in 968 and took and plundered the city.[3] Then he went through all Munster, killing the Scandinavian troops scattered about the province. When Mahon died in 976 Brian took up the fight. By that time he had outgrown the role of a guerilla chief and become an astute planner, more aware of the possibilities of unification than the scions of the older dynasties. Breaking the laws of succession he also managed to achieve the old ambition of the Munster kings by becoming árd-rí. Máelsechlainn, one of the Southern Uí Néill, held the high kingship at the time. Brian, having already defeated and subjected the king of Leinster and Sitric, king of Dublin (A.D. 1000), defeated him also and usurped the high kingship, unifying the whole country under his rule. This was the time when, conscious of his power, he had himself described in the entry made in the Book of Armagh as 'Imperator Scottorum'.[4] For ten years he ruled over Ireland, everywhere asserting his authority by the levy of tributes (boromha, boru in modern Irish), from which he derives his nickname: 'Brian Boru – Brian of the tributes'. This was a time of relative peace during which the century-old wounds of foreign occupation began to heal.

But the apparent calm was deceptive. Outside Ireland all the Scandinavian colonies of the West were in turmoil. In 991 the Norwegian Olav Tryggvason landed in England, soon followed by the Dane, Svein.[5] Their armies were living off the countryside and reducing it to starvation. After a while, the Norwegians left, but in 1011 the Danes succeeded in occupying most of the south of England, took Canterbury and massacred the archbishop. Two years later the Saxon king Ethelred

[1] *A.U.*, 941; and not sixteen years earlier, as indicated in *A.F.M.*, 925.

[2] *War*, pp. 58 sqq.

[3] For this and the subsequent events, see: *War*, pp. 79 sqq.

[4] See p. 4. Cf. *A.U.*, 1014 where he is described as 'arch-King of the Gaedhil of Ireland, and of the Foreigners and Britons, the Augustus of all the north-west of Europe (august iartair tuaisceirt Eorpa uile)'.

[5] *Anglo-Saxon Chr.*, 991 to 1017; see Kendrick, *Vikings*, Shetelig, *V. Ant.*, I.

fled to Normandy and Svein took his place. This is the threatening back-ground against which the battle of Clontarf must be measured.[1] It was fought in March 1014, between Brian and a significant gathering of Scandinavian forces. The Annals of Inisfallen speak of an army 'of all the Foreigners of the Western World'. In this light, even if it is difficult to evaluate the importance of Sitric's intrigues and those of the Earl of Orkney, it would be futile not to see in the attack a deliberate attempt at subjecting Ireland to the fate which had just overtaken England. From this angle the traditional view of the battle as ending the domination of the Northmen in Ireland is perfectly legitimate. What matter if the king of Leinster fought with the Vikings; he was only playing the old game of dynastic rivalry. It is more than likely that this third massive Scandinavian attack, had it succeeded, would have brought to Ireland an equivalent of the thirty years of foreign rule which England had to endure under the Danish kings Svein and Canute (1013–42).

The battle was fought on Good Friday of the year 1014 at Clontarf, on the northern shore of Dublin Bay. The Four Masters speak of 10,000 men in mailcoats gathered by the Scandinavians. The struggle lasted all day. The army of Brian was victorious and 3,000 Vikings met their death; but the old king was killed while praying in his tent on the evening of the battle; his son, his brother and one of his grand-sons were also amongst the dead. The abbot of Armagh came, brought back the body of the king in solemn procession and buried it in his monastery.[2]

However, if the outcome was the end of Scandinavian rule, the cities of the Northmen remained and started to play an important role in the

---

[1] For the battle of Clontarf and the texts concerning it, see: J. Ryan, S.J., 'The battle of Clontarf', *J.R.S.A.I.*, 1938, pp. 1 sqq. One of the important texts is the *Saga of Burnt Njal*, vol. III, *Icelandic Sagas* (Rolls Series; trans. G. W. Dasent; London, 1894). For some interesting suggestions see: E. Linklater, 'The Battle of Clontarf', *Viking* (Oslo), 1951.

[2] *A.F.M.*, 1013 (*recte* 1014): 'Maelmuire, son of Eochaidh, successor of Patrick, proceeded with the seniors and relics to Sord Choluim-Chille (Swords, Co. Dublin, to the North of Clontarf), and they carried from thence the body of Brian, king of Ireland, and the body of Murchadh, his son, and the head of Conaing, and the head of Mothla. Maelmuire and his clergy waked the bodies with great honour and veneration; and they were interred at Ard-Macha (Armagh) in a new tomb.' See also *A.U.*, 1014.

life of the country. This new aspect will have to be examined in the third part of this study of Irish art.

What was the effect of these two centuries of invasion and foreign occupation on life in Ireland and on the conditions of artistic production? First of all the effect on the monasteries has to be examined, because, as we have seen, they were the centres of civilisation and of artistic patronage. On them, the impact of the Vikings was catastrophic. We hear of nothing but churches set on fire, broken shrines, books destroyed by fire and water. Everywhere the pattern is the same. The Vikings knew very well that the churches contained an accumulation of gold and silver objects. The hoard found in the ruins of a church on St Ninian's Isle in the Shetlands, which consists of silver bowls and brooches probably hidden for safety at the time of an attack, gives an idea of what they were seeking.[1] Silver or gold objects melted and made into coins, or simply cut up into fragments of a given weight, were an immediate source of wealth. As for gilt bronze ornaments, they could be brought home: Viking ladies loved them and were wont to have them mounted as brooches.

Viking tombs of the ninth and tenth centuries supply clear confirmation of the literary evidence.[2] The women's graves especially, have produced a number of such objects brought back as souvenirs: three portable shrines transformed into caskets by their new owners once the relics had been thrown away, fragments of croziers, several enamelled bronze bowls which had been originally church lamps, a censer, pails for holy water, etc. There are also a great number of fragments of decorated gilt bronze torn from the objects they had adorned, and often hacked into several pieces, perhaps for division amongst plunderers. Even in the absence of texts, the Viking graves would be clear evidence of the Scandinavian invasion of Ireland and the ruthless plundering that accompanied it. Treasures which had been gathered over centuries were scattered and whole libraries went up in smoke.

[1] A. C. O'Dell, *St Ninian's Isle Treasure* (Aberdeen University Studies 141); Id., *Antiquity*, 1959, pp. 241 sqq.

[2] *Viking Antiquities in Great Britain and Ireland*, ed. by Haakon Shetelig (Oslo, 1940), vol. V (Jan Petersen, *British Antiquities of the Viking Period found in Norway*).

This wholesale destruction is by no means confined to Ireland and the history of Continental monasteries presents exactly the same picture. There also treasuries were scattered and monks fled, carrying with them everything they could. One need only mention the well-known exodus of the community of Noirmoutier, abandoning its island, which then became one of the Viking bases on the coasts of France, carrying the relics of St Philibert, the founder, first to Grandlieu, then here and there for years, until they found a final resting place at Tournus in Burgundy.[1]

In the same way the 'Congregation of St Cuthbert', uprooted from Lindisfarne, wandered for years.[2] A semi-legendary story shows it trying to reach Ireland. For some time it was established at Chester-le street. It finally found security on the high rock partly surrounded by water where Durham was built. Meanwhile, Lindisfarne had fallen to ruin and it was only in the twelfth century that a priory depending on the cathedral of Durham was built on the old site.

At Iona, as we have seen, departure had been decided on almost immediately. Only two years after the record of the first attack on the monastery the Columban order acquired the site of Kells.[3] While the new city ("nova civitas') of Columba was building the pirates re-appeared and massacred sixty-eight members of the 'familia' of Iona, lay and ecclesiastics. By 813 the transfer of the metropolis of St Columba had taken place, and the Annals of Ulster tell us that 'Cellach, abbot of Iona, the church ("templum") of Kells being completed, resigned from the abbacy, which passed to Diarmait'.

The transfer fulfilled its purpose and Kells seems to have been spared all plundering[4] until 919.[5] One may wonder at the choice of Kells as the

[1] See: Cabrol-Leclercq, art: *Grandlieu*.
[2] See: *Relics of St Cuthbert*, pp. 27 sqq.
[3] See the references p. 6 note 2.
[4] The mention of a plunder of Kells around 850 in the *War* (pp. 18–19) is not to be taken into account as this part of the chronicle is completely incoherent from the point of view of chronology – the result perhaps of a displacement of pages in the original manuscript.
[5] *A.U.*, 919 'The "doimliac" of Cenannas was broken by Gentiles and great numbers were martyred there'; cf. *Chr. Sc.*, 919.

seat of the metropolis of the Columban order. Kells was probably an
ancient stronghold called Sibrine, whose situation on the top of a hill,
probably reinforced by mighty fortifications, made it a very safe place.
But when its position on the map is examined, it seems as if Armagh
may have played some part in the new foundation. Armagh had vast

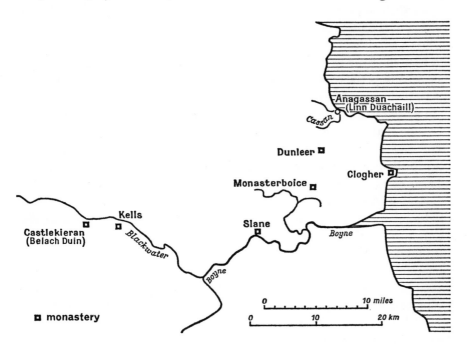

Fig. 1. Territory of 'the Family of Armagh in the South'.

possessions in what corresponds roughly with southern Co. Louth.[1]
The people there seem to have been referred to as 'the Family of Armagh
in the south'. In 831 they are mentioned as defeated by the Norwegians
near Carlingford Lough.[2] A later text clearly establishes the region as
'from Belach–Duin (Castlekieran) to the sea, and from the Boyne to the
Cassan River'.[3] Another text shows Brian Boru meeting representatives

[1] And with the southern part of the archdiocese of Armagh.
[2] *A.U.*, 831.　　　　　　　　　　　　　　　　[3] *A.U.*, 921.

19

of the clergy of Armagh at Castlekieran, the monastery appearing as a sort of frontier post of the possessions of Armagh.[1] It lay only a few miles west of Kells and one may wonder whether it was not Armagh which gave refuge to the community of St Columba. The inscription on the cross of the Tower at Kells, 'Cross of Patrick and Columba',[2] would then appear as commemorating this gift, and the mention of Cellach in the margin of a page of the Book of Armagh would reinforce such as a hypothesis.[3] In these southern territories belonging to Armagh, the two chief monasteries were Dunleer and Monasterboice (Fig. 1). The second is the only one which we need remember; it is important to notice its link with Armagh.

In spite of the transfer to Kells Iona was not completely abandoned. It seems that Cellach, when he had established another abbot in Kells, went back to Iona, where he died in 815.[4] Blathmac who came in his turn to the island with a reliquary of Columba was killed there in 824.[5] There seem to have been other attempts at re-establishing the monastery. According to the Annals of Ulster, in 828 Diarmait, abbot of Iona, went to Scotland 'with the reliquaries of Colum-Cille (Columba)'.[6] Two years later, he brought them back to Ireland.[7] About the middle of the century, Kenneth mac Alpine (840–60), who was at the same time king of the Picts and the Scots, had the reliquaries of St Columba divided into two lots and settled the metropolis of the Columban monasteries of Scotland at Dunkeld, where he had just built a church.[8] It may be that the coming of Indrechtach, abbot of Iona, to Ireland in 848, with the reliquaries of St Columba, was connected with this division.[9] These obstinate attempts to return to the exposed island did not stop there, and in 877, the Annals of Ulster tell us 'the shrine of St Columba and all his reliquaries arrived in Ireland, to escape from the Foreigners'. Finally, when the Dublin Vikings became Christians, they seem to have adopted Iona as a place of retreat and pilgrimage. We

---

[1] *A.U.*, 1005. [2] See p. 138. [3] See p. 7. [4] *A.U.*, 815.
[5] See p. 8. [6] *Chr. Sc.*, 829, *A. Clon.*, 826.
[7] *A.U.*, 830, *Chr. Sc.*, 831, *A. Clon*, 828. [8] Reeves, *St Columba*, p. 316.
[9] *A.U.*, 848; *Fragm.*, pp. 124–5: 'Indrechtach, abbot of Ia (Iona), came to Erin with the relics of Colum Cille.'

have seen that Olav Cuaran ended his life there. Some of his successors followed his example.

As for the monastery of Kells, it was plundered several times during the tenth century : in 919, 946, 949, 968, and in 996, Olav Cuaran himself leading the 968 attack. As in the case of several other monasteries, one may wonder if its century-long immunity did not have a cause which escapes us. Perhaps in order to keep intact one at least of their chief monasteries, Iona and Kells, the 'successors of St Columba' had agreed to pay tribute for Kells to the Dublin Vikings, an arrangement which the dynasty of Ivar, after the re-taking of Dublin in the tenth century, would have ceased to consider valid.

The fate of Bangor was rather different. Established on the shore of Belfast Lough, facing the channel through which the Viking fleets had access into the Irish sea, it was in a very exposed situation. We have seen that the Vikings attacked it around 823. The relics of St Comgall, we are told, were shaken out of their reliquary and 'its scholars and its bishops were put to the sword'. St Bernard of Clairvaux, speaking on the authority of St Malachy who had rebuilt the monastery in the twelfth century,[1] says that 'nine hundred people were killed in a day by pirates' and that, at the time Malachy restored it, it had lain, destroyed 'by pirates', for a long time. He says also that at that time the abbots of Bangor had been for long abbots in name only and that they had gone on administering the lands of the monastery although there had been no community 'for indeed from the time when the monastery was destroyed there was always someone to hold it with its possessions. For they were both appointed by election and were even called abbots, preserving in name, but not in fact, what had once been'.[2] This explains the continuous list of abbots of Bangor which can be compiled from the Annals for the ninth and tenth centuries. They were, however, clearly ecclesiastics and not lay abbots such as existed on the Continent in Carolingian times. It is not very clear when the monastery was finally destroyed. It may have survived the 823 attack. The Annals of Ulster mention an abbot of Bangor 'killed by the Foreigners' in 958. Perhaps it was only then that the monastery was abandoned. It is puzzling to read

[1] *Vita Malachiae*, 13. [2] *Vita Malachiae*, 13.

that in 1065 the king of Ulidia – a territory corresponding to the present counties of Down and Antrim – was killed by his own subjects 'in the daimliag of Bangor',[1] though perhaps this was only a church for the laity which had escaped destruction.

A comparison of what we know of the neighbouring monastery of Nendrum, established on an island of Strangford Lough some twelve miles south of Bangor, may throw some light on this confused evidence.[2] Though the Annals do not mention that it was attacked in the beginning of the ninth century, the excavations have given some indications of a massacre which may well have taken place at the same time as that at Bangor, that is to say about 820. But the monastery was rebuilt and given the protection of a round tower and perhaps of some dry-stone walls. It stood until 874 when the Annals say that the abbot was burned in his own house – a statement which is borne out by the traces of fire and of systematic destruction found in the excavations. It then disappears completely from the records and it was never rebuilt. It is possible, judging from a runic inscription engraved on a slab, that converted Vikings played some part in this second period of the existence of the monastery.

Another monastery in the same neighbourhood, Moville (Magh Bilé) fared very differently. It was plundered at the same time as Bangor. In 824 the Annals of Ulster mention that the 'Pagans' have burned it with its wooden church. Abbots of Moville, 'Coarbs (successors) of St Finnian', appear from time to time in ninth and tenth century annals, though nothing is recorded but the bare fact of their death. Only in the eleventh century can we be sure that their title is not an empty one like that of the contemporary abbots of Bangor, when Marianus Scottus of Mainz, in his Chronicle, tells us that he entered the monastery of Moville in 1052, and that he left for Germany on the advice of his abbot, Tigernach Bairrcech, who is known to have died in 1061.[3]

As for the monastery of Castledermot (Disert Diarmada; Kildare), much farther to the south, on the edge of the Wicklow Mountains, it was

---

[1] *A.F.M., A.U.*   [2] *Vol. I*, pp. 79 sqq.; Lawlor, *Nendrum.*
[3] Henry – Marsh–Micheli, *Illumination*, p. 127.

hardly established when the Viking raids got under way. The Annals of Inisfallen relate its foundation in 812[1] by a certain Dermot who had perhaps played a part in the reform movement of Tallaght and who died in 823.[2] The abbey was plundered in 841 by the Vikings based on Carlingford Lough,[3] and the Annals of the Four Masters say that in 867 Eodois, son of Doughal, was martyred by the 'Foreigners' at Disert-Diarmada. The second half of the ninth century was nevertheless a brilliant time for the monastery, then under the direction of abbot Snedgus, and it was the place where the future king of Cashel, Cormac mac Cuileannáin, was brought up.[4]

Such differences in the fates of individual Irish monasteries were characteristic of the time. Some monasteries disappeared for ever. Inismurray Abbey,[5] on an island off the Sligo coast, is typical of these: attacked at the same time as Iona, at the very beginning of the ninth century, it was never revived. Later churches built on the island were meant for the use of pilgrims and lay people; the monastery itself is never mentioned again.

One would expect the abbeys in the immediate neighbourhood of Dublin to have vanished as soon as the Vikings established themselves at the mouth of the Liffey around 836–40. This is in fact far from true. The case of Clondalkin (Cluain Dolcain) is quite remarkable. It was only four or five miles from the 'Black Pool' (Dubh Linn; Dublin). It was plundered by the Vikings in 832,[6] four years before their first establishment in Dublin, and perhaps again in 840. Nothing more is known of it until 865 or 866. At that time Olav Huite, king of Dublin, was busy fighting the Saxons in York. The Annals say that two Irish chieftains took advantage of this to take 'Olav's fort' at Clondalkin, where they collected a hundred Viking heads.[7] Are we to deduce from the existence of the fort that the monastery had ceased to exist for twenty years or so? Most probably, but it obviously revived as soon as

[1] *A.I.*, 812: 'Foundation of Disert Diarmata'.
[2] *A.F.M.*, 823; *A.U.*, 824.　　　　　[3] *A.F.M.*, *A.U.*, 841.
[4] He may have been buried there also. See *Fragm.*, pp. 205, 215.
[5] Wakeman, *Inismurray*.　　　　　[6] *A.F.M.*, *A.U.*
[7] *A.F.M.*, 865; *A.U.*, 866; *A. Clon.*, 897 (a mistake, no doubt).

the fort was destroyed, as the Annalists enter the death of an abbot of Clondalkin in 879,[1] and similar entries follow at regular intervals.

What happened to Finglas and Tallaght, the twin foundations, the 'two eyes of Ireland' which led the reform movement in the last years of the eighth century?[2] To-day, Finglas is a northern, Tallaght a south-western suburb of Dublin. The last mention of Finglas in the Annals is in 865–7.[3] But the Four Masters continue to record abbots, bishops, lectors and priors of Tallaght all through the ninth and tenth centuries. Despite the presence of such alarming neighbours, the monastic life seems to have continued normally.

Another monastery was completely appropriated by the Vikings. From the end of the seventh century the Annals mention abbots of Linn Duachaill, which Reeves and Todd[4] have located at Anagassan on an estuary formed by the meeting of two rivers, south of Dundalk. Such a site was too good an anchorage for 'long ships' not to be seized by the Vikings. In 840 the Annals[5] record the building of Norwegian forts at Dublin and Linn Duachaill and the plundering raids which originate from them in that year and the following one. The Vikings of Linn Duachaill captured the abbot of the monastery of Clogher[6] who died at their hands in Linn Duachaill. Then the abbot of Linn Duachaill was 'wounded and burnt' by them.[7] The monastery is never mentioned again after this. As for the fort, it prospered, and when the Danes, ten years later, swooped on the Norwegian establishments in Ireland, they attacked at the same time Dublin and Linn Duachaill. In the tenth century, the fort seems to have been still in Scandinavian hands.[8] The Vikings may then have extended their occupation inland, as in 968 we read of an attack on Monasterboice and Dunleer by the high king, who killed there several hundreds of 'Foreigners'.[9]

The monastery on Scattery Island (Inis Cathaig), in the estuary of

---

[1] *A.F.M.*; sometime later, a round tower was built there.
[2] *Vol. I*, p. 43; Flower, *The two Eyes of Ireland.*   [3] *A.F.M.*, 865; *A.U.*, 867.
[4] *War*, pp. LXII–III, note 1; *A.F.M.*, 939, note *h*, 1045, note *o*.
[5] *A.U.* 840.
[6] Probably Clogher (Tyrone), or a monastery at Clogher-head.
[7] *A.F.M.*, 841; *A.U.*, 841; *A. Clon.*, 839.   [8] *A.U.*, 926.
[9] *A.F.M.*, 968. A large mound at Anagassan may be the site of the Viking fort.

the Shannon, was also in a very dangerous position, being only a short distance from the Scandinavian town of Limerick. It seems nonetheless to have survived and after the taking of Limerick by Mahon and Brian in 968, it gave refuge – willingly or not – to the Scandinavian king of Limerick and his sons.

However, of the chief monastic cities enumerated with such pomp in the *Martyrology of Oengus* around 800,[1] not a single one disappeared in the time of the Vikings. There was an extraordinary power of survival in these towns built mostly of wood. After they had been devoured by fire, those of the inhabitants who had been able to escape with the most precious possessions of the churches came back; trees were felled in the neighbouring forests and fairly soon the city was standing again. Houses and churches were built anew and ramparts mended, ready to withstand a new attack. This was true of Clonmacnois, Durrow, Kildare, Clonard, Glendalough, Lismore, all well endowed and with powerful protectors. One can assume that for them the 'Forty year Recess' was a time of rebuilding, enlarging and embellishing.

The position of Armagh is perhaps even more striking. Its resources allowed it to be rebuilt even more quickly and more easily than the other big monastic cities. After any catastrophe, the abbot simply went through the provinces levying the tribute of St Patrick and the treasury of the abbey was filled again with gold and silver; beams and planks were no doubt supplied as part of the tribute and the rebuilding was soon under way.

Meanwhile, beside these Irish monastic cities engaged in a struggle for survival, new towns of a completely different character were developing, the Viking settlements of Dublin, Limerick, Waterford, Wexford, all on estuary harbours admirably suited to sheltering the fleets of a hundred or two hundred ships which sometimes gathered there, and also able to accommodate the trading vessels which incessantly called.

They may have been no more than a gathering of houses huddled closely within the ramparts above the landing quays from which came

[1] Stokes, *Martyr. Oengus*, pp. 24–6; *Vol. I*, pp. 41–2.

their wealth. Unprepossessing as they probably looked they kept in close contact with the world at large. Ships coming from the Mediterranean brought African slaves, silks from China arrived through Byzantium or across Russia and the trading posts on the Baltic. From these towns in Ireland it was customary to go to Iceland, Greenland and even America. The kings of the dynasty of Ivar were minting coins.[1] The description in the *War* of the plunder of Limerick by Mahon in 968 gives some idea of the sort of wealth which was piling up in the warehouses of the city: 'They carried off their jewels and their best property and their saddles beautiful and foreign; their gold and their silver; their beautifully woven cloth of all colours and of all kinds; their satins and silken cloth, pleasing and variegated, both scarlet and green, and all sorts of cloth in like manner.'[2]

All this introduced a different kind of life into the country. Before the battle of Clontarf it may not have had a very deep influence on the Irish. Later, however, when these towns, drifting slowly away from their original Scandinavian ties, took their place in the normal life of the country, their influence was to be felt in many ways.

Until then, one of the main obstacles to the mixing of the two populations was the difference of religion; but in fact this presented all sorts of varied aspects. Not all the Scandinavians showed hostility on this ground. There is, in one of the Fragments of Irish Annals copied by Mac Firbis an astonishing account of the attitude of the Danes in 851. The author ascribes to them the following reasoning: 'This St Patrick against whom these enemies of ours (the Norwegians) have committed many evils, is archbishop and head of the saints of Erin. Let us pray to him fervently, and let us give honourable alms to him for our gaining victory and triumph over these enemies.'[3] After their victory, 'they had a great wide chest (?) filled with gold and silver to give to Patrick'.[4] Some of the Scandinavian kings, amongst them Olav Cuaran in the tenth century, had become Christians. But it was not until the eleventh century that the whole population of Dublin was converted.

A mixed population was appearing. The Fragments of Annals

[1] W. O'Sullivan, 'The Earliest Irish Coinage', *J.R.S.A.I.*, 1949, pp. 190 sqq.
[2] *War*, pp. 78–89.   [3] *Fragm.*, pp. 120–1.   [4] *Fragm.*, pp. 124–5.

mention the Gaill-Gaedhil who are presented as the 'foster-children' of Vikings,[1] more probably in fact, children of mixed ancestry. Whatever their exact origin, they had certainly adopted the piratical ways of their Scandinavian family. There were also, in the ninth century, some Irish chieftains who, without the same excuse, allied themselves with the invaders, plundering with them and living like them.

One may also assume that in the course of the tenth and eleventh centuries other evils appeared as a consequence of the depredations of the Vikings. The obliteration of some great abbeys, in a country where ecclesiastical life was essentially monastic, brought about a local demoralization which increased as new generations grew up practically without religious guidance. This happened for example in some regions of the north-east after the disappearance of Bangor and Nendrum, and explains the sinister picture which St Malachy gave to St Bernard of the moral state of the diocese of Connor.[2]

Nevertheless, while Ireland was in the throes of her struggle with the invaders she remained in contact with England and the Continent, and some of these contacts did in fact become closer as a result of the new historical circumstances. To understand their nature it is necessary to look back to the eighth century.

During the fifty years which preceded the coming of the Vikings the links between Ireland and Northumbria, so close in the seventh century, seem to have tightened again. They went back originally to the time when the Irish missionaries had played an essential part in the conversion of the north of England.[3] We have seen that they remained very close until the beginning of the eighth century, in spite of the 'Easter controversy'.[4] It would seem that Lindisfarne never lost contact with Ireland. In the second half of the eighth century, Alcuin gives us very

[1] 'They were a people who had renounced their baptism, and they were usually called Northmen, for they had the customs of the Northmen and had been fostered by them, and though the original Northmen were bad to the churches, these were far worse, in whatever part of Erin they used to be' (*Fragm.*, pp. 138–9).

[2] *Vita Malachiae*, 16. This passage has too often been used out of context. It applies only to the diocese of Connor at the time when Malachy took charge of it.

[3] *Vol. I*, pp. 33 sqq.   [4] Id., pp. 36–7.

curious glimpses of the presence of Irishmen in the north of England. Alcuin had an Irish master, Colgu, probably at York where he was brought up. An Irish pupil of Colgu, Joseph, settled with Alcuin on the Continent.[1] Amongst the letters of Alcuin which have come down to us is one addressed to Huigbald, abbot of Lindisfarne, another to Colgu, still another to Joseph,[2] who had remained on the Continent while Alcuin was detained in England in 790 by the accession of Ethelred to the throne of Northumbria.[3] About the same time there lived in a monastery of the north of England connected with Lindisfarne, which may be Craike near York, an Irish painter called Ultán.[4] A poem written at the beginning of the ninth century and dedicated to Egbert, bishop of Lindisfarne, praises him as a great master of illumination.

[1] See p. 29.

[2] Asking him, among other things, to send him colours.

[3] *Mon. Alcuiniana*, pp. 146 sqq. The hypothesis that Alcuin was a pupil of Colgu in Clonmacnois is now completely abandoned. It still remains possible that Colgu, and perhaps Joseph, were members of the community of Clonmacnois before settling in England. They were both alive in 790 when Alcuin wrote to Joseph from England giving him news of his master Colgu. In a slightly later letter, Alcuin speaks of the bad state of Joseph's health. Then, between 791 and 796, in a letter to Remedium, abbot of Chur, appears this sentence : 'Direct prayers, I beseech you, for the soul of Joseph, my disciple.' The Irish data are as follows : the death of 'Colca the Wise' is recorded in *A.F.M.* in 791; that of Colgu Ua Duineachta, lector of Clonmacnois, in 789 (*A.F.M.*) and 795 (*A.U.*); he may be the author of the Scúap Chrábaid (Broom of Devotion), a well-known prayer (Kenney, *Sources*, pp. 725–6); the death of Joseph Ua Cearnaigh, abbot of Clonmacnois, is variedly recorded at 789 (*A.F.M.*), 791, (*A. Clon*), 793 (*A.U.*) and 794 (*A.I.*). There is a possibility that Alcuin's master had been lector at Clonmacnois before settling in York. But, as Joseph seems to have been a pupil of Colgu, he is hardly likely to be the abbot of Clonmacnois who died between 789 and 794 (see Kenney, *Sources*, pp. 534–6).

[4] Kenney, *Sources*, p. 234 (No. 70); *Symeonis Monachi Opera Omnia*, ed. Th. Arnold, I (London, 1882), pp. 265 sqq. and 273 sqq.

> 'E quibus est Ultan praeclaro nomine dictus
> Presbyter iste fuit Scottorum gente beatus,
> Comtis qui potuit notis ornare libellos,
> Atque apicum speciem viritim sic reddit amoenam,
> Hac arte ut nullus possit se aequare modernus
> Scriptor.'

See also pp. XXXII sqq. I am greatly indebted to Professor Dorothy Whitelock for drawing my attention to this text.

In 781, in Parma, Alcuin met Charlemagne who invited him to come to his court to supervise the reorganization of the Imperial scriptoria. Alcuin took with him Joseph and other scribes whom he had known in Northumbria, amongst them a monk of Lindisfarne mentioned in his letter to Huigbald. They introduced on the Continent a script which they had been using in Northumbria and which derived ultimately from Irish script. They were also responsible for spreading the use of some elements of Irish illumination in the Imperial scriptoria and later in 796, when Alcuin settled in Tours, in some of the manuscripts written there.

These purely intellectual connections with the north of England manifest themselves for the last time in the attempt made, according to tradition, by the monks of Lindisfarne to cross over to Ireland at the time of their flight from the Vikings. As we have seen, they were replaced by the very different ties which in the ninth and tenth centuries, united the Scandinavian kingdoms of Dublin and York.

Several of the monasteries founded by the Irish on the Continent kept closely in touch with the mother country, and also with Northumbria, as the most usual way from the north of Ireland to France was probably through the north of England. There are in the Annals entries like that about Aileall, 'abbot of Slane (Meath) and of other churches in France and in Ireland', who died in 824[1] or 825.[2] Perhaps the most important of these monasteries was that of Péronne which contained the tomb of the Irish monk and visionary Fursa and which was almost certainly governed by Irish abbots until its destruction by the Vikings in 880.[3] The neighbouring monasteries of Corbie and St Riquier (Centula) were obviously also in contact with Irish pilgrims coming to the Continent. A letter written from York by Alcuin in 790 is a witness of the contacts between these monasteries and Northumbria, as it is addressed to the abbot of Corbie and includes a message for the abbot of Centula.[4]

Western Europe was dotted with other monasteries whose origin, directly or indirectly, went back to Irish missionaries or pilgrims

[1] *A.U.*   [2] *A.F.M.*
[3] *Vol. I*, pp. 39–40; Traube, *Perrona Scottorum.*   [4] *Mon. Alcuiniana*, p. 172.

Lagny, Luxeuil, Saint-Gall, Echternach, Würzburg, Honau, Bobbio, etc. The Irish pilgrims, on their way to Rome or the Holy Land, used to venerate the relics of St Kilian in Würzburg, of St Gall near Lake Constance, or of St Columbanus at Bobbio in the Appenines. Sometimes they broke their journey for some time or remained the rest of their life in one of these places, and the roads which they frequented were to become a little later the familiar track followed by the refugees fleeing from the Scandinavian terror. They spread throughout Europe the fame of Irish erudition which induced the Carolingian emperors to surround themselves with pupils of Irish masters such as Alcuin, Sedulius Scottus, Clemens Scottus and Scottus Eriugena.

The ninth century was marked by an exodus of scribes and scholars who settled in various parts of the Carolingian Empire, but chiefly in the Palace School which followed the Emperor from place to place. Heiric of Auxerre, perhaps himself the pupil of an Irishman, summed up in the second half of the century the impression made by that exodus on those who saw it from the Continent. Speaking of Ireland, he says: 'Ireland of which almost the whole people, despising the dangers of the sea, migrate, with their crowds of philosophers to our shores. The more learned a man is the more likely is he to sentence himself to exile that he may serve the wishes of our most wise Solomon (Charles-the-Bald)'.[1] Other documents give a slightly different colour to the story. The *Life* of St Findan of Rheinau says that prior to his arrival on the Continent he had been caught by Vikings and taken to Orkney; having escaped he went on a pilgrimage to Rome and stopped on his way back in an island of the Rhine where he became a hermit.[2] The *Life* of St Donatus of Fiesole contains similar adventures: he went on a pilgrimage because of the depredations of 'evil men'; on his return from Rome he became bishop of Fiesole.[3]

---

[1] Heiric of Auxerre, *Vita Germani*, *AA.SS.Boll.*, Jul. VII, col. 221–5.

[2] W. Reeves, 'On the Céli-dé, commonly called Culdees', *Tr.R.I.A.*, 1873, p. 263.

[3] Kenney, *Sources*, p. 602. He may have written there a *Life of St Brigid*. See: M. Esposito, 'On the Earliest Latin Life of St Brigid of Kildare', *P.R.I.A.*, 1912, pp. 307 sqq.

Several of these pilgrims and scholars have left their mark on Carolingian thought. It is so with Dicuil, a monk of Iona who, in 810, instead of shutting himself up behind the walls of Kells with the rest of his community, went to the court of Charlemagne where he wrote his *De Mensura Orbis Terrae*, a compilation from ancient geographers filled out with the kind of curious information on the isles of the northern ocean an Irishman of his time could gather at first hand. At the court he met Clemens Scottus author of a treatise on Grammar, the butt of Alcuin's satirical wit and his successor as the head of the Palace School, who was to end his life at Würzburg.[1]

At the same time, a certain Dungal, an Irish recluse in the Abbey of St Denis, near Paris, wrote several texts which have come down to us; and another Dungal, with whom he has sometimes been confused, acted as a sort of minister for education in Lombardy.

A little later, in 848, at the time when the árd-rí Máelsechlainn sent an embassy to Charles-the-Bald to announce his victory over Turgeis, Sedulius Scottus, who may have come with that embassy, reached the episcopal palace at Liége where a group of Irish people was to find in the bishop a patient and generous patron. In exile Sedulius displayed his various accomplishments, writing poetry in the tone of flippant begging which was in the tradition of Irish poems, and busying himself with theology, philosophy, grammar.[2] Around him gathered a whole colony of Irish poets and scholars who can be identified through a series of manuscripts in which they have left their mark. Some of them were established at Liége, others at St Martin of Cologne which was to remain up to the twelfth century an almost completely Irish monastery. There were scribes and painters among them. Some were set to copy Greek texts, others to transcribe manuscripts brought over by refugees.[3]

The Saint-Gall Priscian, which was in Cologne in the middle of the century arrived probably in the travelling bag of some refugee coming

---

[1] M. Esposito, 'An Irish teacher at the Carolingian Court', *Studies*, 1914, pp. 651–76; Manitius, *Lat. Lit.*, I, pp. 647–53.

[2] Bieler, *Ireland*, pp. 120 sqq.

[3] Kenney, *Sources*, pp. 553 sqq.; Micheli, *Enluminure*, pp. 128–9.

to join Sedulius. And one of the poems added in its margins tells something of the memories these travellers carried with them :

'Bitter is the wind to-night
It tosses the ocean's white hair
To-night I fear not the fierce warriors of Norway
Coursing the Irish Sea.'[1]

About 850, the monastery of Saint-Gall was visited by an Irish bishop, Marcus, who was on his way back from Rome with his nephew Moengal or Marcellus. They decided to remain there, but they had difficulty in separating themselves from their companions who were trying to induce them to return to Ireland.[2] They kept their books with them and these passed after their death into the Abbey Library. The Irish Gospel-book (Saint-Gall Ms. 51) may well have been amongst them.

There was at about the same time another group of Irishmen at the Palace School of Charles-the-Bald gathered around Scottus Eriugena, whose personality towers high above this crowd of scholarly travellers.[3] This is not the place to discuss what his knowledge of Greek may owe to the teaching of the Irish school where he had studied. It is enough for us to note the presence of these Irishmen at the court of the emperor for whom Ms. Latin 2 of the Bibliothèque nationale – the 'Second Bible of Charles-the-Bald' – was copied, a manuscript where the hand of an Irish painter can probably be detected here and there.

This complex and changing setting, ranging from burning monasteries to all the luxury of court life, forms the background of the art of these two chaotic centuries, and the very contradictions and incongruities help to explain the variety of its aspects.

[1] *Thesaur. Paleohib.*, II, p. 290.   [2] J. Duft, in *Irish Min. of St Gall*, pp. 33 sqq.
[3] Bieler, *Ireland*, pp. 126 sqq.

2. Sites and Architecture

In ninth- and tenth-century Ireland (as in the eighth century), the most common types of habitation were the rath and the crannog.[1] Many of the previously occupied sites remained in use. Lagore crannog (Meath), for example, although 'razed to the ground' in 848 was rebuilt and went on being occupied until the tenth century.[2] Other establishments which do not go back to a period earlier than the ninth century have also been excavated. One of them is the rath of Lissue, excavated in 1946 by Gerhard Bersu.[3] In it were found fragments of pottery, fairly well preserved wooden vessels and a stone tablet covered on both sides with sketches (Pl. 57).

One of the most important excavated sites for this period is Crannog No. 1 at Ballinderry (Westmeath),[4] an artificial island built close to the shore of a lake now dried up. It has yielded some remarkable objects: a sword whose blade carries the mark of a German workshop and which probably belonged to a Viking, a yew-wood gaming-board (Pl. 15) and a bronze lamp with enamelled handles (Fig. 14). It is unfortunately impossible to establish a clear relation between these objects and the buildings on the artificial island. The gaming-board and the lamp were discovered in the muddy ground outside the crannog, as if they had been discarded by being thrown in the water, while the sword was found prior to the excavations, during drainage operations. The crannog was built according to the usual method: alternate layers of brushwood and peat, about one hundred feet in diameter were piled up on the lake bed and held in place by a stockade of strong posts stuck vertically in the

---

[1] *Vol. I*, p. 4.   [2] Id., pp. 76–7; Hencken, *Lagore.*
[3] G. Bersu, 'The Rath in Townland Lissue, Co. Antrim', *U.J.A.*, 1947, pp. 30 sqq.
[4] H. O'Neill Hencken, 'Ballinderry Crannog No. 1', *P.R.I.A.*, 1936 (C), pp. 103 sqq.

ground and reinforced with planks. Nothing was left of the walls of the houses which had been erected on this platform, and this makes it difficult to ascertain their size and plan. An area about thirty to thirty-five feet wide which at the time of the excavation was described as a 'hearth', is more likely to have been the floor of a hut. It was established over a substratum of beams and all the surface was covered with ash which had piled up gradually as happens in habitations of that time when the hearth is not clearly defined by erect slabs. This house seems to have been in use throughout the occupation of the crannog. The remaining part of the surface of the crannog was covered by a layer of wattles. At some time there was a subsidence in the crannog; new material was then piled up and two smaller houses were built on it. The tenth century seems to be the chief period of habitation, but there was a sporadic occupation up to the sixteenth century. Beside the objects enumerated above, some wooden vessels similar to those found at Lissue have been discovered there as well as some Viking objects and a few gilt bronze and silver pins.

We have seen that beside these traditional types of habitation some towns were developing which were either monastic cities or Scandinavian trading establishments. It is not easy to conjure up their appearance out of the few data given by the texts combined with a critical study of whatever traces they have left on the ground and the conclusions reached thus are of necessity in the nature of hypotheses.

The Scandinavian towns, Dublin, Limerick, Cork, Waterford, Wexford, have suffered from the fact that they have all continued as cities up to our own time, the modern houses covering up the traces of the Viking settlements.

Dublin (Figs. 3,4) is probably the only one which repays study. The modern town and its harbour are built on both sides of the estuary of the Liffey, now a narrow river confined between the straight walls of its quays, tidal for a mile and a half. In older times the tidal river was certainly much wider especially at its meeting with the tributaries on the south side, the Poddle and the Camack. The erratic course of the Poddle, which nowadays runs below the streets has been carefully studied.[1] Coming from the south and meeting the long low hill which bordered the Liffey, it spread out in a vast marsh with a few islands of higher ground. Then, at the eastern end of the hill, it joined the Liffey, the confluence probably forming a small natural harbour. This harbour and the marsh were referred to as the Black Pool (Dubh Linn). The hill is one of the boulder clay moraines left by prehistoric glaciers which are so common in the central Irish plain. As they drain easily they were favourite sites for raths in the early Middle Ages. This was probably the case here, and the eastern end of the hill seems to have been the site of an establishment combining the characteristics of rath and crannog as it was threatened with infiltrations of water at the spring tides. To overcome that disadvantage, its floor was probably covered with mats of wattle similar to those which covered the platform of the Ballinderry crannog. Nearby, a ford (ath) made it possible to cross the river at low tide on the way towards Tara and Armagh. The name of the place – 'Ath cliath, the ford of the wattles' – may derive either from the structure of the rath or from the presence of wattles in the ford itself.

There was, on one of the islands in the marsh of the Poddle, below the hill, a small monastery which took its name from the Black Pool. Very little is known about it, though it figures twice in the Annals of the Four Masters. In 650 they relate the death of St Bearaidh, abbot of Dubhlinn; in 785 that of another abbot, Siadhal.[2] One of the churches of the monastery was probably on the very site where a dedication to St Patrick has survived to our own day in the thirteenth-century cathdral. The present building stands only a few feet from the subterranean course of the Poddle, but the original lay-out of the ground is well

[1] M. V. Ronan, 'The Poddle River and its Branches', *J.R.S.A.I.*, 1927, pp. 39 sqq., and *J.R.S.A.I.*, 1948, pp. 5 sqq.; J. Warburton, J. Whitelaw, R. Walsh, *History of the City of Dublin* (London, 1818), p. 1077. On problems connected with the ancient topography of Dublin, see also: C. Litton Falkiner, *Illustrations of Irish History and Topography* (London–New York, 1904); M. V. Ronan, *Dublin* (Dublin, 1953); G. Little, *Dublin before the Vikings* (Dublin, 1957). I have been greatly helped in these researches by Seán Nolan, of the Ordnance Survey of Ireland, whom I want to thank here.

[2] 650: 'St Bearaidh, abb. of Duibhlinn d.'; 785 (*recte*, 790) : 'Siadhal, Abbot of Duibhlinn, died.'

defined by a twelfth-century text which mentions 'Ecclesia s. Patricii de Insula – the church of St Patrick of the Island'.[1] Another neighbouring church, whose Norman name was St Michael le Pole, was dedicated not to the archangel but to Mac Tháil, a sixth-century saint, so that it also could be a very old foundation.[2] Both churches probably belonged to the monastery in the island of the Poddle and were no doubt re-erected in the eleventh century, after a century and a half of Viking occupation. It is possible that some carved stone slabs which have been found on various occasions near St Patrick's cathedral may be all that remains of the early foundation.[3]

Some distance upstream (Fig. 3), still on the south bank of the Liffey, there was another small monastery at Cill Maighnenn (Kilmainham) also going back to the sixth century. The death of a 'sage' belonging to it is recorded at the end of the eighth century, but nothing more.[4] Its site is marked by the shaft of a curious stone cross. Farther to the south-west, still to the south of the Liffey, stood the monastery of Clondalkin, and, near the spring of the Poddle, that of Tallaght, founded at the end of the eighth century by Máelrúan, which, around 800, together with its twin monastery of Finglas, had been a great centre of spiritual and ascetic activity. We have seen[5] that the latter, which was about two miles north of the Liffey, disappeared shortly after 865. The imposing plain stone cross there may then date back to the end of the eighth or the first half of the ninth century. Farther to the north-east, at Swords, there was a Columban monastery of considerable importance.

It is in this diffuse pattern made up of different types of establishments that the Scandinavian colony of Dublin took its place. In 836 the

[1] In 1179; see Little, *Dublin*, p. 111 and T. Drew, 'Surroundings of the cathedral Church of St Patrick de Insula', *J.R.S.A.I.*, 1890–1, pp. 426 sqq., 1899, pp. 1 sqq.

[2] Cf. *A.F.M.*, 937 : 'The Foreigners deserted Ath Cliath by the help of God and Mac Tháil' (see footnote *y*).

[3] M. V. Ronan, 'Cross in circle stones of St Patrick's Cathedral', *J.R.S.A.I.*, 1941, pp. 1 sqq, also : J. Drew in *J.R.S.A.I.*, 1901, pp. 293 sqq., and 296; Little, *Dublin*, pl. p. 112.

[4] *A.U.*, 786 : 'Fidhcain, a wise man of Cill-Maghnenn (died)'; *A.F.M.*, 782 (*recte* 787) : 'Learghus Ua Fidhchain, a wise man of Cill-Maighnenn (died)'.

[5] P. 24.

Four Masters say that 'Ath cliath was taken for the first time' by the Norwegians. In 840, the Annals announce that the 'Foreigners' are building a fort at Dubhlinn.[1] This fort probably superseded the Irish settlement of Ath cliath, but may have covered from the start a much wider portion of the promontory. It was already a walled city and it is probable that, at that time or shortly afterwards, it occupied the same area as the medieval city which was enclosed in fortifications of which some much re-built and restored fragments still subsist below the church of St Audoen and along Lamb Alley (Fig. 4).[2] It stretched from there as far as the place where the east wing of the castle was erected in the thirteenth century, that is to say on a length of about 660 yards and a width of 330 yards.

This has always been known as the site of the old city, but what was hitherto only vague hypothesis has now been confirmed by excavations. These have been made at two points : in 1961–2, Marcus Ó hEochaidhe excavated for the National Monuments Branch of the Office of Public Works the ground below the east wing of the Castle,[3] while in 1962–3 Brendan Ó Ríordáin explored a patch of cleared ground to the south-west of Christ Church. In the Castle a great number of superimposed layers of habitation dated from a period prior to the construction of the stone fortress of the thirteenth century. The top layers were made of the remains of houses built of boards and beams whose clay hearths were sometimes lined with stones. They had been re-built three times after successive destructions. Below that were found at least four layers of debris of houses whose floors were covered with wattle mats.

The other excavated site, at the corner of High Street and Nicholas Street, has yielded the ruins of houses whose walls were built of wattle and which probably belong to the eleventh and twelfth centuries, perhaps even to the late tenth. Underneath was an earlier layer which contained a few Scandinavian objects, amongst them a spear-head of a

---

[1] 'Another fortress (was erected) by them (the Foreigners) at Dubhlinn, out of which they plundered Leinster and the Ui-Neill, both territory and churches as far as Sliabh Bladhma (Slieve Bloom)' (*A.F.M.*, 840).

[2] D. A. Chart, *The Story of Dublin* (London, 1932), p. 226.

[3] This wing was being reconstructed at the time.

typical shape and a lead weight decorated with a gold stud. This layer lay directly on the boulder clay, so that it seems that the Irish eighth-century settlement did not spread this far.

From these excavations,[1] which may still have surprises in store for us, one can begin to get some idea of the appearance of the town in the first centuries of its existence : a city of elongated shape, more than 600 yards long, watching over its harbour from the top of a promontory surrounded by water on three sides. It probably consisted chiefly of houses built of planks like those in Scandinavia, crowded along narrow streets. We do not so far know anything of the wall which surrounded them, nor of the habitation of the kings of Dublin which is also likely to have been built of wood, nor of the wharves where the goods brought from the four corners of the world were piled up.

A complement to our knowledge of the city and its inhabitants is supplied by the Viking tombs discovered from time to time about a mile up stream near Kilmainham, which seems to have been the burial place of the citizens of the new town.[2] The first discoveries were made by chance about the middle of the nineteenth century, and there is unfortunately no record of the way in which the objects were associated in the tombs. Around 1933 however, other tombs came to light and three of them which were systematically excavated gave some more precise data. The men were buried with iron swords whose decorated pommels have parallels in the Viking cemeteries of Norway and with other weapons such as spears, daggers and axes. The women's graves have yielded pairs of those 'tortoise-brooches' which were an essential element of the costume of Norwegian women of that time. But there were also some Irish objects, penannular brooches, fragments of gilt bronze ornaments mounted as brooches, etc. The most striking is a series of lead weights, each bearing on top a piece of glass or of Irish metalwork, which were found with a pair of scales.[3] For all of these there are close analogies in Scandinavian graves. Judging from the

[1] They have not been published yet, and I am very grateful to the excavators for putting their results at my disposal, and showing me their work in progress.

[2] *V. Ant.*, III, pp. 11 sqq.

[3] Coffey, *Guide*, p. 90.

objects which can be easily dated, such as swords and tortoise-brooches, the Kilmainham graveyard must have been in use from the middle of the ninth century to the tenth, that is to say for the greater part of the time when the city was officially pagan. One of the most striking objects, perhaps dating from the tenth century, is a little gilt-bronze animal which was part of one of those metal weather-vanes which hung from the tops of the masts of the Viking long ships.[1]

Some of the monastic cities were at least as large as this Viking emporium but, as might be expected, they developed on a different pattern. We have seen that many had their origin in small hermitages and had grown gradually into large settlements as crowds of students arrived in the seventh century. The original establishments had then to be remodelled in order to fit the new conditions, and in some cases had to be moved to new and more convenient sites. In the course of the eighth century many of the monasteries tended to become 'cities' with a lay village attached to and serving the ecclesiastical settlement. When in 806–10 the centre of the Columban order was moved to Kells, we are told of the building of the 'nova civitas – the new city'.

Kells and Armagh were both metropolises, Armagh tending to become the head of all the Irish monasteries and Kells governing the order founded by St Columba, both in Ireland and, for a time, also in Scotland. It was to be expected that they would grow to an unparalleled size far out-distancing other contemporary abbeys, even when these had schools and lodgings for the students attending them. Both have remained inhabited to our day and the buildings of the modern towns hamper to a great extent efforts at reconstructing their appearance in the early Middle Ages. It is however possible to get some idea of it by using the Annals, together with old maps and, in the case of Armagh, there are additionally some traditions collected in the middle of the nineteenth century by Reeves.[2]

Armagh – Ard Macha – succeeded Emain Macha, the capital of

[1] A. Mahr, *Ancient Irish Handicraft* (Limerick, 1939), Pl. 24, 10.
[2] J. Stuart, *Historical Memoirs of the City of Armagh* (Newry, 1819); W. Reeves, *The Ancient Churches of Armagh* (Lusk, 1860).

Ulster which plays such an important part in the Táin Bó Cúailgne. This was probably, like Tara, a sanctuary and place of assembly in pagan times, and its ruins (Navan Fort) are still to be seen two or three miles to the west of Armagh.[1] Its name and that of Armagh, 'the Hill of Macha', derive from that of a legendary figure. Thus the religious centre which prided itself on its foundation by St Patrick was also heir to an earlier fame. The town of Armagh is built in very hilly country, and to this day greets the visitor with the sight of two steep hills topped with clusters of trees and church spires : one, to the south, bearing the old cathedral which now belongs to the Church of Ireland and the other, to the north, carrying the modern Catholic cathedral. Both hills have their place in the legend of St Patrick, but the southern was the centre of the old monastic city (Fig. 2). In spite of the silting which must have affected the lower parts of the town, the steepness of its slopes remains. They rise to a flat terrace about 270 yards wide obviously corresponding to the central enclosure which contained the chief ecclesiastical buildings. This was circumscribed by a rampart perhaps surviving from the prehistoric fort in which the first monks of Armagh had settled. In the middle of the terrace stands the thirteenth-century cathedral built on the site of an earlier church. This hill-top enclosure is referred to as 'the Rath' in the numerous annals which from the ninth to the twelfth century allude to the topography of Armagh.

Of all these texts, those describing the fire of 1020 give the most complete description of the city. The Four Masters say : 'Ard Macha was burned with all the fort, without the saving of any house within it, except the Library (teach screaptra) only, and many houses were burned in the trians; and the Daimhliag-mor was burned, and the Cloictheach, with its bells; and Daimhliag-na-Toe, and Daimhliag an-t-Sabhaill; and the old preaching chair, and the chariot of the abbots, and their books in the houses of the students, with much gold, silver and other precious things.' The more cursory text of the Annals of Ulster for the same year manages however to give an interesting detail : 'Ard-Macha was all burned, viz., the great "Damliac", with its roof of

---

[1] Navan Fort has been excavated since 1964 by D. Watermann and P. Collins. No report has appeared so far.

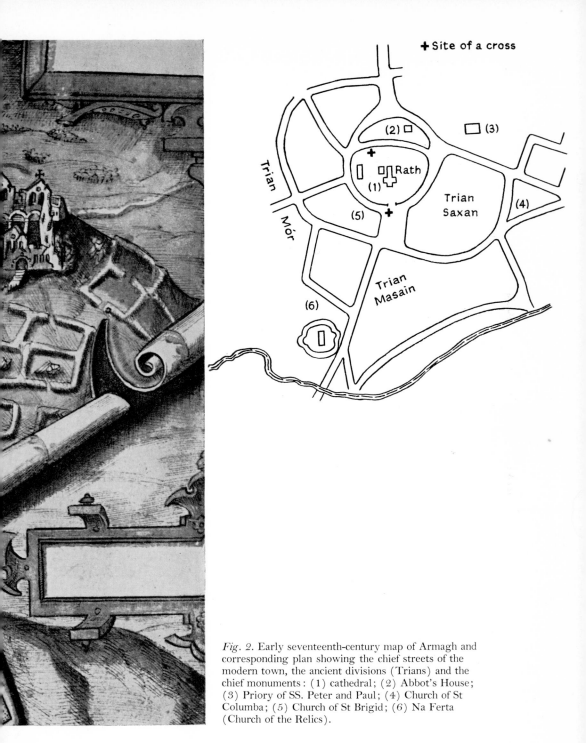

+ Site of a cross

Trian Mór

(2) □

□ (3)

□
□∩ Rath
(1) ⊕

Trian
Saxan

(4)

(5) +

Trian
Masáin

(6)

□

Fig. 2. Early seventeenth-century map of Armagh and corresponding plan showing the chief streets of the modern town, the ancient divisions (Trians) and the chief monuments: (1) cathedral; (2) Abbot's House; (3) Priory of SS. Peter and Paul; (4) Church of St Columba; (5) Church of St Brigid; (6) Na Ferta (Church of the Relics).

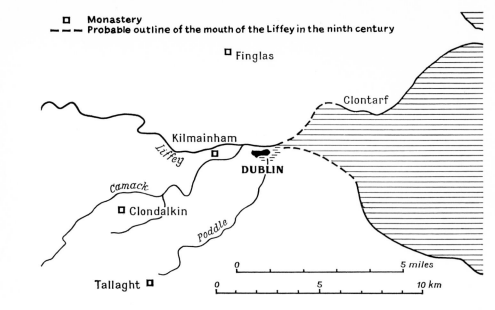

Monastery
Probable outline of the mouth of the Liffey in the ninth century

Finglas

Clontarf

Kilmainham

Liffey

DUBLIN

Camack

Clondalkin

Poddle

0   5 miles

0   5   10 km

Tallaght

Fig. 3. Surroundings of Dublin in the ninth century.

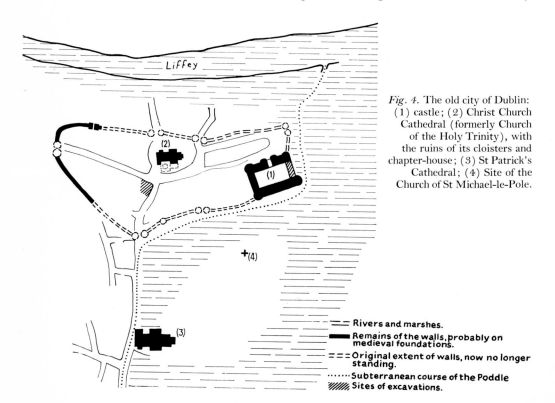

Liffey

(2)

(1)

+(4)

(3)

Fig. 4. The old city of Dublin:
(1) castle; (2) Christ Church
Cathedral (formerly Church
of the Holy Trinity), with
the ruins of its cloisters and
chapter-house; (3) St Patrick's
Cathedral; (4) Site of the
Church of St Michael-le-Pole.

Rivers and marshes.
Remains of the walls, probably on medieval foundations.
Original extent of walls, now no longer standing.
Subterranean course of the Poddle
Sites of excavations.

lead,[1] and the bell-house with its bells, and the Saball, and the Toi, and the abbots' chariot, and the old preaching chair.'

Thus, within the walls of the Rath, there was a large stone church (Daimliag mór) which is mentioned already in the second half of the eighth century and which probably stood on part of the space covered by the nave of the present cathedral. Nearby stood a round tower (cloictech) in which hung several bells. There were also inside the Rath two other churches which are referred to in 1020 as being built of stone but which may have been wooden structures a short while before: the Sabhall (barn) and the Toi. They may be the 'wooden oratories' (dertech) mentioned in the description of the attacks on Armagh in 839.[2] From the texts dealing with the 1020 fire one gathers that there were other wooden buildings in the Rath, and amongst them the Library (house of the manuscripts) where the Book of Armagh was probably kept at that time. If we try to relate these data with the objects shown in a perspective map of Armagh drawn at the very beginning of the seventeenth century by Richard Bartlett and now kept in the National Library of Ireland (Fig. 2),[3] we may identify the Sabhall with one of the buildings to the south of the cathedral. The Toi is figured very nearly in the position which Reeves had suggested for it: parallel to the nave and abutting on the south transept. Near the rath there seems to have been another enclosure (lis) in which was the abbot's house. It is mentioned in the Annals of Ulster in 832 (Foruth na Abbadh), in 915 (Lis nAbbadh) and in 1116 (Teach nAbbadh mór). There again Reeves had placed it correctly though nothing remains at present of the building or its enclosure. The Abbot's house is shown on Bartlett's map as an imposing building somewhat behind the Rath, perhaps Romanesque in style and surrounded by thatched huts. The other large construction indicated by Bartlett to the north of the cathedral is obviously the Priory of SS. Peter and Paul, but since this was established in the twelfth century it will not be considered in this volume.

[1] The lead roof had been put on the church only a few years earlier: *A.U.*, 1008 (*recte* 1009): 'The "oratorium" of Ard Macha was roofed with lead in this year.'

[2] *A.U.*, 839; *A.F.M.*, 839.

[3] G. A. Hayes McCoy, *Ulster and other Irish maps* (Dublin, 1964).

Below the Rath – the essentially ecclesiastical part of the city – were the 'Trians' or 'thirds' where the students probably lived and which also housed the craftsmen and tradesmen connected with the monastery. The areas occupied by each of them can be determined more or less from the Annals and from some data gathered at the end of the eighteenth century. The Trian mór (great third) is mentioned already in 1009.[1] so that it can be accepted that at that time the two other thirds, Trian Masain and Trian Saxan, were already in existence. Trian Saxan (the Saxon third) is mentioned in fact as early as 1091 in the Annals of Ulster. The main gate of the Rath was below the apse of the present cathedral, to the east of the rampart. South of this gate as far as St Brigid's church and above the oldest foundation of St Patrick – the Church of the Relics (Na Ferta) – the houses of Trian Masain were huddled in a few streets. North of the gate, at least as far as St Columba's church, extended Trian Saxan whose name survives in that of the street circumscribing this part of the town: English street. Trian mór lay to the south of the Rath. The Annals of Ulster give a series of landmarks based on the positions of various crosses: they mention a cross at the gate of the Rath, those of St Columba, of bishop Eogan, of Sechnall, and the crosses of St Brigid.[2] Some of these crosses mentioned in the twelfth century may have been late, but two of them, which can still be examined: the fragment to the south of the cathedral (cross of Sechnall?) and the cross which was originally at the gate of the Rath, and which is now in the cathedral, belong stylistically to the ninth century or the beginning of the tenth.[3]

It is extremely difficult to estimate the population of such a town. When, in 868, Olav Huite plundered Armagh, the Annals of Ulster speak of a thousand people killed and taken captive and yet one does not get the impression that this was the whole population of the city. In 894 or 895, seven hundred and ten people were again taken prisoner in the town,[4] so that one must not be afraid of exaggerating in estimating a minimum of 3000 or 4000 inhabitants as the ninth-century

[1] *A.U.*, 1008 (*recte* 1009); 'the Trians' are mentioned in 1020 (*A.F.M.*); see p. 40.

[2] *A.U.*, 1166.　　　　[3] See pp. 136 and 154.　　　　[4] *A.U.*, 894 (*recte* 895).

population. In the twelfth century it is likely to have been more numerous.

The size and lay-out of Kells are so similar that one may wonder if they were not the result of a deliberate imitation of St Patrick's city. There also old ramparts on the top of the hill were adapted to the needs of the 'nova civitas' when it was erected between 806 and 810. The present-day churchyard in which stand the ruins of the medieval church, three carved crosses, and a round tower, obviously occupies only a part of the old enclosure, which has not left such definite traces as in the case of Armagh and through which run two modern streets, Cannon Street and Church Lane. As it is likely to have occupied the top of the hill whose highest point is somewhere to the west of 'St Columba's House', it was probably about 350 yards across.[1] There also the secular town seems to have been to the east of the ecclesiastical enclosure. Its extent in the twelfth century is known, as Hugh de Lacy, after the Norman conquest, surrounded it with walls whose position can be roughly ascertained[2] and which obviously took in only the area built up at the time. This area was about the same size as in Armagh and it may well be that it corresponded with limits already fixed at the time of the foundation of the town in the ninth century.

These two cities were of course of quite unusual importance and it would be wrong to imagine that all the great Irish monasteries were on the same scale. Many, probably most, had a more rustic appearance and a more scattered lay-out. Of some one knows nothing. It is nearly impossible, for example, to estimate the space covered in the tenth century by the monastery of Clonmacnois. It certainly extended over a very much wider area than that of the present cemetery, but this is all that can be said. One of the Irish triads, however, gives a hint as to its appearance when it lists 'the three great collections of stone buildings in Ireland, Armagh, Clonmacnois, Kildare'.[3]

[1] As a point of comparison to this 315 m by 315 m, the city of Rouen in the tenth century was about 430 m by 300 m (*Revue de Normandie*, 1864, p. 66).

[2] R. C. Simington, 'Valuation of Kells (1663) with Note on Map drawn by Robert Johnston', *An. Hib.*, 1960, pp. 233 sqq. Hugh de Lacy's walls may well have been only a stronger version of fortifications already in existence.

[3] 'Tri clochraid Hérenn'; Kuno Meyer, *The Triads of Ireland* (Dublin, 1906), triad 34; the triads are considered, on linguistic grounds, to date to around 850–900.

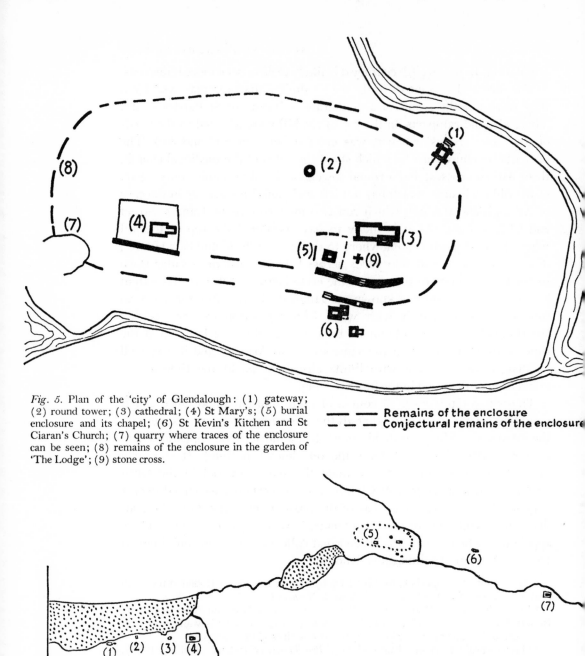

Fig. 5. Plan of the 'city' of Glendalough: (1) gateway; (2) round tower; (3) cathedral; (4) St Mary's; (5) burial enclosure and its chapel; (6) St Kevin's Kitchen and St Ciaran's Church; (7) quarry where traces of the enclosure can be seen; (8) remains of the enclosure in the garden of 'The Lodge'; (9) stone cross.

——— Remains of the enclosure
– – – Conjectural remains of the enclosure

Fig. 6. Plan of the valley of Glendalough: (1) Temple-na-Skellig (church and huts); (2) 'St Kevin's Bed' (hermitage-cave); (3) ruin of a hut; (4) Reefert (church and graveyard); (5) The 'city' with the Round Tower, the cathedral and the churches of St Mary, St Kevin and St Ciaran; (6) Trinity Church; (7) St Saviour's Priory.

In the case of Glendalough, one may venture some suggestions as to the situation and size of the monastic enclosure (Fig. 5). The primitive foundation which was on the steep edge of the upper lake had been transferred in the beginning of the eighth century to a wider stretch of ground.[1] This is a sort of little plateau forming a promontory at the meeting of two streams which surround it on the north, east and south. To the south-west, the lower lake, larger at that time than it is now, stretched as far as the edge of the plateau. To the north-west, the ground rose suddenly towards the mountain side. The piece of ground thus delimited is about 270 yards long and it was probably partly enclosed by a stone wall and partly by wattle fences and earthen banks. The entrance was by a stone-built gate-house which still stands. As its arches are very similar to the chancel arches of two of the Glendalough churches, Reefert and Trinity church, which probably date back to the tenth century or the beginning of the eleventh, the gate may be considered as of the same date. The rampart in which it was inserted probably had, in some places at any rate, two parallel walls. The present cemetery, in which are the ruins of the cathedral and of a small church, a round tower and an undecorated granite cross, no doubt occupies only a small part of the original enclosure. The two parallel walls can be seen clearly to the south, above the small building called 'St Kevin's Kitchen' and one of them, farther west, forms part of the enclosing wall of St Mary's. Elsewhere, their course is marked only by a slight rise in a field and in the garden of 'The Lodge'. All the ground to the west of the present graveyard and to the north of St Mary's was probably occupied by various wooden buildings. This represents the equivalent of the ecclesiastical enclosure in Armagh and Kells. Was there also a lay town? It is not impossible, as some indications would suggest, that there was a village to the north of the enclosure beyond the stream.[2] It has also to be remembered that in Glendalough there were several groups of habitations scattered through the valley, which are still marked by the ruins of various churches (Fig. 6).

[1] Liam Price, 'St Kevin's Road', *F.-S. MacNeill*, pp. 244 sqq.
[2] L. Price, 'Rock Basins or "Bullauns" at Glendalough and Elsewhere', *J.R.S.A.I*, 1959, pp. 161 sqq.

Nendrum, which for convenience's sake has been studied in the first volume,[1] although it continued to be occupied until the end of the tenth century, can give some idea of the appearance of the smaller monasteries. We have seen that a round tower and a stone church with antae were probably erected after the first attack by the Vikings at the beginning of the ninth century and the stone plaques found in the 'school' date probably from the ninth and tenth centuries.

Very little is known of the non-ecclesiastical architecture of the time as nothing remains to indicate what houses or palaces looked like. The only important surviving monument is the Glendalough gate, which does not properly speaking belong to ecclesiastical architecture. In its present state it appears as a quadrangular stone building opening widely in two rounded arches and buttressed by antae on the outside. Originally it had two storeys. The upper is known to have still existed in 1795, and the corbels of the floor can be seen in the surviving walls.[2]

Nothing could be deduced about the appearance of the walls of Armagh from the scribbles which represent them in Bartlett's map. They had probably been already knocked down when he drew his plan, which shows the town in ruins after a period of war.

All that we know of Brian Boru's constructions is what the author of the *War* tells us about them: 'By him were made bridges and causeways and high roads. By him were strengthened also the duns and islands and celebrated royal forts of Mumhain (Munster). He built also the fortifications of Cashel of the kings' and of many other cities.[3]

The ecclesiastical architecture[4] in this period, is in every way the

[1] *Vol. I*, pp. 79 sqq.

[2] R. Cochrane, *Glendalough, Co. Wicklow* (Extr. from the 80th report of the Commissioners of Public Works in Ireland; Dublin, 1911–12); H. G. Leask, *Glendalough, Co. Wicklow* (Dublin, no date). The idea that there was a round tower above the gate is based on a misinterpretation of an eighteenth-century drawing which shows the round tower *behind* the gate in a slightly warped perspective; see: M. V. Ronan, *Glendalough and its ruins* (Enniscorthy, 1962), p. 17, Fig. 1.

[3] *War*, pp. 140–1.

[4] On the ecclesiastical architecture, see: George Petrie, *The Ecclesiastical Architecture of Ireland anterior to the Norman Invasions* (Dublin, 1845); Dunraven, *Notes on Irish Architecture* (London, 1875, 1877, ed. by M. Stokes); A. Champneys,

continuation of what we have seen at the end of the eighth century.[1] There were certainly still wooden churches (durthech). They are frequently mentioned in the Annals. One of the Fragments copied by Mac Firbis shows us Queen Flanna, Flann Sinna's mother, when she was getting a church erected in St Brigid's monastery at Kildare, having 'many tradesmen in the wood felling and cutting timber'.[2] Though they could have been merely cutting beams for the roof, one may assume that they were preparing timbers for a wooden building.

The stone churches (daimliag) were mostly rectangular buildings with antae at both ends, similar to the cathedral built at Glendalough towards the end of the eighth century. In the beginning of the tenth century, Flann Sinna and Abbot Colman built a stone church at Clonmacnois.[3] This was probably on the site of the present cathedral but only its foundations survive below the more recent walls which follow the same plan. It was a large rectangular church with antae, almost as wide as the cathedral of Glendalough but much longer (about 66 by 24 feet), in front of which stands the cross of the Scriptures also probably erected by Flann and Colman.

The *War* mentions churches erected by Brian Boru at Killaloe and Inis Cealtra as well as the tower at Tuamgreiney.[4] In this last case the evidence is confirmed by the obit, in the Chronicon Scottorum, of Cormac Ua Cillín, abbot of Clonmacnois, of Roscommon and of Tuamgreiney, 'by whom the great church at Tuamgreiney and its cloictech were constructed'.[5] Abbot Cormac died in 964, so that it was prior to the death of Mahon that Brian contributed to the erection of the tower. It has vanished now, but the western front of the church remains practically intact showing that traditional arrangement of antae and rectangular doorway which we have met already.[6] The church of St Caimin erected by Brian in Inis Cealtra has been modified by the insertion of a choir and a later doorway, but the walls, with the antae,

---

Irish Ecclesiastical Architecture (London, 1910); H. G. Leask, *Irish Churches and Monastic Buildings*, I (Dundalk, 1955).

[1] *Vol. I.*, pp. 84 sqq.
[2] *Fragm.*, pp. 178–9.
[3] See text p. 12, note 5.
[4] *War*, pp. 138–9, 140–1.
[5] *Chr. Sc.*, 964.
[6] Leask, *Ir. Churches*, I, p. 69.

probably go back to the time when Marcan, brother of Mahon and Brian, was abbot of Killaloe and Inis Cealtra[1] (Pl. 4).

Other churches devoid of antae, whose rectangular doors have a sort of frame in relief, probably go back to the late tenth or early eleventh century. There is one at Aghowle (Wicklow), which has kept three of its walls almost intact (Pl. 5). Its door (Pl. 6) is framed by a thick moulding in high relief. Inside, it has a relieving arch above a blank tympanum. The church at Banagher (Derry) has a door of exactly the same type.[2] There is another at Maghera (Derry) which is of the same general shape, but is covered with an elaborate carved decoration.[3] This may be slightly later than the others and perhaps belongs to the eleventh century.

Beside these plans which still follow the extremely simple scheme of eighth-century architecture there seem to have been others which show a tendency towards setting the choir apart. Two churches at Glendalough, Reefert and Trinity,[4] belong to this new type. They are both outside the city itself, Trinity somewhat farther down the valley, Reefert near the upper lake. In size they are nearly identical, roughly 29 feet long by $17\frac{1}{2}$ feet wide. In both cases, the choir opens onto the nave with a large chancel arch with granite coping-stones (Pls. 10 and 11). These churches have no antae, perhaps because those of the east wall would have been difficult to fit in with the choir, but instead they have stone corbels which obviously played the same part in supporting the end beams of the roof. Reefert was buried under a mass of debris until the nineteenth century when it was excavated at the suggestion of Sir William Wilde.[5] The arch was then re-built, but with the original coping-stones, so that its reconstruction is perfectly satisfactory. The same cannot be said of the door of the church where some stones have obviously not been put back in their proper order. As for Trinity, it was

[1] *A.U.*, 1009: 'Marcan, son of Cennetigh, comarb of Colum son of Crimthann (Terryglass) and of Inis Celtra, and Cill-Dalua (Killaloe) ..."fell asleep" in Christ.'
[2] Henry, *Sc. irl.*, Pl. 111, 3.   [3] This doorway will be studied in *Vol. III*.
[4] R. Cochrane, *Glendalough, Co. Wicklow* (Dublin, 1911–2), H. G. Leask, *Glendalough, Co. Wicklow* (Dublin, 1951).
[5] Sir William Wilde, *Memoir of Gabriel Beranger in his labours in the cause of Irish Art and Antiquities from 1760 to 1780* (Dublin, 1880), p. 125.

greatly modified by the addition of a round tower at its western end, now collapsed. The alteration manifestly took place a good while after the building of the church and was carried out in a masonry of different type, and anyway these round towers incorporated into churches date generally from the twelfth century, so that one must conclude that the church itself was built well before 1100. A date in the tenth century is the most likely. One of the windows of the choir has a triangular head, a shape which occurs often in windows of round towers, in particular on that at Monasterboice (Pl. 2) which was burned in the late eleventh century and had probably been built a good while earlier. It is noticeable also that the two-band frame of the Monasterboice doorway is nearly identical with that of the door of Reefert.

Round towers built in stone stood beside many of these churches (Pls. 2, 3 and 7). They present one of the strangest problems in the history of Irish architecture. Though the question of their purpose is now solved, several other points connected with their erection will have to be examined. George Petrie, over a century ago, showed that they must be identified with the 'cloictech – house of bells', which often figures in the Annals, always in connection with a monastery.[1] At the beginning of the nineteenth century nearly a hundred of them were still standing, about half of which have now disappeared.[2] Before discussing other matters, it is necessary to review what is known of their structure.

Those which are still nearly complete – ten or so – are usually 33 to 40 yards high. They are about 5½ yards in diameter and their walls are 3 to 4 feet thick. These last measurements are approximate, as the tower tapers towards the top and the thickness of the walls decreases. Most of those whose walls have been cleared down to the base are found to have a plinth at the bottom about 3 feet high on the outside, or even several plinths forming a series of steps. The conical roof seems always to have been made of stone.

[1] Petrie, *Round Towers* (1845).
[2] Margaret Stokes has given in her *Early Christian Architecture of Ireland* (Dublin, 1878), a very useful survey of round towers and of the texts concerning them (pp. 52 sqq., and the tables inserted between pp. 150 and 151).

One of the most striking features of these towers is the fact that the door opens a few yards above the ground. The tower on Scattery Island may be an exception, though the walls not being cleared to the base may account for the door seeming to be at ground level. This is certainly the case at Castledermot where the door is level with the floor of the modern church which has been built beside it, but stands probably a yard or two above the original ground level. The door of Lusk round tower (Dublin) is 2 yards above the ground. Elsewhere distances vary between 3 and 6 yards. The tower was divided inside by wooden floors, normally five, six or seven, connected by ladders. Each storey had a window differently oriented from those of the other storeys with a sill about two feet above the floor. The storey immediately under the roof usually has four openings facing more or less the four cardinal points. These windows are very narrow, with a triangular head or a lintel and in a few cases with a rounded arch. The floors are supported in various ways, either by a continuous cornice in the masonry or by beams inserted into sockets or laid on corbels. There are only two examples of stone floors and it is likely that in most cases beams and planks were used. There seem to have been double doors, one on the inside and the other on the outside of the opening. The doorway is sometimes rectangular but more often ends in a circular arch frequently with a slightly raised border. Where the remains of the church have survived, the tower generally stands about 7 to 8 yards from its western front, to the north-west or south-east, the door of the tower opening towards the church.

These towers, as their name shows, were meant for housing bells. The Irish, however, like all pre-Romanesque bells, were small.[1] The most usual type made of beaten iron is hardly more than 4 to 6 inches high. Such bells are shown on carvings like that at Killadeas (Pl. 9) as hand-bells. There are also a few bells of cast bronze which reach up to a foot in height. Even these would hardly produce much volume of sound. Therefore the bells were either rung by hand from each of the openings of the top storey in succession, or, as Margaret Stokes

[1] M. Stokes, op. cit., and *Early Christian Art in Ireland* (3rd ed., Dublin, 1928), pp. 49 sqq.

has suggested on the analogy of representations in Continental carvings and illuminations, they were hung from a horizontal beam and sounded with a hammer. It is necessary to point out, however, that, contrary to a widespread belief, the Irish bells had tongues and consequently would seem to have been made to be sounded either by hand or the pull of a rope. In any case the sound would hardly carry very far, and the analogy is more with a muezzin's cry shrilling out of a minaret than with the peal of bells which roll down over the countryside from a modern church tower. All that was required of the Irish bells was that they should ring the monastic hours for monks working nearby and not summon a scattered congregation.

But why, then, raise these high beacons, and what is more, why build them in stone in a country where timber was the most usual building material? The answer is that the towers served several purposes, some of which explain their robust construction and the inaccessible doors. They must have been used in case of emergency as watch towers, and this justifies their great height. Several texts give hints of another use. The Annals of the Four Masters, at the date of 948, tell us that: 'The cloictech of Slane was burned by the Foreigners with its full of relics and distinguished persons together with Caineachair, Lector of Slane, and the crozier of the patron saint, and a bell, the best of bells.' In 1097, the same Annals relate that 'The cloictech of Mainistir (Monasterboice) with books and many treasures, was burnt'. So the bell-tower was also a sort of keep where all the precious possessions of the abbey were stored in case of danger together with the inmates and any important visitor who might be about. In 1076, an árd-rí was killed in the cloictech of Kells[1] and several other texts mention important persons burnt in towers. When the round tower of Kilkenny was excavated in 1847, there was found in it a thick layer of charcoal mixed with human bones. Similar discoveries were made in other towers and confirm the testimony of the Annals.

The doorway raised at least two yards above the ground which could only be reached by an easily removed ladder, the way in which it was heavily shuttered, all this becomes understandable in such conditions.

[1] *A.F.M.*, 1076.

The round shape made the building nearly proof against attacks with a battering-ram and such a very simple fortress was hardly vulnerable at all from the long-range fighting methods of the time which consisted chiefly in showers of arrows. The only danger was from burning. If the enemy succeeded in setting fire to the floors, then the besieged would be caught in an inescapable trap, as the long stone cylinder ending in openings to the four winds of heaven made a perfect chimney from which nothing could rescue them.

The frequent presence, at the level of the middle storey, of stone hooks from which book-satchels or reliquaries could be hung comes as a confirmation of the texts. One may in fact wonder if in many cases the cloictech was not permanently in use as a library and muniment room. Several of the Mount Athos monasteries have tower libraries and the medieval tradition of keeping books and precious objects in a tower has occasionally also survived to our day in western Europe. To quote only one example, the Chapter of the cathedral of Bayeux in Normandy still keeps its books and manuscripts in one of the enormous western towers of the cathedral. It may be that in some cases the scriptorium was actually in the tower or in a wooden building adjoining it. A Spanish manuscript written in 970, the Apocalypse of Tavara, shows in section a tower divided into storeys connected by ladders exactly as in an Irish round tower; in a room beside the tower, two scribes are shown at work.[1]

In spite of all the efforts which have been made it is almost impossible to establish a chronological sequence of round towers. It is true that some of them are built in rough, unhewn and badly mortared stones. But these are not necessarily the oldest. There are cases like the great tower at Clonmacnois or that at Drumlane (Cavan) where the lower storeys are built of stones carefully cut to fit the curve and no less carefully joined, whilst the upper part is made of rough blocks. They show that the most elaborate construction can well be the earliest or, at least, that a splendidly built tower has occasionally been repaired hastily and carelessly. Other towers, built under pressure of immediate danger,

---

[1] Grabar-Nordenfalk, Pl. p. 173.

may have been made of undressed stones, whatever their date. Again, the presence of the rounded arches does not help the dating, as there is no reason to think that the method of constructing an arch was unknown in Ireland in the ninth century. However some towers have carvings which clearly belong to the Romanesque period and these can be dated consequently to the twelfth century. This applies to the towers of Kildare, Timahoe (Leix) and Devenish (Fermanagh) and gives at least one fixed point when the towers were in use.[1] It remains to be discovered when they first appeared in Ireland. A late text mentions the erection of a cloictech in 917 by Donnchad, the son of Flann Sinna.[2] It would be tempting to accept the tradition which ascribes the erection of the tower of Castledermot (Kildare) to abbot Cairbre who died in 919,[3] as this tower whose doorway is very close to the ground would then become a useful chronological landmark. However the first really reliable text mentioning a round tower is the description of the fire in the tower of Slane in 948 quoted above.[4] Other annalistic references to towers come in rapid succession during the second half of the tent century:[5] 964, 981, 994–6. The text of 964 mentions the erection, sometime before that date, of the tower of Tuamgreiney (Clare); the others deal with destructions. Similar texts are to be found right through the eleventh and twelfth centuries. The towers which were burnt or knocked down in 948, 981 or 994–6 had probably been in existence for some time. One may therefore assume that round towers were built from the beginning of the tenth century, but in the present state of our knowledge it seems hardly possible to push the enquiry further. In fact it seems likely that a good many of these towers were erected during the 'Forty year Recess' which came after half a century of

[1] The Romanesque doorway of the Kildare tower may be an insertion, but it remains that the tower was in use in the twelfth century. The existence of towers in twelfth-century Ireland is moreover asserted by Giraldus Cambrensis who speaks of those he saw as 'ecclesiastical towers which, according to the custom of the country are slender and lofty and round'.

[2] Keating, *Hist. of Ireland*.

[3] M. Stokes, *Early Christian Arch.*, first chronological table at end of volume.

[4] *A.F.M.*, 948; *A.U.*, 949; *Chr. Sc.*, 949; *A. Clon.*, 945; see p. 51.

[5] *Chr. Sc.*, 964; *A. Clon.*, 981; *A.F.M.*, *Chr. Sc.*, *A. Tig.*, 994–5–6.

struggle which must have impressed the monks with their urgent need for some kind of fortification or refuge.

In many cases they seem to have been built on ground which had formerly been part of a graveyard. Some have been excavated. In several of them, once the debris of jackdaws' nests was cleared away, a sort of floor was found to mark the lower level of the foundations–either flags or clay, or a layer of mortar. Below that were graves, generally oriented east-west. So these towers were erected when the monasteries had been already so long in existence that part of the graveyard had been abandoned and forgotten. This comes as a confirmation of the comparatively late date.

Let us see now what parallels there are in other countries and, as the type seems to show so little evolution in Ireland itself, where it could have been imported from. We need not consider the Scottish examples which are only outlyers of the Irish series. Margaret Stokes has already looked for Continental equivalents, but she did not discriminate sufficiently between thin applied turrets containing spiral staircases, towers included in fortifications, and the round towers which have really affinities with the Irish ones through being divided into several storeys and built near a church. The fact that a tower may be detached and at some distance from the church is not quite so essential a characteristic, as we shall see.

First of all there are in East Anglia about one hundred and seventy round towers.[1] Many of them date from the twelfth century but between twenty and thirty are prior to the Norman invasion. They are not detached but are usually built against the west gable of a church. They also differ from the Irish towers in the very poor quality of stone, usually flint, used in their construction. In fact, scholars who have studied them are of the opinion that the absence of good building stone with which the corners of a square tower could have been made accounts for their great number in Norfolk. Their proportions are completely different from those of the Irish towers. Instead of the one to six relation between diameter and height which prevails in Ireland, the English towers are squat in appearance and their diameter is only half

---

[1] Not to say anything of a few others in the rest of England. E. A. Fisher, *The Great Anglo-Saxon Churches* (London, 1962), pp. 316 sqq.

or a third of their height. But the similarities are even more striking. The English towers which date from the Saxon period generally have a door opening 2 or 3 yards above the ground and are divided into several storeys connnected by ladders about 6 to 7 yards long. It seems that they were often added to existing churches and that they may have played the same role of keep-treasury as the Irish towers. Very little is known of their chronology. Fisher suggests that they may be one aspect of the re-building of monasteries which took place in England at the time of St Dunstan (middle of the tenth century). This is only a hypothesis, but a very likely one, and suggests that this kind of tower appeared at about the same time in England and in Ireland.

A feature never found in the Irish towers which is characteristic of the English ones erected before the Norman conquest is the presence at the top of what the Italian archaeologists call 'bifore' – openings divided by a column, sometimes of baluster type, which are frequently found also in the upper storey of the large square Saxon towers. Because of this they have a remarkable analogy with the Ravenna round towers where such openings of two, three or four bays are commonly found.[1]

It is probably in this milieu and consequently in the context of the 'First Romanesque Art' that the origin of these towers is to be sought. The seven or eight towers surviving in Ravenna and those which still exist or existed a short while ago in northern Italy are obviously not all of the same date. A chronological landmark is supplied by the tower of S. Apollinare Nuovo in Ravenna, which is dated by the monogram of Archbishop Giovanni (850–78) carved on the capital of one of the windows. Others are obviously of later date. They do not belong to the original construction of the churches they are connected with, and several are isolated campaniles standing a few yards from the church, at the south-west corner or on the north side. They are divided into storeys but their doorway is usually at ground-level.[2] While some are

[1] G. Galassi, *Roma o Bisanzio*, I (Rome, 1953), pp. 226 sqq.

[2] This may be because, like all Ravennate monuments, they have sunk into the marshy ground. That of Sant' Agata, which is cleared to the base has a door about two yards or more above the ground, but not opening towards the church. The interior of the tower of S. Apollinare in Classe shows continuous cornices in the masonry, supporting the wooden floors, as is the case in some of the Irish towers.

only small bell-towers, others, probably the oldest, have heavy and massive lower storeys devoid of windows except narrow slits. It is obvious that these were very efficient defence towers as well as belfries and that, erected in the troubled times of the ninth and tenth centuries, they were meant to watch over the churches and their possessions. They were the equivalent of the square towers in the same neighbourhood such as those of Aquileia or Pomposa or indeed the campanile of St Mark in Venice. It would be difficult to say whether they are adaptations of Byzantine towers or successors of the round towers figured on several paleo-christian monuments. But they may well be amongst the forms of building which Ravenna passed on to the 'First Romanesque Art'. The round belfry, of Romanesque date, of the church of Santa Coloma in Andorra would seem to suggest it. It is difficult to extend these comparisons to the rest of western Europe as it would be dangerous to use as examples the round towers figured in the old drawing of the monastery of St Riquier in the north of France whose internal structure is unknown and – however tempting – the round turrets figured on both sides of one of the apses in the ninth century plan preserved at St Gall,[1] as in spite of the oratories which may have existed on their top storey, they are nothing but narrow spiral staircase towers.[2]

On the whole this architectural fashion was probably an imitation of Continental prototypes of north Italian origin first appearing in the ninth century and giving rise to two nearly parallel and contemporary types in England and Ireland. As elsewhere at the time, these towers were both a means of defence and a 'house of bells'. Though the round shape is constant in Ireland, the type of monument is akin to those enormous keeps, the pride and privilege of some of the most powerful Continental abbeys of the tenth, eleventh and twelfth centuries, of which the towers of Cuxa in the Pyrenees, of Vendôme, of Marmoutier near

[1] J. Duft, *Studien zum St. Galler Klosterplan* (St Gall, 1962).

[2] For St Riquier (Centula), see two reconstitutions by K. J. Conant, one in his *Benedictine Contribution to Church Architecture* (Latrobe, Pen., 1949), p. 49 and the other in: *Carolingian and Romanesque Architecture, 800–1200* (Pelican H. of Art, 1959), Pl. IIA. The side towers of San Vitale at Ravenna are only wide stair-cases and so were those of Saint Benigne at Dijon.

Tours, and the isolated belfry of the monastery of St Aubin in Angers are a few surviving examples.

Thus the stone architecture of ninth- and tenth-century Ireland shows new forms and greater variety than that of the eighth century. One of its outstanding features is the remarkable skill and precision of stone cutting. Some of the round towers, made of trapezoidal blocks which go through the whole width of the wall are masterpieces of fitting and even of geometrical calculation, and so are some of the church doorways, such as that at Aghowle (Pl. 6). The architects however still show very little interest in structural problems. Their churches are no more than large rectangular boxes in which the choir is only beginning to have a separate space and they will remain that way well into the twelfth century. Whether, however, there were wooden columns dividing this inert space and giving it articulation is something which cannot be decided in the present state of our knowledge, though the complicated subdivisions of the church of Kildare as described by Cogitosus in the late seventh century leave plenty of scope for such speculations.

3. The Decoration of Manuscripts

A.D. 800–1020

THE PREVIOUS study of manuscript illumination in the Irish style[1]
brought us to large Gospel-books decorated in the second half of the
eighth century: Ms. 51 of St Gall and the Book of Mac Regol, and to
smaller volumes like the Book of Dimma and the Stowe Missal. The
first were made for the use of the altar, the others were simply reference
books. Both kinds have an elaborate decoration at the beginning of each
Gospel. The St Gall manuscript had the distinctive feature of two pages
of illustration, one of the Crucifixion, the other of the Last Judgment.
None of these books shows the same minute treatment of detail which is
found in a group of slightly earlier manuscripts whose masterpiece is the
Lichfield Gospels. Obviously a great number of manuscripts has disappeared and this probably deprives us of those which might have
represented the transition between this early eighth-century group and
two works of outstanding quality that we meet on the threshold of the
ninth century, the Book of Kells and the Book of Armagh.[2]

The manuscripts to be described now form a very varied collection.
There are some Gospel-books (Book of Kells, Book of Armagh, Mac
Durnan Gospels, Turin Fragment). But, unlike the surviving eighth
century manuscripts, they include also several psalters (Cotton Ms.
Vitellius F.XI, Ms. 24 of Rouen, Southampton Psalter, Edinburgh
Psalter), and beside these liturgical books, there are two copies of the
Grammar of Priscian, obviously books meant for study.

[1] *Vol. I*, pp. 159 sqq.
[2] For the general problems dealt with in this chapter, consult (besides Kenney,
Sources): E. H. Zimmermann, *Vorkarolingische Miniaturen* (Berlin, 1916); G. L.
Micheli, *L'enluminure du haut Moyen-âge et les influences irlandaises* (Brussels,
1939); A. Grabar–C. Nordenfalk, *Early Medieval Painting* (Skira, 1957). For
chronological reasons, only a few of the manuscripts mentioned are dealt with in:
E. A. Lowe, *Codices Latini Antiquiores* and P. McGurk, *Latin Gospel-Books from
A.D. 400 to A.D. 800* (Paris, etc., 1961).

Several of these manuscripts can be dated fairly precisely: the Book of Armagh has colophons which show it to be the work of a scribe of Armagh, Ferdomnagh, who died in 846, working under the direction of Torbach, who was abbot of Armagh for only one year (807–8). The two Priscian manuscripts, one in Leyden, the other in St Gall, are slightly later (838 and around 850 respectively). The Book of Mac Durnan was in existence when Maelbrigte Mac Durnan was abbot of Armagh (888–927) and was probably written during his time. So all these manuscripts belong to the ninth century. The Book of Kells, which has more than one feature in common with the Book of Armagh, can be added to them and, in all probability, the fragmentary Gospel-book in Turin Library also. The other manuscripts can only be dated by comparison, but it seems likely that only the Rouen and Cotton Psalters belong to the tenth century. The Southampton Psalter (St John's College, Cambridge, Ms. C.9), probably belongs, on linguistic and stylistic grounds, to the beginning of the eleventh century and the Edinburgh Psalter, which is very close to it in decorative style, can hardly be much later.

This great scarcity of surviving manuscripts, due probably to the depredations of the Vikings in the tenth century, brings to mind the complaints of the author of the *War*. According to him, Brian Boru 'sent professors and masters . . . to buy books beyond the sea, and the great ocean; because their writings and their books in every church and in every sanctuary where they were were burned and thrown into water by the plunderers, from the beginning to the end'.[1]

To understand the background of the first stages of this development and more especially to conjure up the atmosphere in which the decoration of the Book of Kells evolved, it is necessary to turn again, as for the seventh and eighth-century illuminations, to Irish foundations outside Ireland, in this case Lindisfarne and some abbeys in the north of England as well as monasteries imbued with Irish influence in the north of France particularly those, such as Corbie, which were in contact with the Irish monastery of Péronne.

[1] *War*, pp. 138–9.

We have seen[1] how Alcuin in the north of England lived in an atmosphere where Irish teaching was still alive and that an Irish manuscript painter was at work in a monastery there, probably a dependency of Lindisfarne, in the second half of the ninth century. Learned travellers like Colgu and Joseph, the master and the friend of Alcuin, no doubt brought books with them from Ireland when they came to settle in England. This milieu, where Irishmen lived, taught and painted, produced some manuscripts which show a mixture of Irish decoration and English features. One of the most important is a Gospel-book now in the Vatican Library (Barberini Ms. Lat. 570); another is the Prayer-book of Cerne (Cambridge, University Library, Ms. Li. I.10), very close to it in some respects. Another Gospel-book, formerly in the Abbey of St Germain-des-Prés in Paris and now in the Leningrad Library, belongs to the same series; and also a fragment of a Gospel-book perhaps written on the Continent and now kept in the church of St Catherine in Maeseyck (Belgium). These manuscripts deserve study because they embody memories of Irish books which have now disappeared, and so help to fill out what we can learn from the few surviving Irish manuscripts. They explain also how, in exchange, some foreign influences penetrated into Ireland.

The Vatican Gospel-book[2] has the usual plan of the luxury Insular Gospel-book and is hardly smaller than the manuscripts of the Lichfield group (it is 10 by 12½ inches). Its prefaces and arguments have decorated capitals and some of its canon-tables are framed in monumental arcades. There is the usual decorative scheme at the beginning of each Gospel: 'portrait' and ornamented page of text. But everything is curiously chaotic and the script itself wavers between the great majuscule of Irish tradition and a script coming very close to minuscule. The canon-tables begin with an arcaded page finely wrought with interlacings (Pl. IV), but this is followed by pages with only sketchy arches of childish tracery. The small decorated initials in the text vary

[1] See p. 28.
[2] Barberini Ms. Lat. 570; Zimmermann, pp. 300 sqq., IV, Pls. 313–17; Lowe, *C.L.A.*, I, No. 63; McGurk, pp. 106–7; Micheli, *Enluminure*, pp. 28–9, Pls. 66, 75.

constantly in style, quantity and importance. At first glance the ornament seems to belong to the normal Irish repertory, the prominence
given to the spiral helping the illusion (Pl. 34). A closer study, however reveals animals of very unusual type in the compartments of the
letters and a whole crop of flippant and grotesque heads emerging from
the spirals and grinning at the corner of a frame or the end of a letter.
Such animated endings are not uncommon in the Lichfield Gospels,
but the crawling and sneaking of comical characters belongs to another
world, that of the English manuscripts with semi-Irish decoration of
the type of the Codex Aureus from Canterbury now in the Stockholm
Royal Library. Some of the small initials and the little beasts which
wander about the text – a horned sphinx, a lanky pink and green
cat – are even more caricature-like (Pl. V). The book has a colophon:
'Ora pro Uigbaldo – pray for Uigbald,'[1] which connects it most probably
with Huigbald, abbot of Lindisfarne, the friend of Alcuin, who governed
the monastery from 760 to 803 and lived through the anguished days of
the Viking attack of 793.[2] He may have directed the work, as obviously it
must be ascribed to several hands.

The manuscript in the University Library in Cambridge referred to
above comes from the Abbey of Cerne in Dorset.[3] It is a collection of
Gospel extracts and prayers which is paralleled in several manuscripts
(prototypes of the medieval Books of Hours) which have strong Irish
textual affinities but seem to have been written in England. It has on
Fol. 21 an acrostic which yields the name Eadeluald Episcopus, and the
heading of the abbreviated psalter it contains attributes it to 'Oethelwald
Episcopus'. Aedelvald or Aethelwold was a much more common name
than Huicbald. Several attributions have been suggested in consequence.
One is to an eighth-century abbot of the monastery of Sherborne whose
geographical closeness to Cerne would lend some likelihood to the
hypothesis. But manuscripts travel widely and the analogies between
the decoration and that of the Vatican manuscript would seem rather to

---

[1] On fol. 153r.   [2] See pp. 28–9 and 6.

[3] Dom A. B. Kuypers, O.S.B., *The Prayer-Book of Aedelvald the Bishop commonly
called the Book of Cerne* (Cambridge, 1902). See also: Kenney, *Sources*, pp. 720–2
(576); Zimmermann, p. 294, IV, Pls. 293–6; Micheli, *Enluminure*, pp. 32–3, Pl. 28.

indicate a northern origin. An Aethelwold who was bishop of Lichfield from 818 to 830 has also been suggested. But the date seems too late, so that the most acceptable hypothesis remains that proposed by Bishop,[1] who thought that the 'Book of Aethelwald' was only the source from which the Book of Cerne was copied and that 'Aethelwald' was the bishop of Lindisfarne who governed the monastery from 721 to 740.[2] This would imply a similar background to that of the Vatican Gospels and one might accept a date for both of them somewhere between 770 and 790.

The Book of Cerne is written in Anglo-Saxon miniscule which, deriving from Irish script, had by that time acquired a flavour of its own. It is presented like an unusually fine 'pocket-book'. It begins with the texts of the Passion and the Resurrection from the four Gospels which, from the ornamental viewpoint, are treated like Gospels: each starts with a large capital and a decorated line of text (Pl. II); on the opposite page, unexpectedly, the Evangelist's symbol takes pride of place under an arcading, whilst the Evangelist himself appears only as a small bust framed in a circle in the middle of the arch.[3] Prayers and hymns have a few finely drawn initials. Then comes an abbreviated psalter in the text of which are found little animals similar to those of the Vatican Gospel-book (Pl. V). They are usually meant to point out the end of verses which have been thrown back on the preceding or following line. Signs of reference are not rare in other parts of the book, but, apart from the psalter they are no more than a sort of Z-shaped mark, so that one cannot help suspecting that the model for the psalter had this feature.

In the Leningrad Gospels[4] we have another luxury manuscript. It has

[1] E. Bishop, *Liturgica historica* (Oxford, 1918), pp. 192–7; W. Levison, *England and the Continent in the Eighth Century* (Oxford, 1946), pp. 147, 295 sqq.

[2] He was responsible for the 'binding' or 'shrine' of the Book of Lindisfarne; *E.Q.C. Lindisfarnensis*, pp. 5 and 17.

[3] A similar arrangement is found in a manuscript emanating from Canterbury, Royal Ms. I E.VI in the British Museum (Zimmermann, IV, Pl. 289).

[4] Leningrad, Public Library, Ms. Lat. F.V.I. No. 8; Dom A. Staerk, O.S.B., *Les Manuscrits latins du Vᵉ au XIIIᵉ siècle conservés à la Bibliothèque impériale de St Petersburg* (St Petersburg, 1910), pp. 25–6, Pls. XXI–XXIII; Zimmermann, pp. 304–5, IV, Pls. 321–6; McGurk, pp. 101 and 122–3; Micheli, *Enluminure*, pp. 28–9, Pls. 13, 50, 77.

monumental canon-tables and very large capitals at the beginning of each Gospel. The arcades of the canon-tables are of a splendid fantasy, all in bold curvilinear lines, but, as in the Book of Cerne, there are few spirals and the animals are anything but Irish (Pl. 35).

Only the Vatican Gospels have Evangelists' portraits. Their Mediterranean inspiration is manifest not only in the pose of the figures, which are shown sitting sideways writing, but also in the decoration of light foliage outlined on the coloured ground of the page. They are neither in the hard pseudo-Byzantine style of the Lindisfarne Evangelists, nor are they subject to ornamental simplifications like those of the Lichfield and St Gall Gospels. They are modelled in beautifully rounded volumes which have a touch of classical serenity. They have a close relation in the only surviving Evangelist's portrait in a dismembered Gospel-book whose fragments are preserved in the church of St Catherine in Maeseyck (Belgium).[1] It comes from the monastery of Alden Eick founded in the early eighth century under the direction of Willibrord. It has been generally attributed to the late eighth century. Recently, Nordenfalk, struck by the classical flavour of the Evangelist figure, has suggested that it might be a product of the school of York at the time of Wilfrid (late seventh century).[2] However a close examination reveals that some of the bases of the canon-table columns are decorated with animals very similar to some in the same position in the Leningrad Gospels, and others have little impertinent beasts like those in the Book of Cerne (Pl. IV). So the traditional date may not be very far wrong. Nevertheless all these figures of Evangelists, both those of the Vatican Gospels and that at Maeseyck, may well go back to prototypes of the time of Wilfrid.

[1] Dom D. de Bruyne, O.S.B., 'L'évangéliaire du VIIIe siècle conservé à Maeseyck', *Bull. Soc. Art et Hist. du Diocèse de Liège*, 1908, pp. 385 sqq.; Zimmermann, pp. 142–3, IV, Pls. 318–20; McGurk, pp. 47–8; Micheli, *Enluminure*, pp. 49–50, Pls. 37, 159; *Art Mosan et Arts anciens au Pays de Liège* (catal. exh.; Liége, 1951), pp. 64 (F. Masai) and 43; *Karl der Grosse* (catal. exh.; Aachen, 1965), pp. 236–7, Pl. 42. What is under discussion above is a small fragment consisting in an Evangelist portrait (the three others have disappeared since 1858), and eight pages of canon-tables which go with it. This fragment is inserted in an incomplete Gospel-book also including a set of canon-tables.

[2] Grabar-Nordenfalk, p. 122.

Some of the canon-tables of the Maeseyck Gospels (Pl. IV), like those of the Vatican Gospels, have the heads of the Evangelists' symbols above each list of references. In the middle of the arch a bust is enclosed in a circular frame, as in the Book of Cerne. In some of the spandrels of the arcades, there are vivid sketches of birds, obviously imitations of Oriental models. Whether it was written in Alden Eick or brought there from the north of England, it is closely connected with the group we have just examined and completes it in some ways. It is only partly dependent on Irish influence and its connections with Mediterranean models cannot be doubted.

It will be necessary to refer to these manuscripts when trying to outline some of the characteristics of the Book of Kells. They are the product of a renewed interest in Irish illumination at Lindisfarne, and possibly also in the neighbourhood of York, due to the presence there of Irish painters and Irish books. The imitation is much less faithful than it was in the Lindisfarne Gospels, showing clearly how rapidly an impulse from outside can wane. Except in the Vatican manuscript, spirals are rare and poorly drawn. The animals are very different from the Irish ones, and have only in common with them the way in which they are combined. In the north of England this was the last episode in the evolution of the Irish manner, which was soon to be swept away in the violent changes brought about by Scandinavian rule. Whilst the Book of Kells embodies the full flowering of Irish art, these manuscripts are no more than a pale reflection of it. Still, they show the influence of Irish manuscripts which have now disappeared and can give many useful clues to the problems of the symbol canon-tables, of the small animals in the text and even perhaps of some of the borrowings from Mediterranean art. They are also interesting in that they show the sort of north English illumination which Alcuin may have known when he was at the head of the school of York (766–80) and at the time of his visits to England around 790.

The other centre of manuscript illumination which has obvious connections with Irish painting is that of the neighbourhood of Amiens. These connections are easily explained by the fact that Péronne, where

aum reg

rem &comr

&mmoodbeec

onnoeius ii
il snaounc

s male ha

the Irish monk saint Fursa was buried, remained an Irish monastery late into the eighth century and perhaps even until its destruction by the Vikings in 880.[1] The nearby monasteries of St Riquier and Corbie had Irish contacts from their foundation and no doubt kept in touch with Ireland through Péronne.

A psalter which belonged to the Corbie Library (Amiens, Bibl. municipale, Ms. 18),[2] another which is now in Stuttgart (Ms. Bibl. Fol. 23),[3] a Gospel-book kept in the Library of the Cathedral of Essen,[4] which came there probably from Corvey, a daughter-house of Corbie in Germany, and which may have been illuminated in Corbie, the 'Psalter of Charlemagne',[5] and the uncial Gospel-book in the Municipal Library at Poitiers (Ms. 17),[6] which originated in the region of Amiens, form a rather miscellaneous group united nevertheless by a few common features. They come from a centre where the Merovingian fashion of fish-and-bird initials was still in favour but was combined with obsessive insular traditions imposing the use of interlacings, animal interlacings and a certain tendency to abstract decoration. People from the eastern Mediterranean were familiar figures there. As a proof of it one could mention a Latin translation of the Greek text of the Alexandrian Chronicle attributed by a note to a certain George, no doubt a Byzantine settled in Gaul, who was bishop of Amiens at the end of the eighth century. This manuscript has an initial of the same style as those of the Amiens Psalter.[7]

The whole series of manuscripts belongs to the late eighth or the

---

[1] Traube, *Perrona Scottorum*; see *Vol. I*, pp. 39–40.

[2] Leroquais, *Psautiers*, I, p. 6, Pls. III–VI; J. Porcher, 'Le Psautier d'Amiens et l'Évangéliaire de Charlemagne', *Revue des Arts*, 1957, pp. 51 sqq.; Grabar-Nordenfalk, p. 142; *Les manuscrits à peintures en France du VIIe au XIIe siècle* (catal. exh., Paris, Bibl. nat., 1954), pp. 84–5; *Byzance et la France médiévale* (catal. exh., Paris, Bibl. nat., 1958), p. 57.

[3] E. T. de Wald, *The Stuttgart Psalter* (Princeton, 1930) (the volume of plates only has appeared).

[4] Micheli, *Enluminure*, pp. 84–5.

[5] Paris, Bibl. nat., Ms. Lat. 13.159.

[6] Dom P. Minard, O.S.B., 'L'évangéliaire oncial de l'Abbaye Sainte-Croix de Poitiers', *Revue Mabillon*, 1943, pp. 1 sqq.

[7] *Byzance et le France médiévale*, pp. 57–8 (No. 103).

F

ninth century. It comes from a milieu alien to the majestic elaboration of official Carolingian art, but rich in talent, in bold curiosity, in the taste for decorative experiments. Though it retains archaic features, it looks towards the future and in a way by-passes Carolingian art on a direct route to Romanesque. There can be little doubt that the painters of the Book of Kells were aware of its existence and familiar with the work of these Continental scriptoria. Péronne was a normal stopping place for all the Irish who landed on the Continent or left it and one can assume that there was in the late eighth century constant communication between Péronne and Corbie on the one hand, and such centres of illumination as Lindisfarne–York and Ireland–Iona on the other. We shall come back to these manuscripts later. It will be enough to define here their chief characteristics.

The decoration of the Amiens Psalter consists essentially in initials (Pls. 24, 26, 31) lightly drawn with the pen and occasionally picked out in colour. It is a continual fantasy where real and imaginary animals intermingle and nimble, ironical, emphatic little figures move about freely, sometimes in commentary upon the text. It is an enchanting world, full of decorative invention; in a way the same world as that of the initials of the Book of Kells, on a slightly larger scale and with a less rigorous stylization. The analogies are so close that one may well speculate about the link between the two works. Jean Porcher has pointed out some Byzantine features in the psalter.[1] To these can be added human hands and feet emerging from the letters as in the Sacramentary of Gellone, a mannerism which is also Byzantine. Are we to see in the three manuscripts, the Sacramentary, which modern criticism tends to locate in the north of France, the Amiens Psalter, and the Book of Kells, several attempts to imitate Greek initials, the two last manuscripts showing different combinations of Byzantine data and the Irish decorative system (Pls. 22, 24, 26, 31, 32)?

The Psalter of Charlemagne and the Essen Gospel-book contain many fish-and-bird decorative letters in the Merovingian tradition but this is combined in the psalter with interlacings of Irish origin, and in the Gospel-book with stray fragments of acanthus incorporated into

[1] See J. Porcher, op. cit.

66

the rhythm of the interlacing (Pl. III). These broken leaf patterns reappear in some of the initials of the Stuttgart Psalter. This last manuscript (Pls. VI–VII) has literal illustrations of the text, some with the same iconographical content as those of the nearly contemporary Utrecht Psalter. They appear as rectangular panels, the width of the page, inserted in the text like the illustrations of some later Byzantine Psalters or Gospel-books such as the eleventh-century Ms. Grec 74 of the Bibliothèque nationale in Paris. Ebersolt has suggested that the last was an imitation of a pre-iconoclastic manuscript and it is probably from a book of that type also that the author of the Stuttgart Psalter derived his inspiration. The imitation is no doubt coarser in style than its model but it is at times singularly expressive and gives some precious iconographical data.

It remains to examine briefly the relationship of Carolingian manuscripts proper, or at least the oldest of them to the Irish manuscripts. This is especially important as some sweeping statements have been made from time to time about Carolingian influence on the Book of Kells. In this connection it is useful to remember that the problem is twofold and that beside a possible Carolingian influence on Irish work, the presence of Irish elements in Carolingian manuscripts has to be considered. This point will be studied later, but it is necessary to indicate here its relevance to the first great manuscript which marks the beginning of the Carolingian Renaissance, the Lectionary written by Godescalc before 783 for Charlemagne and Queen Hildegard who died in that year. Porcher has shown[1] that the decoration seems to be the work of an artist trained in Insular methods who is striving to imitate Italian models. If one could be sure that Alcuin came to Charlemagne's court immediately after their meeting in Parma in 781 it might be considered as the first work of that Insular workshop which he governed until his death in 804, first at the court and afterwards in Tours. In later manuscripts of this school such as the Gospels of St Medard of Soissons (Paris, Bibl. nat. Lat. 8850) and the Harley Gospel-book (Br. Mus., Harley Ms. 2788) the canons with Evangelists' symbols appear as a continuation of those in the Vatican Evangeliary and the Maeseyck

[1] J. Porcher, op. cit.

fragment. The Mediterranean models give the general flavour: the purple backgrounds, the gold and silver script, the elaborate arrangements of portraits and architecture. But the large initials and a few other features like the symbol canons are manifestations of the style which Alcuin and his companions, especially Joseph the Irishman, had known and practised from childhood. In fact, several of the problems involved are unfortunately much more complicated than this simplification would suggest. That of the canons, in particular, is full of difficulties of all kinds, partly perhaps arising from the use of models now lost. Still, this crude outline will provide us later with a useful framework for the study of the problem, raised by Friend, of the relation between the Book of Kells and the Harley Gospel-book.

Having thus gathered some notions of the varied related manuscripts, we can turn our attention directly to the Book of Kells, the manuscript of the Gospels which, until the seventeenth century, was preserved in Kells (Meath).[1]

It is a large codex. It measures at present 13 by $9\frac{1}{2}$ inches, but it must have been originally, before its pages were trimmed, about 15 by 11 inches, so that it was slightly larger than the books of the Lichfield–Lindisfarne series. It is also thicker, and had about 350 pages, instead of the 258 of the Lindisfarne Gospels. The difference is accounted for partly by picture pages which do not occur in the Book of Lindisfarne, and partly by the prodigal magnificence of the lay-out of the text set in wide margins, with generous spacing and interspersed with exuberant initials. It is written on a thick vellum whose surface appears almost polished but which is of uneven quality. The majesty of its appearance has been partly spoiled by the binder who, in the early nineteenth century, clipped the pages, sometimes cutting away the edges of the illuminations. Otherwise, it is in fairly good condition, in spite of its adventures. There is a record in the Annals of Ulster of the way in which, in 1007, 'The great Gospel of Columkille, the chief relic of the Western World,

T.C.D. Libr. Ms. No. 58. The Book has been published in a complete facsimile: *E.Q.C. Cenannensis*, vols. I and II; vol. III contains studies by E. H. Alton, P. Meyer, G. O. Simms. See also: E. Sullivan, *The Book of Kells* (London, 1914); Lowe, *C.L.A.*, II, No. 274; Zimmermann, p. 72, III, Pls. 166–84.

was wickedly stolen during the night from the Western sacristy of the great stone church at Cenannas on account of its wrought shrine'. It was recovered a few months later, deprived of its gold, 'under a sod'[1]

A few leaves are missing and seem to have been missing for centuries. After the dissolution of the Columban monastery of Kells in the twelfth century, it remained in the monastery church which became the parish church of Kells.[2] In the sixteenth century it was examined by a Gerald Plunkett of Dublin who wrote some notes in it, one of them showing that pages were already then missing at the end of the book. It was examined also by the famous Irish historian James Ussher, when he was the protestant bishop-elect of Meath, and he wrote in it: 'August 24, 1621. I reckoned the leaves of this book and found them to be in number 344'. The manuscript passed about forty years later to the Library of Trinity College, Dublin,[3] having meanwhile probably lost four more pages, as it now has only 340. The missing leaves are thus a few folios at both ends (including the last four chapters of the Gospel of St John) which were probably lost as a result of the theft of 1007 when they may have been ripped away with the binding, and the four leaves which have disappeared since Ussher's reckoning, most probably full page illuminations, among them the two missing Evangelist's portraits.

There is no earlier mention of the manuscript than the annalistic entry of A.D. 1007 quoted above. However there is no serious reason to doubt that it was written and decorated in the monastery's scriptorium.

From several features of its decoration, it appears to date from the late eighth or early ninth century, its lavish decoration having taken very many years. But this was a critical time in the history of the Iona–Kells community. It seems more than likely that the decoration was far from finished at the time of the Viking attack on Iona. The unfinished

---

[1] *A.U.*, 1007; I have followed partly Bieler's reconstruction of the sentence (*Ireland*, p. 113), more logical than the version given in the translation in *A.U.*; see also *Chr. Sc.*, 1005.

[2] For new light on this part of the history of the Book of Kells, see: E. J. F. Arnould, 'Enigmas in the Book of Kells', *Annual Bulletin of the Friends of the Library of Trinity College, Dublin*, 1953, pp. 4 sqq.; A Gwynn, S. J., 'Some notes on the History of the Books of Kells', *I.H.S.*, 1954, pp. 131 sqq.; W. O'Sullivan, 'The donor of the Book of Kells', *I.H.S.*, 1958, pp. 5 sqq.

[3] It was given to the Library by Henry Jones, like the Book of Durrow (see last reference note 2 above, and *Vol. I*, p. 167).

book was no doubt brought to Kells, where the scriptorium started work again in its new surroundings. We need not accept A. M. Friend's drastic assumption of the 'dispersion' of the Iona scriptorium at the time of the Viking attack.[1] The Annalists mention sixty-eight members of the community massacred in 805. A few probably died also in 802. This obviously represents a very small proportion of the inmates of the monastery and its various annexes. It remains possible, however, that one of the painters of the Book disappeared then, as the Annals of Ulster have for A.D. 802 an entry on the death of Connachtach, 'eminent scribe and abbot of Ia (Iona)'. One cannot help wondering if it was he who established the decorative plan of the manuscript and whether he had started work on it. Nevertheless, the monastery of Kells shows from the start a vigorous artistic activity and among the carved crosses surviving there, the one near the tower has points in common with the decoration of the manuscript. So we can assume that other painters proceeded with the work, most of which was done in Kells.

The script, a formal majuscule, not always easily legible, with words often imperfectly separated, is in the tradition of the early eighth-century manuscripts and of the Book of Mac Regol. The text is the Irish 'mixed version' and often differs substantially from the Vulgate. In spite of the imposing aspect of the lay-out the transcription is often careless; misspellings are innumerable, there are copyist's errors, and the negligence of the scribes is such that the colophons are practically unintelligible. This carelessness is in no sense a novelty, but is often found in the work of the Irish scribes. Correctors have intervened as a consequence, but loath to mar the beauty of the written page, rather than erase or cross a mistake, they prefer to mark it with an ornamental sign as something to be omitted; thus the corrections and their references are transformed into an added pattern.

The decoration itself is affected by these empiric methods. It seems

[1] Friend, *Canon-tables*, p. 639: 'It was in process of completion when suddenly the Northmen swooped down upon the monastery. The splendid scriptorium was dispersed . . . the hand of the artist of Kells is never seen again in any illuminated Celtic manuscript. The fleeing monks took his glorous unfinished gospel book with them to Kells, where later they completed the necessary canon tables as best they could. . . .'

to have started in all directions at the same time. At least two pages intended for illumination have remained blank. Others are unfinished. One passes without transition from one style to another. But this impulsive presentation contributes to the feeling of teeming sumptuousness which is one of the most attractive features of the manuscript.

None of the Irish manuscripts, so far, had ever shown so ambitious a plan of decoration as the Book of Kells. The main lines of the usual layout subsist, but complicated by innumerable additions. It is impossible, in its present state, to discover how the opening of the Book was decorated. Because of the disappearance of the first few pages, it now begins, rather clumsily, in the middle of one of the lists of Hebrew names. This is followed immediately by the canon-tables, framed in heavily ornamented pillars supporting arched tympana where the symbols of the Evangelists pass in fantastic cavalcades (Pl. 23). After eight such arcades, each different from the others in style and colour scheme, the remainder of the tables, always difficult to accommodate in an architectural setting because of their miscellaneous character, are framed simply by coloured ribbons similar to those around the Echternach Gospels canons. Prefaces and summaries of the Gospels follow; these last all start with wide decorative labels (Pl. II) of the same type as those at the beginning of the Gospel extracts in the Book of Cerne, possibly a common device in Ireland at that time, of which the artist of the Book of Cerne may have learned through a travelling painter or a wandering book.

After this comes the usual decoration of the introductory pages of the Gospels : first the 'portrait' of the Evangelist (Pl. J), then a page with a few initial letters smothered with ornament and enlarged to such a size that there is hardly room for a word or two of the text. In the Lindisfarne Gospels these opening pages were balanced on the left by carpet-pages. Here, in three cases one finds instead pages carrying the four symbols of the Evangelists accommodated each time in a different kind of frame (Pl. 28). The Chi-Rho – the monogram of Christ at the beginning of the Nativity story in St Matthew (Matt. I,18) – is treated as in most Irish manuscripts like the beginning of a Gospel (Pl. 20) and is given a carpet-page, the only one in the Book (Pl. C).

71

There was also a series of full-page pictures scattered through the text and illustrating it on a much more lavish scale than the two picture pages at the end of the St Gall Gospels.[1] In most cases they are associated with a page of ornamented text. A Virgin and Child surrounded by angels is found opposite the 'Nativitas Christi in Bethleem' page of the summaries of St Matthew (Pl. 17). The Arrest of Christ in St Matthew's Gospel (Pl. G) is followed by the decorated text: 'Tunc dixit illis ISU – then Jesus said to them.' Though the Arrest itself is not described until a later paragraph, its figuration comes here quite naturally as a beginning to the text of the Passion.[2] Still in the same Gospel, a page which remains blank beside the ornamented text: 'Tunc crucifixerant (sic) XPI – then they crucified Christ.' had no doubt been meant for a Crucifixion which was never painted, towards which faced three groups of human busts inserted in the frame of the text. No illustrated page proper is now to be found in the Gospel of St Mark, but there may have been one originally, possibly another Crucifixion facing the decorated page where is written: 'Erat autem hora tercia – it was the third hour.' In St Luke's Gospel, the picture of the Temptation on the Temple faces: 'Jesus autem plenus SS – And Jesus being full of the Holy Ghost' (Pl. B) and a blank page at the end may have been intended for an Ascension. The Gospel of St John is devoid of illustrated pages, but its last chapters are missing and it is conceivable that it may have ended, as in the St Gall Gospels, with a representation of the Last Judgment.

Beside this ambitious decorative programme, there is a constant stream of ornamentation in the text itself. There is hardly a paragraph, a sentence even which has not its initial either drawn in a few bold black lines enlivened by touches of colour, or made by the bent and twisted body of a man or an animal, or even by an intricate jumble of animals, birds, snakes, fishes, fighting, biting, devouring each other (Pls. 22, 24, 26, 32). Other animals walk about the page. Their function is

---

[1] Ms. A. II. 17 of Durham, which dates probably of *c.* 700, has a full-page figuration of the Crucifixion (*Vol. I*, Pl. 99). It is thus possible that the use of full-page illustrations went back to a fairly early date in Irish illumination. Our knowledge of early manuscripts is too fragmentary to allow any definite statement on the subject.

[2] See pp. 81–2.

usually to attract attention to words and syllables which continue the text on another line, and they do so by pointing energetically at them or by curling around them (Pls. H, 33). The process is the same as in the psalter of the Book of Cerne (Pl. V) and some parts of the Vatican Gospels (Pl. V), and may have been developed in Ireland and imitated in the two other manuscripts, unless all three draw on similar models, possibly Oriental. Some of the manuscripts of the School of Tours where Alcuin's direction left its mark, for example the Grandval Bible,[1] show a similar intrusion of small animals into the text. Still, there is little in common between the crawling, humped and distorted worms of the Prayer-Book and the alert company of brightly coloured, sharply edged little beasts of the Book of Kells. It happens occasionally that the painter, wanting to stress an important sequence in the text, links together a series of initials into a vertical chain: as in the Genealogy of Christ in St Luke's Gospel and in the Beatitudes in St Matthew's.

The decoration of the Book is not from a single hand. It is the collective work of a whole scriptorium where a few great artists were supported by less skilled helpers and, as a consequence, it remains difficult to define the personality of each painter. One has to keep in mind that pupils may have filled in some of the compartments of a page designed by a master. And the best artists in the confined atmosphere of the scriptorium were bound to influence each other, and occasionally to collaborate in the decoration of a page. Several of the ornamental pages are single leaf additions to the vellum quires and these could be distributed to the painters without upsetting the work of the scribe. Consequently, as could be expected, each Gospel shows examples of the work of several hands.

One artist was obviously entrusted with the cruciform carpet-page known as the 'page of the eight circles' (Pl. C); the great Chi–Rho (Pls. 20, 25) and the initial page of each of the Gospels, except the

---

[1] Br. M. Add. Ms. 10.546; Fol. 7r; Koehler, *Karol. Min.*, I, Pl. 52. The use of little animals in the text is not limited to this period. They are found in later Irish manuscripts, for example in some pages of the St Ouen Psalter (Henry, *Three Psalters*, Pls. XVII–XVIII) and in an Irish twelfth-century psalter in the British Museum, Add. Ms. 36.929 (Henry – Marsh-Micheli, *Illumination*, Pl. XLI).

'Quoniam' of St Luke. One feels tempted to call him 'the Goldsmith', for his work at first sight seems wrought in precious metals, in enamel and niello. He composes a page by drawing a few wide patterns, the irregular shape of letters or the outline of the cross, in broad bands of golden yellow, silvery blue, purple or red. Inside these legible frames, out of them, around them, flows in a continuous stream a fantastic decoration of minute spirals endlessly interlocked with each other, animal bodies plaited and knit, snakes twisted into patterns of eight, little men so ingeniously folded and bent inside a circle that they look like geometrical figures gone crazy. The delicacy of his work is incredible. He can wind spirals to such a point that their thread is only barely visible. He never blunders over an interlacing, however microscopic, and keeps his string going imperturbably up and down. But with all the care he gives to details, he never loses sight of an ultimate purpose, and reaches it undeterred. His work, in spite of all its intricacy, is never confused. It gives only an impression of extraordinary richness, of a world so complex that it promises endless fields of exploration. He does not aim at symmetry and is seldom found balancing two equal motifs exactly. He may start to draw identical patterns, but he destroys their similarity in a subtle manner before he has finished, either by an irregular arrangement of the colours or by the sudden alteration of a few curves. His repertory of ornament is absolutely traditional: spirals, elongated animals, birds, threads. His only innovation is the constant use of ribbon-shaped snakes. But he never uses any vegetal ornament. He draws human beings with complete unconcern for their real shape, seeing them only as decorative material. Two or three times he is more or less forced to respect their natural appearance; this may result in extreme awkwardness as in the case of the figure holding a book – probably the Evangelist – in the margin of the opening page of St Matthew or, on the contrary, in a most impressive hieratism as when he depicts St John in a purple dress edged with flashes of bright red, surrounded by the palm-leaf pattern of yellow and blue flames. Sometimes he unbends to unexpected fantasy, representing the second 'I' of Principio by a little bright blue man playing the harp on the C which is itself represented by a twisted animal body (Fig. 13). But generally his

74

mood is grave, a mixture of violence and subtlety, a sort of decorative intoxication.

Another painter was the official portraitist of the Book. He made the two big figures of Evangelists, that of the teaching Christ (Pl. 27) and perhaps those of the symbols in square frames and the 'Quoniam' at the beginning of the Gospel of St Luke. He seems to have been trained in the same methods of ornamentation as the Goldsmith. He works as minutely when he chooses, but without the poetical meandering virtuosity of his colleague. Like him he uses spirals, animal interlacings and knotted threads. But occasionally he adds to that traditional series of patterns the novelty of some vegetal scrolls. He does not try to vary his motifs or to surprise us. His feeling for symmetry is rather deadening. One cannot help thinking that, if there is to be ornamentation, he will make it, and to the best of his ability, but that his heart is really in the drawing of figures. And rightly so, for he is able to draw them with a grand monumental feeling. The great St Matthew draped in wide folds of purple and gold, the figure before the Chi–Rho, probably of Christ teaching, standing between two bright-coloured peacocks, a red book in his hand, and the St John on a blue throne, his head surrounded by a whirling halo, are the most impressive effigies ever designed by an Irish artist. His Evangelists' symbols fulfil their decorative purpose, but without any surprising display of imagination. He sometimes amuses himself by drawing little men, half real, half fantastic. The twenty little figures sleeping, crawling and falling between the letters of the 'Quoniam' give the measure of his invention (Fig. 8).

He cuts a rather tame figure beside the Illustrator, the wild, erratic painter who made the Arrest (Pl. G), the Temptation (Pl. B) the Virgin and Child (Pl. 17), the 'Tunc crucifixerant' and probably the symbols at the beginning of St John's Gospel (Pl. 28). This artist does not pause much over the niceties of elaborate ornament. He cares nothing for beautiful architectural frames. He casually weaves a few ferocious-looking beasts in a border, twists luxurious branches sprouting out of a vase, sets two lions snarling at the keystone of an arch or on the side of a frame, and knots another one into the shape of a T. His notion of colour sets one's teeth on edge. A combination of purple and apple green is one of his favourite devices, and he loves it so much that he uses it even in superposed layers showing through one another, often combined with an aggressive cherry red. With that brutal idea of colour and a savage notion of drawing, he manages to create the most astonishing pages of the Book, because he is audacious, sure of himself, dares to set his figures in motion, and is at times almost a visionary.

Beside these chief painters, there is a very attractive fourth who has composed little more than one or two big pages – the 'Nativitas Christi' (Pl. D) and perhaps one page of the canons – but who has displayed all his graceful fantasy and his dashing verve in many of the small capitals, in the cartouches of the text, in the border of the Genealogy, and in the animals drawn between the lines. He has certainly collaborated with the Goldsmith and added the little animal scenes in the big Chi–Rho page (Pl. 24). He is a fastidious draughtsman. He combines a delightfully smiling sense of observation where shape is concerned with a breathless impetuousity in the description of movement. He sketches with a sharp pen cats (Pls. 32, 33), cocks and hens, a goat, a greyhound, all roaming through the pages, draws a horseman riding over a word (Pl. 21), a warrior with a shield and spear sitting on a line, a cormorant nesting on top of a letter. Thanks to him there is a note of everyday life in that haughty universe of the Book of Kells. Though his original inspiration can be traced back to Greek manuscripts where scattered animals cover the margins, he clothed his borrowings in the garb of a familiar reality[1] and he must have often wandered, waxed tablets in hand, towards the farm of the monastery. He sketched the hens, made friends with the dogs and the goat and marvelled in bewilderment at the perpetual metamorphoses of a cat's body.

In the shadow of these strongly marked personalities all the lesser

---

[1] He may have been helped in his emancipation from abstract formulas by the example of the more realistic animal art of the Picts of Scotland, which he certainly knew pretty well. See in: C. Curle, 'The Chronology of the Early Christian Monuments of Scotland', *P.S.A.Sc.*, 1939–40, Pl. XIX, the close analogy of his drawing of a wolf with wolves engraved or carved on Pictish slabs. His birds would lend themselves to the same comparisons. The contacts of Iona with the mainland of Scotland are sufficient to explain such a knowledge in a member of the Iona–Kells community.

breed of young painters and muddlers were allowed from time to time to leave their mark on the Book. There are awkwardly balanced pages, initials betraying a complete lack of imagination, and the decoration of the canon-tables is strangely uneven. But this hardly affects the total impact of the volume.

Leaving the pleasant task of description, it is now time to turn to the hardest of the problems connected with the Book of Kells, that of its relation to other manuscripts, especially those of the north of England and the Carolingian manuscripts of the Palace School (or Ada School). A detailed study of all the complex facets of this problem is impossible here as it would be out of proportion in such a short study. Nevertheless, even a slight analysis of this aspect of the history of the manuscript can help to establish its date and affinities.

Both Bruun[1] and Friend[2] tried to show that the non-Celtic elements in the Book of Kells could be linked with the Carolingian Renaissance. In this blunt form the proposition is practically untenable. Even toning it down and saying that the non-Irish elements of the Book can be traced back to the sources which inspired the Carolingian Renaissance, one would be obliged to gloss over some of the Book's most original features. Koehler[3] has pointed out the rarity and small size of the illustrations of Biblical subjects in the large manuscripts of the time of Charlemagne. Even the illustration of the Utrecht Psalter (c. A.D. 820) is nothing but a multiplicity of tiny sketches. Only around 835–45 do fairly large Biblical illustrations make their appearance in the Bibles of the School of Tours (Grandval Bible, Br. M. Add. Ms. 10546; Vivien Bible, or First Bible or Charles-the-Bald, Paris, Bibl. nat. Ms. Lat. 1, c. A.D. 846). The concept of illustration remains however very different from that of the two surviving pictures of the Book of Kells – the Temptation and the Arrest of Christ – or of the page with the Virgin and Child surrounded by angels. In consequence, keeping an open mind

---

[1] J. A. Bruun, *An Enquiry into the Art of the Illuminated Manuscripts of the Middle Ages*, I, *Celtic illuminated Manuscripts* (Edinburgh, 1897).

[2] A. M. Friend, 'The Canon Tables of the Book of Kells', *Medieval Studies in Memory of Kingsley Porter* (Cambridge, Mass., 1939), II, pp. 611 sqq.

[3] W. Koehler, 'An illustrated Evangelistary of the Ada School and its model', *J.W.C.I.*, 1952, pp. 48 sqq.

about conclusions, it seems essential to re-examine the chief points of the problem.

First, let us take the Virgin and Child page (Pl. 17). Kitzinger has studied in great detail the attitudes of the two chief figures in order to compare them with the similar group engraved on the wooden reliquary of St Cuthbert which may have been decorated at Lindisfarne in 698.[1] He has stressed a feature they have in common: the fact that the Child is not seated facing the onlooker as in most of the representations of the time but is flung across his mother's lap in a much more casual way. In the Book of Kells, far from looking at us, he is turned towards his mother so that his face is seen in profile. A very keen perception of the enormous gaps which exist in our knowledge of pre-Romanesque art brought Kitzinger to conclude, on the strength of some faint clues, that there had existed in the East – to which the style of the Kells picture seems to point – representations of the Virgin and Child more familiar than hieratic in their presentation.

Since this study was written, the publication of the Sinai Madonna has supplied us with one element at least of such representations: the Child seated across his mother's lap.[2] Moreover, Kitzinger has pointed out that the Child shown in profile, or at least turned towards his mother, is often found in the sarcophagi carvings representing the Adoration of the Magi. Sarcophagi from Rome and a few from Spain supply ten examples or more.[3] This tradition seems to have survived in Rome, as the Child in the Santa Maria Nuova icon, cleaned in 1954, was certainly turned towards his mother.[4] This familiar figuration of the Child, perhaps originating in the Magi figurations, may have been more

---

[1] E. Kitzinger, 'The Coffin-Reliquary', *Relics of St Cuthbert*, pp. 202 sqq.

[2] G.-M. Sotirou, *Les Icones du Mont Sinaï* (Athens, 1956), Fig. 4; E. Kitzinger, 'On some Icons of the Seventh Century', *Late Classical and Medieval Studies in Honour of A. M. Friend Jr.* (Princeton, 1955), pp. 132 sqq.

[3] Wilpert, *Sarcofagi*, II, pp. 284 sqq., Pls. CCXIX, CCXXII, CCXXIV, LXXXXIII, etc. See also for later examples (early eighth century): Wilpert, *R. Mosaiken*, IV, Pl. 161 (Sta Maria Antiqua) and III, Pl. 113 (Sta Maria in Cosmedin); see: V. Lasareff, 'Studies in the Iconography of the Virgin', *Art Bulletin*, 1938, pp. 26 sqq. and A. Grabar, 'Note sur l'iconographie ancienne de la Vierge', *Cahiers Techniques de l'Art*, 1954.

[4] P. Cellini, 'Una Madonna molto antiqua', *Proporzioni*, 1950, pp. 1 sqq.

common in icon painting than now appears. It is found in a Roman context, though Kitzinger was right to suspect in the case of the Book of Kells an Oriental inspiration to which all the stylistic details point and which is also indicated by similarities to the representation of the Virgin and Child in Saqqarah frescoes.[1]

All this becomes still more obvious if the composition is considered as a whole. The Madonna is surrounded by four angels, two of which at the top are especially striking. Turning to us, they point towards the central group with a slightly ineffective gesture which brings our eyes a little too high (Pl. C). Their wings provide the composition with a series of triangular patterns. A very similar arrangement is found on a carved block of stone from Thalin (Armenia),[2] which dates probably from the seventh century, and in a page from a ninth-century Coptic manuscript in the Pierpont–Morgan collection (Fig. 7).[3] The similarity between these two compositions is enough to make us suspect how widespread the theme may have been. The Virgin is seated on a very elaborate throne. In both cases she is in an absolutely frontal position, different from that which she is given in the Book of Kells. In the Coptic illumination, the angels stand on the sides of the throne and their outstretched hands are just level with the head of Christ. In the Armenian carving, they stand erect on both sides of the throne, and their gestures are again perfectly appropriate. One cannot help thinking that the painter of the Book of Kells imitated some illumination of the same type as that of the Coptic manuscript, but that he placed his angels slightly higher, without realizing that their gesture was thereby rendered almost meaningless. Another surprising feature of the Kells picture is the absence of a glory around the Child's head, but the Coptic painter has drawn such a tiny one that it could easily be confused with the outline of the head, which suggests perhaps the source of the omission. So, far from emanating from a Carolingian milieu, this page of the Book of Kells takes us back to Oriental prototypes.

[1] K. Wessel, *Koptische Kunst* (Recklinghausen, 1963), figs. 5, 6, 33, pl. II, etc.

[2] J. Strzygowski, *Die Baukunst der Armenier und Europa* (Vienna, 1918), II, fig. 680, p. 717.

[3] [H. Hyvernat], *Bibliothecae Pierpont Morgan, Codices Coptici Photographice expressi* (Rome, 1922), t. XX, pl. 2 (Codex M. 612 (Fol. lv); dated A.D. 893).

a

b

Fig. 7. The Virgin and Child between angels : *a*, Coptic manuscript (ninth century), Pierpont Morgan Collection; *b*, carving, probably of the seventh century, Thalin (Armenia).

80

Colour plates between pages 80 and 81

A. Book of Kells, angel (see Pl. 17)
B. Book of Kells, Temptation of Christ
C. Book of Kells, detail from the Page
    of the eight circles
D. Book of Kells, detail from the
    Nativitas Christi page

E. Book of Kells, detail from one
    of the canon-tables (see Pl. 23)
F. Book of Kells, animal in the text
G. Bok of Kells, Arrest of Christ
H. Book of Kells, symbol of St Luke
    (see Pl. 28)

The two illustrations in the Book, the Temptation and the Arrest, are remarkable from several points of view (Pls. B and G). The Temptation of Christ is rarely figured in Early Christian iconography and is scarcely found before the Carolingian period.[1] It appears in the Sacramentary of Drogo where the three temptations are represented on the same page.[2] Christ in the Temptation on the Temple seems, in this case, to be on the slope of a roof, and the Devil, white-faced, and wearing a sort of black coat, is very different from the smoky-faced, cricket-like figure of the Kells painting. These sooty coloured and nimble devils are essentially a Byzantine type. The margins of the 'Monastic Psalters' are full of their gambols and so are the pages devoted to the Last Judgment of Ms. Grec 74 of the Bibliothèque nationale (Pl. VII). In the Stuttgart Psalter, Christ in the Temptation on the mountain is shown standing between two devils of this type, though perhaps slightly stouter, and two angels with veiled hands (Fol. 107v; Pl. VI). After this period the subject appears more and more often. One of the most interesting versions is to be found in the Echternach Codex Aureus (Nuremberg Museum; late tenth century),[3] where the Temple appears as a simplified representation of a church and the Devil is a little ink-black, gesticulating figure (Pl. VI). The popularity of the subject clearly corresponds with the time of our manuscript though it still has the flavour of novelty and, judging by the style of the figures, the model followed by our painter would seem to have been Byzantine.[4]

The Arrest is not figured near the text which describes it; it comes as a sort of prelude to the Passion, and this aspect is emphasized by the

[1] L. Réau, *Iconographie de l'art chrétien*, II (*Nouv. Test.*, Paris, 1957), pp. 304 sqq.
[2] Paris, Bibl. nat. Ms. Lat. 9428, Fol. 41r (ninth century); Koehler, *Karol. Min.*, III, Pl. 83.
[3] On p. 32; P. Metz, *Das Goldene Evangelienbuch von Echternach in Germanischen National-Museum zu Nurnberg* (Munich, 1956). It is found also in the tenth-century Gospel-book of the Emperor Otto at Aachen.
[4] Cf. the mosaics of Byzantine style of St Mark in Venice (Galassi, *Roma o Bisanzio*, I, p. 247, Fig. 139) and those of Monreale, in Sicily (O. Demus, *The Mosaics of Norman Sicily* (London, 1949), Pl. 66B). The Temptation appears also at Sant' Angelo in Formis. It is found in several eleventh and twelfth-century Greek manuscripts (see Demus, loc. cit.), among them the Studion Psalter (Br. M. Add. Ms. 19.352, Fol. 123v).

un-realistic treatment of the scene. Christ towers above the two figures whose efforts to hold him seem completely ineffective. The voluntary character of the offering of the Passion is thus stressed, and the analogy, indicated by Macalister, with the representations of Aaron and Hur supporting Moses' arms is probably not accidental either. The parallelism between the two scenes is suggested on the cross of Muiredach at Monasterboice, where the Arrest is figured on the lowest panel of the west side of the shaft (Pl. 79), while Moses, Aaron and Hur appear in the top panel on the same side, with the symmetrical arrangement always given to the scene, which, because of the outstretched arms of Moses is usually considered as prefiguring the Crucifixion, though it is also a figure of the efficacity of prayer.[1] So the story of the Passion is prefaced by a picture laden with a multiple symbolical meaning. It is harder, however, in this case to suggest the origin of the model used by the artist than in the case of the other two pictures.

The 'portraits' are more complex than they seem at first glance. The two figures in the Gospel of St Matthew seem to be standing in the traditional attitude of the semi-classical figure holding a book in his hand (Pl. 27). Though they have the same frontal presentation, their clothes are not as uncompromisingly reduced to a series of patterns as those of the Evangelists in the Lichfield and St Gall Gospels. One detail betrays their ultimate derivation from classical models : the red lines of the sandal straps on the feet. However, on a closer inspection, these figures which seem to be standing and in fact have been drawn as if standing, have chairs behind them. In the Matthew portrait it is behind the side columns and it is really only a misunderstood adaptation of a seat which the painter has not tried to connect with the figure; similarly the curve above the halo is a vestigial memory of an architectural frame. In the portrait of Christ (Pl. 27), the seat is almost absorbed in the draperies which have become part of it.

The third figure, at the beginning of St John's Gospel (Pl. J) is clearly seated, the knees spread out in that overemphasis of a difficult foreshortening found in so many apsidial mosaic figures. A. M. Friend[2] has compared this 'portrait' of St John with that found in a Carolingian

[1] Cf. p. 181.   [2] Friend, *Canon Tables*, p. 629, Pl. XX.

manuscript of the Palace School (Br.M. Ms. Harley 2788). The two figures certainly have some points in common, and the pattern of red lines in the background of the Kells figure is explained by the drapery flung on the back of the throne in the Harley manuscript. But on the whole the similarity is slight. The seats are totally different, the feet are not in the same position; above all there is a world of difference between the clean-shaven, strongly classical face of the Harley St John and the long face tapering to a pointed beard of the Kells figure. Both are shown dipping a pen in ink, but while the Evangelist of the Harley manuscript uses a little square ink-pot of surprisingly modern appearance the painter of the Book of Kells has carefully depicted an ink-horn similar to that which he, no doubt, was using himself, and of a type shown nearly a century earlier beside St Mark in the Book of Lichfield.

Friend's comparison of the two figures in the Gospel of St Matthew in the Book of Kells with those found in another Palace School manuscript, the Lorsch Gospel-book, now divided between Alba Julia (Rumania) and the Vatican Library,[1] is more fruitful, as it explains the significance of the two Kells figures. In the Lorsch Gospels, St Matthew's portrait is at the beginning of the prologue to the Gospel, while at the beginning of the Gospel proper, there is a figure of Christ between the Evangelists' symbols and angels framed in medallions. This is closely similar to the arrangement in the Book of Kells where one portrait is at the beginning of the Gospel and another, framed by four angels and two peacocks, symbols of resurrection, is amongst the decorated pages immediately after the Genealogy (Pl. 27).

The Book of Kells has therefore enough features in common with the earliest of the great Carolingian manuscripts to be their contemporary and to have been decorated in a milieu where the same models were available. This general similarity is however all that one can accept and it would be dangerous to push the comparisons too far, as direct imitations from Oriental manuscripts can also easily be detected in the Book of Kells. This brings us to the knotty problem of the Kells canon-tables which have also been linked up with canon-tables in some of the Palace School manuscripts.

[1] Koehler, *Karol. Min.*, II, Pls. 94–116.

Here it may not be superfluous to outline a few basic facts. The canons are lists of corresponding passages in the four Gospels, presented in parallel columns, compiled in the fourth century by Eusebius of Caesarea, who first divided the texts into numbered sections for easy reference. There are ten canons, the first giving the passages common to all four Gospels, the following (second to fourth) those found in three of the Gospels, five others (fifth to ninth) those found in two Gospels and the last (tenth) the texts which occur in only one Gospel.

Fairly soon, it became the custom to copy these lists at the beginning of Gospel-books and to place them under arcades which gave rise to a lavish decoration of the opening pages.[1] This architectural framing, however pleasing to the eye, had its drawbacks, as the uneven length of the lists hardly lends itself to a symmetrical arrangement. The artist found himself faced first with the problem of passing from an even number of parallel lists (four or two) to an uneven number (three). Several solutions could be envisaged : either to change the arcades from four to three, then again to four (placing two series of double lists on the same page), or else to keep the fourfold arcades, leaving one arcade blank for the second, third and fourth canons. In fact, from the fifth canon on endless difficulties may arise from the very irregular length of the lists. To avoid the worst pitfalls, the artist needs a good deal of space. Twelve pages seem to be the safe minimum. But there still remain two stumbling blocks where scribe and painter in despair may well give up the use of arcades : at the beginning of the fifth canon they may be overwhelmed by the difficulty of accommodating all the explicits and incipits of the following canons; and even if they persevere at this point they may abandon the architectural frame before the ninth canon where a series of short lists, some of which are not even comparisons, renders the system of parallel spaces meaningless. The work of the decorator becomes infinitely more difficult if he has to include the symbol corresponding to the Gospel excerpts quoted below, as this makes it impossible to put one short list under another from a different Gospel, so the work of painter and scribe has to be synchronized with great care.

[1] C. Nordenfalk, *Die Spätantiken Kanontafeln* (Göteborg, 1938).

It is not easy to determine when the arcaded canons were introduced into Irish manuscripts. In the Book of Durrow, the lists are simply framed by thin bands of interlacings, and in the Echternach Gospels by large coloured ribbons. As the Lichfield Gospels and Rawlinson Ms. G.167 have lost their preliminary pages, nothing can be known of the arrangement of their canons. We have seen that arcaded canon-tables of Oriental inspiration are found in both the Gospels of Maihingen and those of Trier.[1] In the Book of Lindisfarne, the canons are spread out on sixteen pages under Insular style arcades. The painter of an English manuscript with Celtic affinities, Royal Ms. I.B of the British Museum, succeeds in compressing them into twelve pages, and so does the painter of the Vatican Gospels. However, in this last case, the artist does not seem to be very sure of what he is doing : on the seven first pages he had drawn four arcades on each page and thus fits the first four canons. At the first critical point mentioned above, he gives up the arcades and leaves the remaining lists unframed. A Gospel-book in Irish script of which only two pages have survived, Royal Ms. 7.C.XII in the British Museum abandons its arcades at the second critical point, between the eighth and ninth canons.[2]

Neither in the Vatican manuscript nor in the Maeseyck Gospels is the series of symbol canons complete. In the former there is a first very magnificent page framed by ornamented arcades whose tympana bear the four Evangelical symbols (Pl. IV). But, on the next page the system collapses. The ornaments vanish, and so do the symbols. They reappaer a few pages farther on, however, under the guise of little heads very awkwardly sketched and hardly ever corresponding with the list below. The painter of the Maeseyck Gospels also wavers (Pl. IV) and does not use the symbols right through. They are mostly busts, very simply drawn, which occasionally give a slightly comical impression of trying to look around the corner of a wall.

Where did this system of putting the symbols at the top of the lists

[1] *Vol. I*, pp. 180–1.
[2] P. McGurk, 'Two Notes on the Book of Kells and its relation to other insular Gospel-books', *Scriptorium*, 1955, pp. 105 sqq.

of references originate? The problem, in spite of much study, is far from settled.[1] In the early Middle Ages, outside the group of manuscripts we are studying at present, the symbol-canons are found, only in a certain number of Carolingian manuscripts of the late eighth and ninth century which have definite affinities with Insular art. The oldest of the series are Harley Ms. 2788 of the British Museum and the Gospelbook of St Médard de Soissons in Paris (Bibl. nat. Ms. Lat. 8850).[2] In the tenth century the symbol-canons reappear in Spanish Bibles where they are handled with a remarkable virtuosity and a minimum of mistakes.[3] There, the symbols are invariably anthropomorphic, a feature which is rare elsewhere. Nevertheless, the very fact of their existence puts the problem on a wider basis and makes it difficult to see in this type of canon-table an Insular invention, as has sometimes been done. It seems more likely that there were prototypes which were known in England and Ireland on the one hand, and in Spain on the other. The theme may have passed, as we have seen,[4] from Insular to Carolingian art, though a common source remains possible.

In the Book of Kells, the symbols are treated with a feeling for their epic character which is altogether absent in the Vatican and Maeseyck Gospels and which is totally alien to the painter of Harley Ms. 2788. The dancing and pirouetting postures of his symbols make them almost laughable. The painters of the Book of Kells, on the contrary, never lose sight of the visionary origin of the creatures they depict. They pass above the arcades in a fantasy of flapping wings and blazing colours. Far from being merely little headings topping lists of figures, their very appearance introduces us from the first page of the Book to the supernatural atmosphere into which the reader is about to step.

[1] R. Crozet, 'Les quatre évangélistes et leurs symboles, assimilations et adaptations', *Les cahiers techniques de l'art*, 1962; Friend, *Canon Tables*, pp. 618 sqq. If one followed Nordenfalk in his early dating of the Maeseyck fragment, one would be tempted to postulate an inspiration from a Greek or Italian manuscript seen by the painter either at Echternach or in Northumbria around 700. Unfortunately no Greek manuscript with symbol canon-tables has come down to us.

[2] Koehler, *Karol. Min.*, II, Pls. 42–52 and 67–93.

[3] Friend, *Canon Tables*, p. 619.   [4] See pp. 67–8.

However, when it comes to a question of accuracy, the painters fall into every trap which opens under their feet – unless a lack of synchronization between their work and that of the scribe is to blame for most of the mistakes.

First of all, for some unfathomable reason, only ten or eleven pages were reserved for the canon-tables,[1] a compression which seems surprising in a book conceived on such an ample scale. As we have seen above, this is definitely too little. Nevertheless, all goes well as far as the fifth page. If there seem to be some irregularities and the symbol of St Luke twice suggests the appearance of a bird,[2] it may be because it is shown full face on the first page, and on the third the bull's head on the eagle's body may be an effort to suggest the symbol of St John which otherwise does not appear on this table. This ambiguous appearance is moreover in full accord with one of the sources of these symbols, the Vision of Ezekiel, where they are described as one fantastic being with four heads. On the fifth page, however, the scribe, possibly afraid of being short of space, suddenly decides to fit the third canon in a remarkably untidy fashion around the bases of the columns.[3] As a consequence, the work of the painter and that of the scribe do not synchronize on the next page. This may account for another composite beast, a lion with a bull's head, meant perhaps to hide the fact that a space reserved for a list from St Luke has been filled with one from St Mark. It is impossible to know what protests this gave rise to, but there must have been a crisis, because the stiff architectural composition on the following page is by a different hand and devoid of symbols.

Then comes the magnificent eighth page which seems to be the work of a hand never found again in the book (Pl. E, Pl. 23). There, as the text includes the sixth, seventh and eighth canons, the symbols are not connected definitely with any of the lists. *Homo* and *Aquila*, their wings

---

[1] The verso of the last canon-table remained blank, and so may have been reserved originally for one of the tables (fol. 6v). This may have something to do with the confusion on fol. 3v (see below).

[2] Fols. 1v and 2v.

[3] Unless, of course, he had forgotten it, so that it had to be added in whatever space was available.

spread in a triangular shape, fill the spandrels, while *Leo* and *Vitulus*, inscribed in a tympanum, are drawn on two opposed curves and outlined on a purple sky. Nowhere does the feeling for majesty expressed by combinations of lines which is the core of these symbol designs, unfold itself more impressively, except perhaps in the Book of Armagh imbued with the same visionary dream (Pls. 18, 33). The next page is an anticlimax. The painter of Kells gave up the architectural system at the point where the painter of Royal Ms. 7.C.XII had abandoned it, and arcades are suddenly replaced by wide coloured ribbons similar to those of the canon-tables of the Echternach Gospels.

From the above analysis it becomes clear that the change was not caused by the 'dispersion' of the Iona scriptorium, as Friend would have it. There are simply several critical points in the arrangement of canons under arcades and even more when symbols have to be accommodated. One is between the fourth and the fifth canons. This is where the painter of the Vatican Gospels stops using arcades; where the painters of the Book of Kells drop the symbols for the first time; where there is a change of style and errors in the use of symbols in Harley Ms. 2788. The other is between the eighth and the ninth canons, where the painters of Royal Ms. 7.C.XII and of the Book of Kells abandon the use of arcades. It seems therefore that the similarities noticed by Friend between the Book of Kells and the Harley manuscript result from an inherent common cause and are not in any way proof of the existence of a common prototype.

The three pages of symbols which have survived in the Book of Kells show this same preoccupation with the Evangelists symbols, this keen feeling for their spiritual nature. The antecedents of these pages are to be found in the Book of Durrow and the Lichfield Gospels,[1] where the four symbols are placed in the four quarters into which a rectangular frame is divided by a cross. While, however, their figures float in space, in the Book of Kells they are more intimately mixed with ornament. Each time also they are presented in different fashion, whether they are in the traditional rectangular frames (St Matthew), or within the compass of a circular gold and purple frame which forms a halo around

[1] *Vol. I*, Pl. 98.

them (St Mark), or in the triangular spaces outlined by the saltire which suggests ornamental bands running across the surface of a vault (St John) (Pls. 28, H).

Before leaving the Book of Kells it remains to examine the types of decoration used in its pages. On the whole, they belong to the usual repertoire of Irish eighth-century art: spirals, interlacings, key-patterns. But there is a constant interpenetration of motifs. The lines

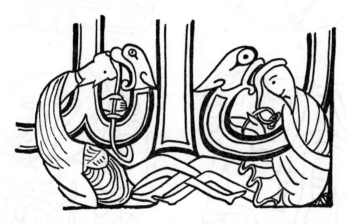

Fig. 8. Book of Kells, detail from the first page of the Gospel of St Luke.

connecting the spirals, those which outline the neck of an animal or a bird (Pls. 24, 25, 27), may suddenly blossom into an intricate inter-lacing, which does not destroy the pattern but is absorbed into the continuity of its tracery. In a curvilinear pattern the largest spirals may be occasionally replaced by discs containing human or animal inter-lacings (Pl. 25). This is remote from the invariable discrimination between different categories of ornament found in the Book of Durrow. Here long familiarity leads to their mixing and fusion and the painters produce remarkable effects from these combinations. We have seen[1] that several monuments of the middle and late eighth century – Ahenny crosses, crosses and pillars of the Clonmacnois–Bealin group – showed

[1] *Vol. I,* pp. 140 and 144.

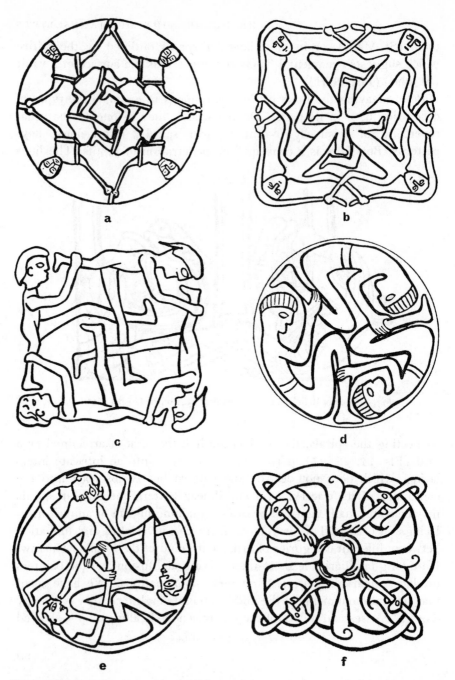

Fig. 9. Wheels of figures or animals; *a*, bronze from the Luristan; *b*, Old Kilcullen cross; *c*, Kells, Market cross; *d*, gilt bronze disc found at Togherstown (N.M.D.); *e*, Book of Kells, detail; *f*, open-work bronze plaque (Trondheim Museum).

the same tendency to run one ornament into the next and also to mix spirals and interlacings. The decorative background is the same in the manuscript and the crosses and in both combinations of little human figures appear beside animal-interlacings. Sometimes they are inscribed within circular or square frames and form decorative wheels (Fig. 9) of which examples from a remote antiquity are found in the East (Fig. 9, *a*); or they are arranged in a sort of weave on the model of animal interlacings (Pl. G, Fig. 13). There are already examples of this type of ornament in the Gospels of Mac Regol and in Ms. 1395 in the St Gall Library.[1]

Fig. 10.
Book of Kells, foliage.

Some of the late eighth-century crosses also employ vegetable ornament, for example the cross at Old Kilcullen. On the South cross at Clonmacnois[2] there is a vine pattern inhabited by little animal figures. A similar motif is found on the Tower cross at Kells.[3] This affection for foliage pattern is manifest also in the Book of Kells. It contains vine patterns not very different from those found in the Vatican Gospels (Pl. 34) and in the Amiens Psalter (Fig. 11). Other plant motifs are of a rarer type. They come from vases, which are represented either straight or sideways, in complete disregard of the laws of gravity. The stems are twisted in all directions and carry large clover-like leaves and sometimes little bunches of fruit (Figs. 10 and 12). There are few contemporary parallels for this type of vegetation. The only striking ones are again to be found in the Amiens Psalter (Fig. 11) and the Vatican Gospels (Pl. V), which have so many other points in common with the Book of Kells. Besides this type of foliage which is part and parcel of the decoration, there is another, found chiefly in the early part of the Book; it consists of slight branches sketched with a great economy of means in the intervals in the text: a curve for the stem, a couple of leaves, a few drops of ink or paint for the fruit, no more. The painters of the Vatican Gospels are also inclined to use this feathery addition to the text, which is likely to be Oriental in its origin.

We have seen already that these decorations probably had a sym-

[1] *Irish Min. of St Gall*, Pl. XVII.   [2] *Vol. I*, Pl. 85.
[3] Henry, *Sc. irl.*, Pl. 54,4; Id., *Irish High Crosses*, Pl. 27.

Fig. 11.
Amiens Psalter,
foliage.

bolical significance going back to a very remote past, of which the painter was still conscious.[1] The vine is a stock Christian symbol. But the spiral which the Celts derived at several periods from vegetable motifs, may well have been used fairly often instead of the vine and with the same eucharistic meaning. As we have seen, interlacing was originally a figure for running water and motifs related to the swastika, such as key-patterns, may have kept from their solar origin all sorts of connections with fire. One cannot resist the temptation of remembering such interpretations when examining the frame of St John's portrait (Pl. J).[2] Though the page has been savagely trimmed, the head, feet and hands of a large figure still show clearly on the four sides, as in those Medieval representations where God is shown holding the world figured as a large disc, marked with the emblems of the four elements, whose centre is occupied by the figure of Man. On this page in fact the different types of ornaments are carefully defined and isolated from each other; water could be figured by interlacings, earth by snakes, air by birds in the four corners, and fire by key-patterns.

Remembering the various parallels which have been mentioned in the course of this study, the Book of Kells is seen to take its place, quite naturally, in the period to which it has usually been assigned: the late eighth and early ninth century. It appears clearly as the continuation of the Irish illuminated manuscripts of the late seventh and eighth century, especially of the Book of Durrow, the Lichfield Gospels and the St Gall Gospels. In its decorative structure, the distribution and appearance of the ornamental pages, it follows the tradition established in these earlier manuscripts. The patterns used are the same, though handled in a more fanciful and imaginative way and generally drawn on a much more minute scale. Its connections with the group of manuscripts of Irish style illuminated in the north of England at the end of the eighth century are not quite so close: these often employ degenerate versions of Irish ornament, and their decorative pages are not always ordered according to the usual Irish standard. Nevertheless they show strong traces of preoccupations which were also in the minds of the painters

[1] *Vol. I*, pp. 203 sqq.   [2] See: *E.Q.C. Cenannensis*, II, fol. 291v.

of the Book of Kells : amongst others, the use of symbols in the canon-
tables, and of little animals and foliage in the body of the text. It was a
neighbouring 'milieu', where Irish influences were still very strong and
which may have supplied, in exchange for the inspiration it received, a
few interesting suggestions. The links with the manuscripts of the
Amiens region are of a different kind. There, we are dealing with a

Fig. 12. Book of Kells, foliage.

stopping-place of the Irish on their arrival on the Continent, where all
sorts of exchanges, enriched by the presence of Oriental manuscripts,
were taking place. Besides the analogies shown by the Amiens Psalter,
which have been indicated in the course of this study of the Book of
Kells, there are other striking and unexpected similarities. A. M. Friend
has likened the scalopped halo of Christ in Ms. 17 of the Poitiers Library,
a manuscript originating from the neighbourhood of Amiens,[1] to that of

[1] See p. 65.

93

St John in the Book of Kells;[1] G. L. Micheli has pointed out how close in their general composition are a page framed by two erect lions in the Gospel-book in the cathedral of Essen, which comes from Corbie or its daughter-house in Germany, Corvey, with the final page of the Gospel of St Mark in the Book of Kells.[2] Several other comparisons could be made.

With Carolingian art the contacts are of a different nature, and are partly the result of exchanges and partly of inspiration from a common source. We have seen that the first stages of this process were dominated by the presence of Alcuin and the semi-Insular scriptorium which he had established for Charlemagne, that scriptorium which produced, in the region of Trier and Lorsch, the first great books of the Palace School. It is well to remember also that they originated in a region which had seen, less than a century earlier, the creation of manuscripts of half-Insular, half-Continental style, such as the Trier Gospels, which betrayed also a strong Oriental influence. This tradition may have been still alive in the area.

It remains to wonder whether the Book of Kells was unique in its lavish and elaborate decoration, or whether a few other books of the same importance were produced at about the same time by some outstanding scriptoria. All that can be quoted is the description of one such manuscript which was still kept at Kildare in the twelfth century, and fragments subsisting from another which had been brought to the Continent and belonged to the library of Bobbio Abbey. There may have been others, but probably not many. Such works monopolizing for years the activity of a whole scriptorium, were only possible in the richest and largest monasteries. Beside Kells and Kildare, Armagh, Clonmacnois perhaps, or Bangor, may also have been able to produce them, but it would be a mistake to imagine each small monastery equipped with books of such grandeur. They were the exceptional culmination of that art and endlessly supplied models for the lesser painters of poorer houses.

The description of the Book of Kildare by Giraldus Cambrensis has often been quoted. The Welsh historian who accompanied the Norman knights in the invasion of Ireland at the end of the twelfth century was

[1] Friend, *Canon Tables*, p. 629, Pl. XX.   [2] Micheli, *Enluminure*, p. 85.

only too inclined to look down on Ireland and to consider its inhabitants as wild savages. His wonder at the book he describes is all the more remarkable: 'Of all the marvels of Kildare, I recall nothing more marvellous than that wonderful book, written, they say, at the dictation of an angel in the days of St Brigid. This book contains the harmony of the four Evangelists according to Jerome, where for almost every page there are different designs, distinguished by varied colours. Here you may see the face of majesty, divinely drawn, here the mystic symbols of the Evangelists, each with wings, now six, now four, now two; here the eagle, there the calf, here the man and there the lion, and other forms almost infinite. Look at them superficially with the ordinary casual glance, and you would think it is an erasure, and not tracery. Fine craftsmanship is all about you, but you might not notice it. Look more keenly at it and you will penetrate to the very shrine of art. You will make out intricacies, so delicate and subtle, so exact and compact, so full of knots and links, with colours so fresh and vivid, that you might say that all this was the work of an angel, and not of a man. For my part the oftener I see the book, and the more carefully I study it, the more I am lost in ever fresh amazement, and I see more and more wonders in the Book.'[1]

It could be the description of the Book of Kells. But as there is no evidence that it was at Kildare at the end of the twelfth century we must assume that there was another book similar to it not only in the elaborateness of the detail but also in the frequent use of the Evangelists' symbols.

Though the Turin Gospel-book may not have been as lavishly decorated and it may not have had much ornament in the text, still its four illuminated pages are the only ones which for the sumptuousness of the decoration can be compared with those of the Book of Kells. It is now no more than a ruin, its history being a succession of tragedies. It reached Bobbio before the ninth century.[2] Later it was brutally used as a source of vellum; its text was erased and replaced by that of the

[1] O'Meara, *Giraldus Cambrensis*, pp. 151–2; I have quoted here Dr Alton's translation in *E.Q.C. Cenannensis*, p. 15.

[2] Kenney, *Sources*, p. 649 (No. 485); Lowe, IV, No. 466; Zimmermann, pp. 102, 108, 246–7, III, Pls. 198, 211; Micheli, *Enluminure*, p. 25.

Esposizione sopra il Credo by Cavalca. Nevertheless four decorated pages were spared as well as a decorated initial and it was still possible to trace some parts of the original text under the new one.[1] Unfortunately the manuscript was lost in the fire in the Turin Library in 1904. The four miniatures, which were exhibited separately, were saved but are now badly shrunk and darkened to the colour of old leather. There are several descriptions of the manuscript as it was before the fire and Cipolla's publication includes photographs which were taken when the pages were intact. They are not very good, but if one compares them with recent photographs taken by letting the light play through the vellum,[2] one can get a sufficiently clear idea of the decoration (Pls. 37–40).

Before the pages were shrunk by the heat they were about $11\frac{1}{2}$ by $5\frac{1}{2}$ inches, so the book was slightly smaller than the Book of Kells and roughly the same size as the St Gall Gospel-book. Although it can be compared to the Book of Kells for the minute treatment of the ornament, the lay-out of the carpet-pages is nearer to that found in the St Gall Gospels and one may wonder if it did not originate in the scriptorium which, some fifty years earlier, had produced the Gospel-book now in the St Gall Library.

Of the four pages which were spared when the vellum was used again, two are carpet-pages and two full page miniatures, one of the Ascension, the other of the Last Judgment. Zimmermann thought that these last were more recent than the others, but there is nothing to justify this hypothesis. It seems unlikely that such a book did not have more than four decorated pages. Others may have got lost before the alteration of the text. When the 1890 catalogue was compiled there were 189 folios in the book,[3] which hardly seems enough for the four Gospels written in

[1] G. Ottino, *I Codici Bobbiesi nella Biblioteca nazionale di Torino indicati e descritti* (Turin-Palermo, 1890), p. 56; C. Cipolla, *Collezione paleographica, Codici Bobbiesi della Biblioteca nazionale universitaria di Torino* (Milan, 1907), Pls. XXXIX–XLI. (See also: F. Carta, C. Cipolla, C. Frati, *Monumenta palaeographica sacra* (Turin, 1899), Pl. X.)

[2] This is the case for the photographs on Pls. 38–9; those on Pls. 37 and 40 are from Cipolla's book.

[3] Or 190; see: B. Peyron, *Codices Italici manu exarati qui in bibliotheca Taurinensis Athenaei ante diem XXVI Januarii MCMIV asservabantur* (Turin, 1904), pp. 381–3; the description is otherwise the same as in Ottino's catalogue of 1890.

96

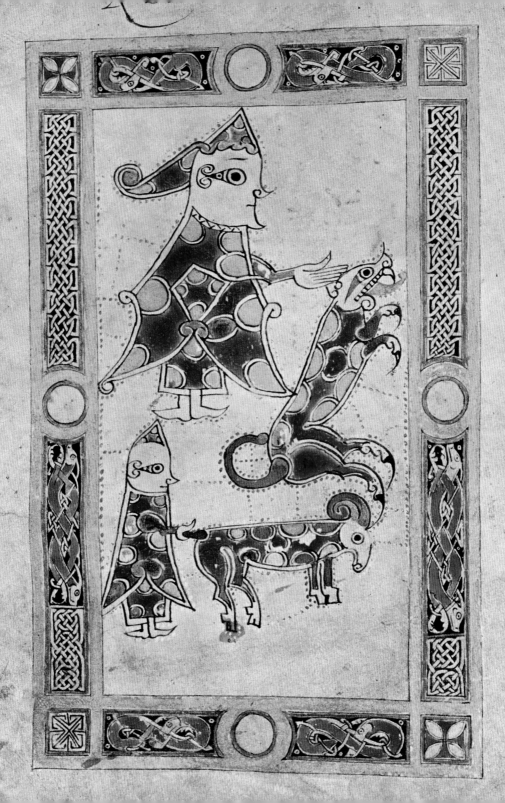

17

nupqone

rahoir th

aidiñ le

decoreþ tī

Onaq

rioi d

aupid

ibrq;

ai aio ud

au uideam

p bapa cor

plapa me

the large script which can be seen faintly on some of Cipolla's photographs. We have to assume that pages of text were already missing at the time of the erasure and it is even more likely that some illuminated pages had disappeared.

The Ascension page, however, raises a problem: the text written between the figures is neither that of St Mark or St Luke, the two Evangelists who describe the scene. It is the text of the Acts of the Apostles. One may then wonder whether the original volume contained a complete New Testament, like the Book of Armagh written at about the same date.

One of the carpet-pages (Pl. 38) bears a large cross covered with circle-interlacings on a background of key-patterns. This is very nearly the same arrangement as that found on the carpet-page of the Maihingen Gospels, though the details are much more intricate. The other (Pl. 39) is more complicated in its general disposition and choice of pattern, with a great variety of animal and bird interlacing, a few string interlacings and five discs of spirals enlivened with lines of dots. In addition there are two panels filled with human interlace, a characteristic feature of the decoration of the Book of Kells, and on each side of the frame appear two strange figures, carrying on their heads a flourish of antler-like interlace which closely resemble the squatting figure on the North cross of Clonmacnois,[1] but here they are accompanied by two birds.

The two picture-pages are closer, in the presentation of the figures, to the sober style of the St Gall Gospels than to the baroque exuberance of the Book of Kells. In the Ascension page (Pl. 37) Christ's bust is framed in a circular glory, with two small angels inscribed above his shoulders in elliptical halos. This disc was partly outlined on a dark background (purple or azure?) against which stand also four angels; they are strangely immobile and hieratic and do not exert themselves in the usual fashion to carry aloft the mandorla. Farther down, also in a circular frame, stands another angel who takes the place of the 'men in white garments' mentioned in the text of Acts, whose words are quoted on either side of the circular frame. Below, twelve little busts represent the Apostles. Their names are inscribed beside each of them and,

[1] *Vol. I*, Pl. 91.

according to an anachronism which is common in Early Christian art, Paul is figured on the right of the angel, symmetrically with Peter who is on the left.

The various representations of the Ascension on Early Christian monuments and objects[1] do not supply any very obvious parallel to this composition. Christ shown in bust, the presence of only one angel, the completely stereotyped figuration of the Apostles, are so many unusual features, or at least features which are never found together elsewhere. The Stuttgart Psalter offers several examples of Christ in bust, holding a book in one hand and blessing with the other, enclosed in a circular frame, but never as part of an Ascension. This presentation of the theme is Oriental in its general lines[2] and contrasts strongly with Western iconography where Christ is shown in profile climbing a mountain and sometimes pulled towards Heaven by the Hand of God – iconography found in Western ivories[3] and in the Sacramentary of Drogo.[4] The Greek endings of some of the words in the inscription[5] point also to a Byzantine examplar. As for the angel, alone in a central position, one may well wonder if a picture where the Virgin was figured above the Apostles, as she is in the ninth-century fresco in the church of San Clemente in Rome,[6] has not been imitated, the painter turning this isolated figure into that of an angel.

The other page (Pl. 40) is obviously a description of the Last Judgment as schematic as that of the St Gall manuscript. This time, however, Christ is not shown in bust, but standing and holding a cross which overlaps the frame. The trumpeter angels majestically accom-

---

[1] Such as those in the Rabbula Gospels, in a fresco of Bawit, on ampullae from Monza, on the Vatican box, on an icon in the Sinai monastery, etc. For the iconography of the Ascension, see: E. T. de Wald, 'The iconography of the Ascension', *American Journal of Archaeology*, 1915, pp. 279 sqq.; S. H. Gutberlet, *Die Himmelfahrt Christi in der bildenden Kunst* (Strasbourg, 1934).

[2] See a Byzantine ivory in Berlin (W. F. Volbach, *Die Bildwerke des Deutschen Museum, Die Elfenbeinwerke*) (Berlin–Leipzig, 1923), p. 14, Pl. 10, and another in the Museo nazionale, Florence (Rice, *Byzantium*, Pl. 114).

[3] See for example: Volbach, op. cit., p. 19, Pl. 21 (ninth cent.).

[4] Koehler, *Karol. Min.*, III, Pl. 88.

[5] 'filios', 'angelos'.

[6] It was painted under Leo IV (847–55); Wilpert, *R. Mosaiken*, IV, p. 210.

panying him in the St Gall miniature have disappeared, being replaced by a small figure blowing a long, straight trumpet in the top right-hand corner. The page is divided into ninety-six rectangular compartments, each framing a small full-face figure holding a book tightly to his breast. The general effect is remarkably similar to that of Byzantine enamelled bindings or reliquaries, which are divided by relief frames into compartments, each holding a figure or two,[1] and the artist probably imitated such a model. Moreover, comparisons have to be made with small identical figures of Apostles in four superposed lines on the Moone cross,[2] or with those, even more similar in their attire, which accompany the Crucifixion on the North cross at Castledermot.[3] These last may very well proceed from the imitation of an illuminated page of the type of the Turin one. The head of Christ flattened at the top against the frame is found in the Judgment miniature and in the Crucifixion of the North cross at Castledermot (Pl. 70).

Thus, from whatever angle one chooses to consider it, the manuscript appears as a continuation into the ninth century of the style of the St Gall Gospels including many features reminiscent of the Book of Kells and showing an obviously Byzantine inspiration in the picture pages. Nevertheless it has a very individual flavour which combines a hieratic presentation of the figures with a somewhat uncertain and flabby definition of the draperies, less incisive and patterned than is usual in Irish manuscripts. Some of the details also are unique as for example the chevron border on the edge of the halo in the Ascension and on the border of the circular frames of the spiral panels in one of the carpet-pages.

Let us now leave the luxury books written in large majuscules and smothered in ornament and turn our attention towards the few surviving works from the Armagh scriptorium. We shall find there a style different in many ways from that of the Turin manuscript, where a linear

[1] As for example the tenth-century Reliquary of the True Cross taken from Constantinople in 1204 and now preserved in Limburg-an-der-Lahn (Germany) (Rice, *Byzantium*, Pls. 124–6.)

[2] *Vol. I*, Pl. 71.   [3] See Pls. 66 and 70.

preoccupation is dominant. The chief works are the Book of Armagh and the Book of Mac Durnan, both written in a fine minuscule script which easily takes an ornamental twist, and the two manuscripts of Priscian's Grammar, written by less accomplished scribes in the same tradition.

The Book of Armagh[1] is a composite manuscript. It has the only complete New Testament text which has survived from Early Christian Ireland – a New Testament whose Gospels seem to have been treated as a privileged section, with separately numbered quires, though they are clearly part of the whole manuscript. But it also contains 'St Patrick's file', painstakingly collected by the monastery of Armagh in order to back its claim to a primacy over the other Irish monasteries, and its right to levy St Patrick's tribute. This includes the *Confession* of St Patrick, the biographical notes compiled in the seventh century by Muirchú and Tirechán, a few other Patrician documents and finally Sulpicius Severus' *Life of St Martin* (thought to be the uncle of St Patrick).

The various quires may originally have been left unbound, though they were thought of from the start as forming a whole and were written by the same hand. It was a current practice in the Middle Ages to enter the most precious documents relating to a monastery in a manuscript of the Gospels in order to ensure their safe keeping, and of this there are other striking examples in Irish manuscripts.

The Book is fairly small ($7\frac{3}{4}$ by $5\frac{1}{2}$ inches) and is written in minuscule script, so that the Gospels fit into the category of 'pocket Gospel-books'.[2] There are several colophons which were altered in order to attribute the Book to St Patrick himself. Charles Graves read them in 1846 with the help of reagents which have unfortunately damaged them to a great extent.[3] There is still, however, enough visible to check some of his readings. The colophons are in Latin, though partly written in Greek characters. That on Fol. 53v indicates that the Book was written

[1] T.C.D. Libr. No. 52; J. Gwynn, *Liber Ardmachanus, The Book of Armagh* (Dublin, 1913); Lowe, *C.L.A.*, II, No. 270; Zimmermann, p. 251, III, Pls. 206–7.
[2] Henry, *An Irish Manuscript*, pp. 151 sqq.
[3] C. Graves, in: *P.R.I.A.*, 1846, pp. 316–24 and 365–9.

by Ferdomnach, under the direction of Torbach 'successor of St Patrick' – that is, abbot of Armagh. The Annals of Ulster have, at the year 846 an entry on the death of Ferdomnach 'a wise and excellent scribe of Armagh', and at A.D. 808, they announce the death of 'Torbach, scribe and abbot of Armagh' who, according to the lists in the Leabhar Breac would have been abbot for only one year. This means that at least a section of the Book dates from 807–8, and the marginal entry in the Gospel of St Matthew which mentions Cellach, abbot of Iona, most probably at the time when he took refuge in Kells around 807,[1] comes as a confirmation of this date.

Ferdomnach is amongst the most accomplished of the Irish scribes whose works have reached us. He handles the minuscule script, in itself an unpromising medium, with incredible virtuosity, giving it a sort of regular rhythmic appearance, then suddenly extracting from it the melody of great curves cutting across the page (Pl. 30). It seems practically certain that he illustrated the Book himself, as the drawings show the same poetic feeling for significant line as the script. The decoration, however, remains very simple. It consists of a few initials and drawings of the Evangelists' symbols. These are of the same epic quality as some of the symbols in the canon-tables of the Book of Kells and reveal the same acute awareness of their visionary origin and their identification with different aspects of the Word of God. The artist is also as conscious of their inter-relation as the painters of the Book of Kells, though he does not express it with hybrid animals or juxtapositions; instead he prefers to place on the wings of one of the symbols medallions containing the heads of the others (Pl. 33). The initials, however small, are drawn with a great delicacy and several of them belong quite clearly to the repertoire of the Book of Kells (Pls. 29, 30).

The two manuscripts of the *Grammar* of Priscian, closely akin to each other, have line initials of the same type as those of the Book of Armagh, and are likely to be the work of scribes trained in Armagh. That in Leyden Library[2] may have been written on the Continent. It is the work

---

[1] See p. 20.
[2] Leyden, Univ. Libr. Ms. Lat. 67; Zimmermann, pp. 251–2, III, Pl. 208; Kenney, *Sources*, pp. 557, 574 sqq.

of a scribe called Dubtach who copied it, according to the colophon,[1] in 838. Judging from a marginal poem probably written by an Irishman, it was taken a few years later to Soissons. The manuscript in the St Gall Library[2] has a text of Priscian in the same tradition, which seems to be Irish. It was written in Ireland by several scribes working around 850, under the direction of a certain Maelbrigte. It is full of Irish glosses and it was probably taken to the Continent fairly soon after its completion. It was in Cologne between 850 and 869 and passed from there to St Gall.

These pen drawn initials, which were a passing fashion of the first half of the ninth century, are not without their analogy with the bold effects of pen drawing so often favoured by the artist who decorated the Lichfield Gospels.[3] This may be a tradition which lived right through the eighth century, though some of the links in the chain of evidence are missing.

In the Book of Mac Durnan,[4] unlike the Priscian manuscripts, the script is of the same type as that of the Book of Armagh. In fact the similarity is such that it has been suggested that Ferdomnach was the scribe.[5] The decoration, however, is so different in style that it is hard to believe that both manuscripts are from the same hand, unless Ferdomnach entrusted the decoration of the Book of Mac Durnan to another painter. But we have seen that Ferdomnach died in 846 and the style of the illuminations seems to fit much better in the latter part of the ninth century, which accords with the known facts of its history.

It belonged to the Library of Canterbury cathedral.[6] An inscription in the style of the Carolingian colophons was added when the Book arrived

---

[1] On Fol. 7v.

[2] St Gall, Stiftsbibl. Ms. 904: *Irish Min. of St Gall*, pp. 72 sqq. (Duft); Zimmermann, p. 252, III, Pls. 208–9; Kenney, *Sources*, pp. 674 sqq.

[3] *Vol. I*, Pl. 106.

[4] Lambeth Palace Library; E. Millar, *Les Manuscrits à peintures des Bibliothèques de Londres*, II (*Lambeth Palace*) (Paris, 1914); N. R. Kerr, *Medieval Libraries of Great Britain, A List of Surviving Books* (London, Roy. Hist. Soc., 1941); Zimmermann, pp. 248–50, III, Pl. 205; McGurk, *Pocket-books*; Henry, *An Irish Manuscript*.

[5] L. Bieler, 'Insular Palaeography, Recent State and Problems', *Scriptorium*, 1949, pp. 267 sqq.

[6] It has the usual mark of Christ Church Library on Fol. 5r.

in England.[1] It tells us that 'MAEIEL BRIDVS MAC DVRNANI ISTV̄ TEXTV̄ PER TRIQVADRV̄ DŌ DIGNE DOGMATIZAT', a somewhat ambiguous sentence, but one which in any case establishes a relation between Maelbrigte and the book which 'he taught excellently'. The end of the inscription is clearer and shows that Aethelstan (924–39) gave the manuscript to Christ Church, Canterbury (the cathedral) 'for ever'. Ethelstan who, after the death of Sitric in York, added Northumbria to his kingdom of Mercia and established a sort of supremacy over all the English kingdoms, was a great collector of manuscripts and made rich presents to the churches of his kingdom. Maelbrigte Mac Tornain or mac Durnan who, as we have seen, was abbot of Armagh probably from 888 on, became as well 'successor of St Columba', that is Head of all the Columban monasteries, and simultaneously it seems, abbot of Raphoe in Donegal.[2] He died at 'a happy old age' in 927.[3] A few facts testify to contacts between Armagh and England at that time. In 913 he obtained gifts in Munster to ransom prisoners from Britain in the hands of the Vikings.[4] Besides, a twelfth-century manuscript which was written either in or for Bangor at the time of its rebuilding by St Malachy, contains a description of an esoteric game, the *Alea evangelii*, of which we are told that its rules were brought back to Ireland from the court of Aethelstan, 'rex Anglorum', by Dubinnsi, abbot of Bangor.[5] It may be that the journey of Dubinnsi, perhaps abbot of Bangor only in name and possibly residing in Armagh, had something to do with the arrival in England of Maelbrigte's book and with its long sojourn on the shelves of Canterbury before passing to those of Lambeth Palace.

It is much harder to piece together the history of the manuscript in Ireland. Maelbrigte obviously used it, but did he commission its writing or even write it himself? It would be hard to say. The only two facts which are certain are that the Book did exist in the time of Maelbrigte and, judging by its script, that it was written by a scribe trained in Armagh and probably a pupil of Ferdomnach who died in 846.

---

[1] See Westwood, *Paleographia Sacra Pictoria*, p. 15.
[2] *A.F.M.*, 927; Reeves, *St Columba*, p. 392.
[3] *A.U.*, 927, *A.I.*, 927.   [4] *A.U.*, 913 *Fragm.*; pp. 244–5.
[5] Henry – Marsh-Micheli, *Illumination*, p. 153.

103

The manuscript is slightly smaller than the Book of Armagh ($6\frac{1}{4}$ by $8\frac{1}{4}$ inches). Its illuminations are in perfect condition and the colours have kept all their intensity (Pls. 36, 42–4, I, K, L). They are vivid shades mostly of purple, green and orange. White is used for the faces, hands and feet of the figures and for some objects such as the croziers. The pigments have a curiously enamelled appearance which may be due to a lead white filler.[1] The drawing is of great firmness and precision but without any of the fine flights of imaginative graphism characteristic of the Book of Armagh. The decorative repertoire is also slightly different as spirals are rare and where they occur appear dessicated and stiff or turn out to be really interlacings. Other interlacings are made of large ribbons with double edges, distant relations of those in the Book of Durrow. The decoration is orderly and well planned. It follows the usual pattern, except for the fact that Matthew I.18 is treated as if it was the beginning of the Gospel of St Matthew. We have already noted the tendency in Irish manuscripts to treat the Genealogy at the beginning of that Gospel as if it were a separate text, but nowhere else is this tendency embodied as uncompromising as here. The Book begins with the four symbols reduced to magnificent coloured mosaics (Pl. K). Then comes the beginning of the Genealogy, with an initial very similar to that in the same position in the Book of Armagh. The Genealogy is followed by the portrait of the Evangelist, who holds a white crozier flung across the whole page (Pl. 44). His draperies are depicted by semi-circular patterns of green ribbon edged with orange and dotted with groups of white spots. He faces the page bearing the Chi–Rho, the monogram of Christ, which is set amidst a burst of bright colours (Pl. I). Each of the other Gospels starts normally with a portrait and a page with a large initial. These initials are very close to those in the Book of Armagh, and may be imitated from it. On the whole, the Book gives the impression of being inspired by the script and initials of an older and much revered book, and not of containing repetitions of forms already used by the same scribe-painter. This formal and well-ordered example

[1] Such as was used in the Lichfield Gospels and the Book of Kells (*E.Q.C. Lindisfarnensis*, pp. 273–4 (Werner and Roosen-Runge)), and probably in the Cotton Irish Psalter (Henry, *Three Psalters*, p. 28).

of the pocket Gospel-book represents what one might expect from the Armagh scriptorium at a somewhat later period than that which saw the production of the Book of Armagh, still marked with the untidy presentation of its immediate predecessors, the Mulling and Dimma Gospels.

By a strange chance the only manuscripts which have come down to us from the tenth and early eleventh-century period are all psalters, while no psalters of the eighth and ninth centuries have survived. The result is that we are faced with a book decoration of an already standardized type, while knowing nothing of the process which brought it into existence. As is the case in all Irish psalters to the end of the twelfth century, the one hundred and fifty psalms are divided into three groups of fifty.[1] This division is not found in the Cathach,[2] the only surviving psalter anterior to the eighth century, so that we have to assume that its use spread in Ireland in the course of the eighth or ninth century. In spite of what has been said, this division does not seem to have had any liturgical significance. One may wonder whether it was first invented in Ireland or came from the Continent, where it appears occasionally.[3] The remarkable fact is that while it became invariable in Ireland, the Continental psalters offer a variety of arrangements and divisions of completely different types adopted for liturgical reasons. This tri-partite plan has important decorative consequences as the three sections of the psalter are treated like the four divisions of a Gospel-book, beginning with a large initial page generally accompanied by a picture page. In addition a psalter demands the use of a great many lesser initials, one at the beginning of each psalm.

These later psalters, like the Cathach before them, are copies of St Jerome's second revision of the Latin text of the psalms, which is known as the Gallican version. In this they differ from the Anglo-Saxon

[1] Henry, *Three Irish Psalters*, p. 24.   [2] *Vol. I*, pp. 58 sqq.
[3] Henry, op. cit., pp. 26–7. As was pointed out to me by F. Wormald, it may derive eventually from divisions into three books of commentaries on the psalter, such as those of St Augustine and Cassiodorus. It is noteworthy that the *Cassiodorus in Psalmos* of the Durham Library (eighth century) is abundantly decorated at the beginning of each of its three books.

psalters which often follow the first or Roman version which was brought to England by St Augustine of Canterbury, or occasionally the third or 'Hebrew' version. There is also an example of a double psalter written in Ireland (Rouen, Munic. Libr. Ms. 24), with the Gallican version on one side and the Hebrew version on the other.[1] Like a small fragment of another double psalter kept in Trinity College, Dublin,[2] it is connected with a series of double and triple psalters written in Carolingian times in France and Spain.

Two examples of illustrated Irish psalters have survived. One is in the Cotton collection in the British Museum (Ms. Vitellius F.XI), the other in the Library of St John's College, Cambridge ('Southampton Psalter', Ms. C.9).[3] The former probably goes back to the beginning of the tenth century, and although the latter is a century later, it follows the first in many of its features. The 'Double Psalter of St Ouen' in Rouen Library and the Trinity College, Dublin, fragment belong probably to the tenth century. Other psalters are connected with that in Cambridge. One, in the University Library in Edinburgh (Ms. 56)[4] probably dates from the early eleventh century. Another, the 'Psalter of Ricemarcus' (Trinity College, Dublin, Ms. 50)[5] can be dated to the end of the century. The Edinburgh Psalter may have been illuminated in Scotland where it was at the end of the eleventh century. The Ricemarcus Psalter was written in Wales by the son of a Welsh scribe who had lived for several years in Ireland.[6] Both are copies of the Hebrew version of the psalms and in this differ from the purely Irish psalters.

[1] Henry, op. cit., pp. 37 sqq.

[2] T.C.D. Libr. Ms. H.3.18; L. Bieler – G. Mac Niocaill, 'Fragment of an Irish Double Psalter with Glosses in the Library of Trinity College, Dublin', *Celtica*, 1960, pp. 28 sqq.

[3] For references concerning these two manuscripts, see: Henry, *Three Psalters*, pp. 27–8 and 33–4. For the Southampton Psalter, see: Zimmermann, III, Pls. 212–213.

[4] C. P. Finlayson, *Celtic Psalter, Edinburgh University Library, Ms. 56* (Amsterdam, 1962).

[5] H. J. Lawlor, *The Psalter and Martyrology of Ricemarch* (London, 1914).

[6] N. K. Chadwick, 'Intellectual Life in West Wales in the Last Days of the Celtic Church', *Studies in the Early British Church* (Cambridge, 1958), pp. 121 sqq.

The Cotton Psalter is in very bad condition, as it was charred in the fire at Ashburnham House which damaged the Cotton collection in 1731. The beginning and the end of the book have disappeared and, in consequence, the decorative opening of the first Fifty is lost. In general, what has survived is shrunken and discoloured. Nevertheless it proved possible with infra-red photographs and special printing, to read even the worst damaged of the illuminations (Pl. 41, Pl. II). The Cambridge Psalter on the other hand is in a perfect state of preservation and has kept all its bright colours (Pls. M, N, O). Both had a picture-page at the beginning of each of the Fifties. In the Cotton Psalter one finds David the Musician (second Fifty) and David killing Goliath (third Fifty); in the Cambridge Psalter David killing the lion, the Crucifixion and David killing Goliath.

The illuminations of the Cotton Psalter have a violence of style which connects them closely with the carvings of the tenth century high crosses, so that it is not surprising to discover a parallel to David the Musician on the cross of the Scriptures at Clonmacnois (Pl. 91) and an even closer one to David killing Goliath on the cross of Muiredach at Monasterboice (Pl. 85). Both pictures show a strange mixture of stylisation and realism. The clothes of the poet-king are reduced to a few wide ribbons, on one side his hair turns into an interlacing. Yet the instrument on which he is playing, half-harp and half-lyre, is depicted with great precision, the painter even indicating by a few light strokes the left hand seen through the strings. David and Goliath are almost reduced to an abstract composition of interlocking red and purple masses. The end of the sling passes under the border of David's clothes. His head is summarized as a square with an eye in the centre. Yet, there is a curious intensity in the way in which the stone is shown travelling towards Goliath's forehead which he tries to protect with his hand. The composition is as massive as in the same scene at Monasterboice, with the same characteristic details: the small crook carried by David, Goliath's pointed helmet, and his large size indicated by the fact that he can only be fitted into the panel with his legs folded. One cannot escape a strong feeling that both works are contemporary, and the early tenth century date given to

107

the manuscript by Westwood for paleographical reasons thus finds its confirmation.[1]

The representation of David and Goliath in the Cambridge Psalter is obviously inspired by the earlier one, but the painter seems hardly to understand what he is copying (Pl. N). David holds his crook as a stroller would his walking-stick and has no sling. Goliath is childishly shown – as happens a few times elsewhere – upside down, as if in falling his helmet had got stuck in the ground. He still protects his face from a stone which is not shown. In fact, everything here is reduced to decorative devices. All the eloquence of the scene in the Cotton Psalter has vanished, leaving only a patterned surface. The picture of David and the lion goes even farther towards a pure playing-card style (Pl. M). The Crucifixion alone retains an echo of the imposing composition of earlier Irish illuminations (Pl. 45). The two painters use pure ornament in much the same way. They both draw decorative frames around their pages, and large initials made of an animal folded up in the shape of the letter, using a method already found in the Book of Kells (Pls. 46, O). The small initials at the beginning of each psalm belong to two different types which also go back to initials found in the Book of Kells. Some are drawn with a thick black line ending in animal heads and enclosing a mosaic of bright dots; the others are made by the coloured ribbon-body of a little animal bent to the shape of the letter (Pl. 48). In the Cotton Psalter, as in the Book of Kells, there does not seem to be any definite order in the succession of these two types. In the Cambridge Psalter on the other hand, they generally alternate, and this method, which Iewan, the son of the Welsh scribe Sulien ignored (Pls. P, 46, 47),[2] became practically invariable in the twelfth century. There is nothing in the initials comparable to the ever-renewed invention of the Book of

[1] J. O. Westwood, 'On the particularities exhibited by the Miniatures and Ornamentation of Ancient Irish Illuminated Manuscripts', *Arch. Journ.*, 1850, pp. 17 sqq.

[2] The 'Psalter of Ricemarcus' was written by a scribe called Ithael and decorated by Iewan. Iewan is the scribe, and probably also the painter of the manuscript of the *De Trinitate* of St Augustine in the Library of Corpus Christi College, Cambridge (Ms. 199) (Pl. P).

Kells, but nevertheless they remain pleasant and well adapted to the decoration of a less ambitious codex.

These few psalters show that a tradition of illumination was able to survive in the Irish monasteries in spite of the destruction wrought by the Vikings and the exodus to the Continent of so many scribes. This tradition was to revive for a time in the Romanesque period and then live on in monotonous repetition into and even beyond the Middle Ages.[1]

An aspect of the history of Irish illumination which can only be briefly indicated here is its influence on Carolingian miniatures.

The part played by Alcuin in the Court scriptorium has already been mentioned. When he settled in Tours his Irish companion, Joseph, was dead,[2] but no doubt the new scriptorium which he organized remained in touch with Insular scriptoria, as Irish features went on reappearing for a long time in the manuscripts it produced.

Then a new influx of Irish influence made itself felt in Carolingian manuscripts. The School which developed in the north of France, long labelled as 'Franco-Saxon' is now more rightly called 'Franco-Insular'. It produced for the successors of Charlemagne, Louis-the-Pious and Charles-the-Bald, some great books in which Irish influence appears blatantly. In the most magnificent of these, known as the Second Bible of Charles-the-Bald (Paris, Bibl. nat. Ms. Lat. 2),[3] some of the decorations, animal-interlacings and spirals with foliated links, betray the hand of an Irish painter, or of a pupil of Irish masters. This new wave of Insular style is explained quite easily by the presence at the time of a number of Irish refugees in the north of France, and especially around Johannes Scottus Eriugena. It is also likely that Péronne and Corbie played their part in this transmission.

However, it is not possible to follow in detail all the complex and

---

[1] Some of the nineteenth-century Irish manuscripts in the British Museum still have a few initials with animal-interlacing.

[2] See p. 28, note 3.

[3] A. Boinet, *La Miniature carolingienne* (Paris, 1913), Pls. C–CII; Micheli, *Enluminure*, Figs. 198–201; A. van Moe, *Illuminated Initials* (London, 1950), Pls. 39, 45, 51, 83.

very rich development of this Irish fashion in Continental manuscripts. Having pointed out its highlights, one can only refer the reader for a detailed study, to the book which G. L. Micheli[1] has devoted to the subject.[2]

Fig. 13. Book of Kells, detail of the first page of St John's Gospel.

[1] Micheli, *Enluminure.*

[2] I can only mention here an article by Anne O'Sullivan, 'The Colophon of the Cotton Psalter (Vitellius F. XI)', *J.R.S.A.I.*, *1966*, pp. 179 sqq., which came out as this book was going to press. In it is quoted a poem addressed to an Abbot Muiredach, which Ussher copied from one of the pages, later burnt, of the Psalter. This comes to strengthen the connection between the Psalter and the monastery of Monasterboice.

4. Metalwork

A.D. 800—1020

THE MEAGRENESS of our information about metalwork is one of the strange features of the period we are studying. Though no more than fragments sometimes remain of objects of the seventh and eighth centuries, they allow us nevertheless to form a general picture, fairly accurate in its main lines, of the Irish goldsmith's craft before the coming of the Vikings. For the ninth and tenth century on the other hand, we have only a few surviving objects and their background remains obscure.[1]

There could be several reasons for this phenomenon. First of all, it is difficult to draw a definite line between the art of the eighth century and that of the ninth. A certain number of objects usually ascribed to the eighth century – amongst them some of the penannular brooches – may be as late in date as 800, or may even belong to the first half of the ninth century. Then, our sources of information are not the same as for the earlier period. In the excitement of the first conquests, the Vikings laid hands on all kinds of church treasures and brought their plunder back to Norway. From their tombs in Norway come about half of the surviving Irish metal objects of the eighth century.[2] Later on the Vikings settled in the towns they had founded in Ireland and obviously went back less and less often to Scandinavia with their loot. At the same time, the Irish, with a wisdom bred of hard experience probably took more care than before to protect or conceal what remained of the treasuries of their

---

[1] The chief references are : *Christian Art in Ancient Ireland* (*C.A.A.I.*), vol. I, ed. by Adolf Mahr (Dublin, 1932), vol. II, ed. by Joseph Raftery (Dublin, 1941), and : H. S. Crawford, 'A descriptive List of Irish Shrines and Reliquaries', *J.R.S.A.I.*, 1923, pp. 74 sqq., which consult for any object which has no special reference in this chapter.

[2] *Viking Antiquities in Great Britain and Ireland* ed. by Haakon Shetelig (Oslo, 1940), vol. V (Jan Petersen, *British Antiquities of the Viking Period found in Norway*) ; see also, vol. III (J. Bøe, *Norse Antiquities in Ireland*).

111

devastated monasteries. Towards the middle of the tenth century the Vikings were gradually converted to Christianity and so ceased to be buried with all their possessions, thereby depriving us of a valuable source of information.

It is more than likely in fact that the manufacture of elaborate metal objects slowed down during this unstable period. But it cannot have stopped completely. We have the example of painters and sculptors to show us that artistic activity did not come to a standstill and there are metal objects which can definitely be attributed to that time. However, the quality of the work is not the same. There were still men capable of creative invention, technicians able to do fine casting; but the work was slightly coarser, the effects more cheaply obtained; the filigree threads were thicker, the animal-interlacing ceased to be quite so accurate, and there appeared a new type of jewellery made for the invaders, showy in size, gaudy in colour, where the cold gleam of silver often replaced the subtle colour modulations and the technical triumphs of the earlier objects. The comparative peace, the prosperity and the rich patronage of the eighth century had been necessary to foster the highest degree of technical and artistic perfection.

Some of the large objects which have survived, seem to represent the last stage of a long process of evolution. For instance the lamp found in Crannog No. 1 at Ballinderry (Westmeath), although rather meagrely decorated, represents a normal continuation of the hanging-bowl series. But there are others which give us a glimpse of objects about which so far we knew very little. This is true of the croziers or fragments of croziers which are the most important large metal objects to survive. A few cast-bronze bells, some of them decorated, also belong to this time. Our knowledge of shrines for the period is virtually confined to the part of the Soiscél Molaise which dates from the beginning of the eleventh century. The trinkets – brooches, pins and fasteners – are fairly well known, but remain rather a puzzle in their appearance.

The Ballinderry lamp (Fig. 14)[1] is not semi-spherical like the majority of earlier hanging-bowls, but has an ovoid shape and the

---

[1] Hencken, *Ballinderry No 1*, pp. 191 sqq.

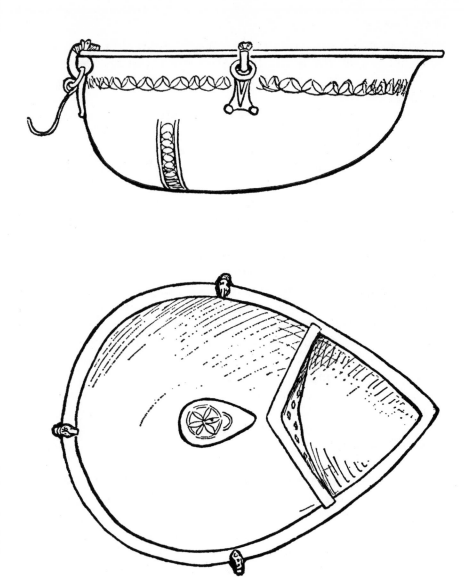

Fig. 14. Enamelled bronze hanging-bowl found in Crannog No. 1 of Ballinderry.

pointed spout is separated from the rest by a vertical filter.[1] The bronze bowl hung from chains by three zoomorphic escutcheon-hooks, the heads of which rest on the edge of the bowl. The ring at the opposite end from the spout has a bronze hook attached which could be hung from different links of the chain in order to tilt the lamp as the oil was going down. Lamps with such a device were still used in the Irish countryside in the nineteenth century. The escutcheons have an enamel decoration which is now dark green but may well have been originally red. The reserved patterns of bronze outlined on the enamel background are no more than rather awkward little zig-zags. The rest of the ornament consists of engravings on the bronze surface of the bowl and in applied bands of bronze bearing deeply incised patterns. The most remarkable is a ring with a foliage ornament (Pl. III) which was dated, at the time of the discovery, *circa* A.D. 1000, by comparison with Scandinavian patterns. However, there is on a page of the early ninth century Gospel-book in the cathedral of Essen[2] an exactly identical motif (Pl. III). Therefore the lamp is probably a good deal older than was thought at first and appears as the end of the series of sixth, seventh and eighth-century hanging-bowls, incidentally confirming the fact that they were lamps.[3]

The general shape of the croziers belonging to this period fits in with the representations of croziers found on a number of carvings : the pillar of Killadeas (Fermanagh) (Pl. 9), one of the statues on White Island (Fermanagh) (Pl. 14) and panels of two of the crosses at Monasterboice (Figs. 35, 40), of the cross of the Scriptures at Clonmacnois (Pl. 91) and of the Market cross at Kells (Pl. 104). Most of them are in very bad condition, and it is obvious that they were broken and repaired by pieces being inserted at various times. It is nonetheless possible to get a clear idea of their general appearance. As in the eighth century, they have the shape of a walking-stick with a slight bend below the hook which was to become more pronounced in the Roman-

---

[1] Two hanging-bowls are triangular in shape; one is in Dublin Museum (found at Kilgulbin, Kerry), the other in Stavanger Museum (found at Hegreberg, Rogaland); the Kilgulbin bowl has traces of the attachment of a strainer.

[2] See p. 65.   [3] See *Vol. I*, pp. 68 sqq.

esque period. The metal plaques are mounted on a core of yew wood which may or may not have been originally the walking-stick of a saint.[1]

At intervals knops of cast bronze serve to hold the metal plaques onto the wood. There were probably four. This is the number found on the British Museum crozier (Pl. 52), though in that case the upper knop is a later restoration. The Prosperous (Kildare) crozier and that in Belfast Museum (Pl. 52), which was found at Toome (Antrim), also have four, and the reason why both the croziers of St Mel and St

Fig. 15. Detail from the British Museum crozier (after M. Mac Dermott).

Dympna have only three is probably that they were shortened when repaired. The British Museum crozier and that found at Prosperous are nearly of the same length, about 4 feet 4 inches, and though in both cases the hook has been greatly modified, this was probably the average length of the ninth and tenth-century croziers. The hook ended in a bevelled panel into which fitted a little reliquary box.

The crozier found around 1840 in a turf-bog near Prosperous (Kildare) is now preserved in Clongowes Wood College (Kildare).[2] It is the only one of the series to have an enamelled decoration, which covers the knops, the foot and the lid of the reliquary-box. The reserved lines

[1] The theory that Irish croziers contain the walking-stick of a saint was first proposed by Petrie and developed by Margaret Stokes in *Early Christian Art in Ireland*, chap. 'Crosiers'. See: F. Henry, 'Les crosses pré-romanes', *Iris Hibernia* (Fribourg, Switzerland), 1956, pp. 35 sqq.

[2] *C.A.A.I.*, vol. II, pp. 145–6, vol. I, Pls. 73, 74, 75.

of bronze running through the enamelled surface are treated in very much the same way as in the eighth-century enamels, and the little cross on the reliquary lid is nearly identical with that on the enamelled bird head in the Ashmolean Museum.[1] Yet the work has not the same crispness and is rather monotonous. It comes fairly near the treatment of the zig-zags on the escutcheons of the Ballinderry lamp with which it is probably contemporary. No indication of date can be derived from the inscription on the crozier which is now completely illegible. There is a bronze crest on the hook where a series of silhouettes of birds is conjured up by the combination of a cut-out process and inlays of silver. It is difficult to say whether this belongs to the same period as the enamels or whether it is a later addition. The hook is of a most extraordinary shape which could perhaps be explained by the late insertion of some fragments from a broken crozier.

The other decorated croziers, that in the British Museum,[2] the crozier of St Dympna and the crozier of St Mel,[3] which have all been studied in detail by Máire Mac Dermott, are devoid of enamelling and have a decoration of small lozenge-shaped or triangular panels, each panel holding a separate ornament, interlace, animal-interlacing, or foliage (Fig. 16). They are probably connected with an early ninth century type which is known only from a few fragments : a piece from a foot and the end of a hook with its reliquary-box, both found probably at Shankill near Belfast (Belfast Museum),[4] and a ferrule from the Petrie collection in the Dublin Museum.[5] They are all covered with chip-carving ornament, mostly interlacings. The two knops of the Dublin fragment are in high relief, with four clearly framed discs standing out on a background of fine interlacing, and appear clearly as forerunners of the third knop of the British Museum crozier which also has a series of circular panels (Pl. 49). But in that last example the tendency to sub-

[1] See : *Vol. I*, Pl. 26.

[2] *C.A.A.I.*, vol. II, p. 158, vol. I, Pls. 71, 72; Máire Mac Dermott, 'The Kells Crosier', *Archaeologia*, 1955, pp. 59 sqq.

[3] *C.A.A.I.*, vol. II, p. 158, vol. I, Pls. 73, 76; M. Mac Dermott, 'The Crosiers of St Dympna and St Mel and Tenth Century Irish Metalwork', *P.R.I.A.*, 1957(C), pp. 167 sqq.

[4] *C.A.A.I.*, vol. II, Pl. 93,4,5.   [5] *C.A.A.I.*, vol. II, Pl. 91,3.

Fig. 16. Details from the croziers of the British Museum and of St Mel (after M. Mac Dermott).

divide into panels has hardened with the isolation of each type of ornament into separate frames. On these croziers spirals are scarce and when
they occur, they are generally combined with interlacings. On most of
them the bronze surface is rubbed and darkened with age and they present
a very poor appearance. To judge them as they deserve to be judged it
is necessary to try, by an effort of the imagination, to visualize their
original brilliance. The hook of St Mel's crozier was gilt and had a
number of coloured settings. All the panels of the British Museum
crozier were plated with a thin silver foil. These were really very richly
coloured objects whose only serious faults were the monotony of execution and the lack of technical variety.

The little we know about the origin of these croziers is not very useful
in locating in time and place the workshops which produced them.
St Mel's crozier was found in the nineteenth century at Ardagh (Longford), a short distance from the old cathedral of St Mel; it is now kept
in St Mel's College, Longford. The so-called 'crozier of St Dympna'
was bought in 1835 by George Petrie from the O'Luans, for centuries
its hereditary keepers. It is now with the Petrie collection in the
Dublin Museum. It was traditionally associated with St Damnat,
foundress of the monastery of Tech Damnata (Tedavnet, Monaghan),
who was identified in the Middle Ages, rightly or wrongly, with St
Dympna of Gheel near Antwerp. As for the British Museum crozier, it
was found behind a cupboard in a solicitor's office in London, with no
indication of how it had got there. Bought in 1850 by Cardinal Wiseman,
it passed finally into the British Museum collections.

St Dympna's crozier has the remains of an inscription which has become practically illegible. The crozier in London, however, has a
perfectly clear inscription: 'OR DO CONDUILIG OCUS DO MEL-
FINNEN – pray for Cúduilig and Máelfinnén.' Both names are very
widespread and their presence on the crozier is not very illuminating.
For long they were identified with a bishop of Kells who died in 969
and a steward of Kells whose death is recorded in 1047. As the decoration is of two different periods, the inscription, if one accepts these
identifications, would record the two patrons who had supervised its
making and re-decorating. But the Annals of Inisfallen at the date of

1039, record the death of a Máelfinnén, bishop of Emly and also of a Cúduilig 'royal heir of Cashel' (heir designate of the king of Cashel) who could perfectly well have ordered the repairs done to the crozier in the eleventh century.[1] Another Cúduilig, working with his sons is described, according to its inscription, as having wrought the shrine of St Patrick's Bell,[2] at the end of the eleventh century. The name could conceivably have been hereditary in this goldsmith family. Faced with such a wealth of possibilities, it may be wiser to accept the fact that, as the inscription does not give any indication of the social position of the people mentioned, no precise date or place can be deduced from it. However, the upper knop was remade at the same time as the casing of the hook (Pl. 52), after the battering of this part of the crozier, the breaking of its wooden core and the scraping of the ornament. From its style there is no great difficulty in dating the new knop to the eleventh century. This gives a *terminus ante quem* for the decoration of the rest of the object which must be earlier and consequently dates back to the tenth and even perhaps to the ninth century. This dating is also valid for the croziers of St Mel and St Dympna which are closely akin to that of the British Museum though their execution is much poorer.

All three have rather dessicated interlacings which occasionally are untied into loose loops. The only two panels of spirals on the British Museum crozier show the curvilinear motifs associated in one case with interlacings, in the other with zoomorphs (Pl. 49). The principal elements of the decoration are small beasts which show on the British Museum crozier a delightful vivacity of drawing (Fig. 16). Little animals with upturned jaws are bent to the shape of the frame without losing any of their liveliness. Sometimes there is a bird with a large round eye and fluffy feathers, or a stag, his legs entangled like those of some horses in the Book of Kells (Fig. 16, Pl. 21). Some aspects of these animals call for comparisons with the Book of Mac Durnan or the Southampton Psalter, where a few beasts sport just such curled-up jaws. But this method of division and especially the balancing of the animal on a sharply folded paw or on the point of the snout is a ninth-

[1] See Mac Dermott, *Kells Crosier*, p. 106.
[2] Macalister, *Corpus*, II, pp. 112–13 (No. 944).

century fashion and parallel examples, though with a very different type of animal, are found on the silver objects, of British manufacture, from Trewhiddle in Cornwall.[1]

A date in the ninth–tenth century for this type of animal ornament is confirmed by the fact that its ultimate development is found on an object belonging to the extreme end of our present period, called traditionally, the 'Soiscél Molaise – Gospel of St Molaise'.[2] It has been modified and re-modelled, like the British Museum crozier, probably also after ill treatment by the Vikings. As Joseph Raftery has shown, it originally consisted of a small bronze box, a house-shaped shrine of a normal seventh and eighth-century type. From this early period comes one of the enamelled escutcheons to which the suspension strap was attached. The other one has been torn off, like the rest of the decoration. From an inscription[3] we learn that the ornament which now covers nearly the whole box is due to Gilla Biathín working at the bidding of Cenfaelad successor of Molaise, who, we know from another source, became abbot of the monastery of St Molaise, on the island of Devenish in Lough Erne (Fermanagh), in 1001, and died in 1025. So we are probably dealing with an object made during the period of comparative peace brought about by the victories of Brian Boru over the Vikings, and with one of the attempts at restoring a venerable object saved from disaster which must have been numerous at the time. The broken shrine seems to have been turned into a *cumdach* – a box made to contain an especially precious book. These were common in Ireland. We have mentioned already that of the Book of Kells,[4] so lavishly covered with gold that it was responsible for the theft of the manuscript in 1007. That of the Book of Durrow, also lost, had an inscription (known by a copy)[5] recording that it had been made to the order of Flann Sinna, king of

[1] D. Wilson, 'The Trewhiddle Hoard', *Archaeologia*, 1961, pp. 75 sqq.
[2] *C.A.A.I.*, vol. II, pp. 119 sqq., vol. I, Pls. 57–8; M. Stokes, 'Observations on two Ancient Irish Works of Art known as the Breac Moedog, or Shrine of St Moedoc of Ferns, and the Soiscel Molaise, or Gospel of St Molaise of Devenish', *Archaeologia*, 1867, pp. 131 sqq.
[3] Macalister, *Corpus*, II, p. 124 (No. 961).
[4] See p. 69.
[5] *E.Q.C. Durmachensis*, II, pp. 31–2.

Ireland from 877 to 915. In 937, his son, Donchadh,[1] enclosed the Book of Armagh in a cumdach which has also disappeared. In the case of the Soiscél Molaise its very name (Soiscél) shows that it must have contained a Gospel-book, and this is confirmed by the fact that the cover of the box bears the four symbols of the Evangelists with inscriptions giving the name of each Evangelist and the appropriate symbol.

These symbols are modelled in very low relief in the four compartments formed by a cross of gold filigree inscribed in a rectangular frame. They are depicted with the same extreme stylisation as those of the Book of mac Durnan (Pl. K). The full face head of St Luke's symbol is almost the same in both but the rest is rather different; and in fact what attracts the attention most strikingly at first glance is the bizarre arrangement of the chevron-like wings. The robustness of the figures, the great decorative feeling with which they are adapted to their frame, and the sensitive modelling all reappear in the only figure remaining of the decoration on the other sides, which may represent an Evangelist (Pl. 58). The cross of Muiredach at Monasterboice, which is a century older, has some figures treated in the same way, conveying the same massive sense of presence. This seems to indicate that the shrine of St Molaise is the outcome and only survivor of a long tradition of metalwork in which cast bronze or silver figures corresponded to the carved ones on the stone crosses. The Evangelist is surrounded by a swarm of knotted and curling animals, and other beasts of the same type are confined in a series of smaller panels. They are not cut out silhouettes like the animals on the croziers, but most of them have the same long curled-up jaws. There also we are probably looking at traditional motifs, but in this case we are able to follow more or less their elaboration on the surviving ninth and tenth-century croziers. This zoomorphic decoration is also occasionally paralleled in the manuscripts and especially in some of the borders of the Southampton Psalter. In both cases there are irregular combinations of two animals and animals shown face to face. The Psalter is most probably contemporary with the

---

[1] *A.F.M.*, 937: 'Canoin-Phadraig was covered by Donnchadh, son of Flann, king of Ireland'; see: W. Reeves, 'On the Book of Armagh', *P.R.I.A.*, 1891–3, pp. 77 sqq.

repair of the shrine and we are thus able to connect a certain number of otherwise isolated objects.

Through the Soiscél Molaise we are also able to appraise the changes in the metalwork. In fact they may leave us in some perplexity. On the one hand this sculptural virtuosity in modelling figures is an interesting novelty, contrasting sharply with the purely geometrical descriptions of volumes in the Athlone plaque and the Aghaboe figure.[1] On the other hand, what are we to think of the thick gold filigree, almost rope-like when compared with the microscopic weaving of gold threads found in the eighth-century brooches and the Ardagh chalice? It is this which brings home to us the disastrous consequences of two centuries of strife. The feeling for effect remains, but the means by which it is attained are now clumsy and unimaginatively monotonous. Technical skill will take some time to reappear and will never again reach the incredible heights attained before the coming of the Vikings.

A few isolated fragments may have belonged originally either to the sides of a cumdach or to the binding of a book. Two of them, identical in shape, obviously decorated the corners of such a recentangular surface. One comes from Clonmacnois and bears an open-work disc of spirals surrounded by animals;[2] the second found near Dublin[3] is entirely covered by two animals similar to those of the Soiscél Molaise, though more vigorously drawn (Pl. 51). The other objects are little openwork plaques with a representation of the Crucifixion which might very well have been in the middle of a book-cover in the same position as so many ivory Crucifixions on Carolingian bindings. As on many of the high crosses, Christ is surrounded by the sponge and lance bearers and two angels.

One of these plaques found at Dungannon (Tyrone) (Edinburgh Museum) and another nearly identical in the Dublin Museum[4] are especially close to the carvings on the crosses of the late ninth and early tenth century and it seems hardly possible to give them a widely different date. Longinus is shown piercing the right side of Christ, a rare feature

---

[1] *Vol. I*, Pls. 46, 47.   [2] *C.A.A.I.*, vol. I, Pl. 50,2.
[3] *C.A.A.I.*, vol. I, Pl. 29,2.
[4] *C.A.A.I.*, vol. II, p. 152, vol. I, Pls. 29,11 and 50,8.

at that time as we shall see, but found on the Arboe Cross which is also in County Tyrone (Pl. I). It may well have existed also on a few crosses in the north of Ireland whose upper parts, carrying the Crucifixion, have now disappeared. On another of these metal plaques Christ is wearing a sort of skirt (Pl. 53).[1] This feature is not unknown on the stone crosses, no more than the long dress found on a plaque from Clonmacnois (Pl. 8)[2] and on another plaque in Dublin Museum (Pl. 54). In the last three, the faces, with their prominent eyes and forked beards, are very close to that of the Evangelist on St Molaise's shrine. On the Clonmacnois plaque, Longinus is on the left side of Christ, as he is on the cross of the Scriptures at Clonmacnois and on all the southern crosses. This shows that there are iconographical variations in these metal carvings parallel to those found in stone carvings. On this last plaque, moreover, the crosses of the thieves, small and without figures, are shown on either side of Christ's cross. The vegetal motif engraved on Christ's dress is not very different from the motif on the Ballin-derry lamp (Pl. III) and like that motif it reminds one of foliage patterns found in some manuscripts of the Carolingian period, particu-larly in the canon-tables of the Essen manuscript and in manuscripts of the School of Tours.[3] All these books came from scriptoria which were in touch with Ireland and so could have supplied the model to the Irish metalworkers. These scrolls will live on. They occur for example on the little binding plaque in the Dublin Museum found at Holy Cross (Tipperary)[4] which, judging from its animal decoration, can hardly be earlier than the end of the eleventh or the twelfth century. They appear also, if a little differently on the figure-mount found in Thomas Street, Dublin (British Museum)[5] which is twelfth-century work.

This is the place to mention another Irish object in the British Museum, a kind of two-faced bronze disc with a wide flat stem (Pl. 55).[6] Its purpose is slightly puzzling, though it might conceivably be the end

---

[1] *C.A.A.I.*, vol. II, p. 152, vol. I, Pl. 50,7.

[2] M. Mac Dermott, 'An Openwork Crucifixion Plaque from Clonmacnoise', *J.R.S.A.I.*, 1954, pp. 36 sqq.

[3] Micheli, *Enluminure*, Fig. 138.   [4] *C.A.A.I.*, vol. I, Pl. 50,1.

[5] *C.A.A.I.*, vol. I, Pl. 24,6.

[6] M. Stokes, *Early Chistian Art*, p. 93; *C.A.A.I.*, vol. II, p. 104; vol. I, Pl. 31.3.

of the arm of a free-standing bronze cross. Its surface has the same division into panels as the knops of the croziers and the ornament is also of the same type, except the angular pattern which recalls the cloisons of some eighth-century enamels.

The border of lozenges alternating with transverse lines on this last object deserves consideration. It looks like an awkward rendering of a classical motif found on some of the sixth and seventh-century ivories and occasionally imitated by Carolingian ivory carvers. It is found on a whole set of Irish objects of the ninth and tenth centuries: the Dungannon and Clonmacnois Crucifixion plaques, the reverse of the Corp naomh,[1] a crozier from the Bell collection in the Edinburgh Museum,[2] and, in a slightly deformed version, on the ring connecting the arms of the cross on the British Museum crozier. One feels tempted to add to the list the chevrons and transverse lines which run in the circular frames of the Turin illuminations (Pls. 37, 39). It would be unwise to give too definite a chronological value to this motif, but it is a remarkable fact that it is never found on any of the dated objects of the late eleventh–twelfth century or on those which can be ascribed to the eighth century.

Some bells are also amongst the outstanding objects of this period. In the seventh and eighth centuries, small hand-bells made of a sheet of iron or bronze coated with iron were a standard element of the equipment of churches and perhaps of the insigna of the Irish bishops.[3] They probably remained in use until a late date. One example was found in Nendrum and seems to have been hidden at the time of the Viking attack, at the end of the tenth century.[4]

Towards the end of the eighth century cast bronze bells of varied shapes and sizes appear. The only reliable chronological indication concerning them is supplied by the Armagh bell in the Dublin Museum,[5] which bears a very beautifully formed inscription in Irish characters requesting a prayer for Cumascach, son of Aillil, who, according to the Annals of Ulster, was a steward of the monastery of Armagh and died

---

[1] *C.A.A.I.*, vol. I, Pl. 69.   [2] *C.A.A.I.*, vol. I, Pls. 27,2, and 71,1.
[3] W. Stokes, *The Tripartite Life of St Patrick* (London, 1887), p. 345; see *Vol. I*, p. 101.
[4] Lawlor, *Nendrum*, p. 149, Pl. XIV.   [5] *C.A.A.I.*, vol. II, p. 144, vol. I, Pl. 49.

in 908. However, two large bells nearly 14 in. in height, one found in Bangor and now in the Bangor town hall (Pl. 51), the other from one of the islands of Lough Lene (Westmeath)[1] (Pl. 50) where it may have been concealed at a late date, have a decoration which suggests the early ninth century. They are very simple in shape, rather massive and with a strong handle. On both there is a key-pattern border around the lip and a cross on the wider sides – a cross with hollowed angles on the Bangor specimen and a cross with circle on the other. One likes to imagine that bells of this type were rung from the round towers, as they are large and thick enough to give a deep peal, though certainly not a very loud one.

Some bells which had belonged to a saint were enshrined. Several bell-shrines were made during the Romanesque period. It is not easy to decide whether any example of the ninth or tenth century has survived.[2] The reliquary called the 'Corp naomh – holy body'[3] may have been originally a bell-shrine (Pl. 55). It was found at Temple Cross (Westmeath) and is now in the Dublin Museum, where it is mounted on a block of wood. The lower part of the decoration is mostly late medieval, though the nielloed bronze cross on one of the sides may have belonged to the original object. The upper part, which is wide enough to have covered the handle of a bell, is cast in one piece. On one side it bears a figure holding a book, reduced to a few simplified lines, flanked on each side by a horseman and a bird. All this is in very low relief and the surfaces are covered by an overall guilloche, either the hatchings and interlacings of the background or the surface of the figures themselves, where the ornament is now partly rubbed. The head of the central figure is almost modelled in the round and belongs to the openwork crest of the object. The horsemen are akin to those found in the Book of

[1] *C.A.A.I.*, vol. II, Pl. 144; vol. I, Pl. 47; W. B. Smythe, 'On the Bell from Lough Lene in the Academy Museum', *P.R.I.A.*, 1878–88, pp. 164 sqq.
[2] The eighth-century shrine-mount from the Killua Castle collection in Dublin Museum (*Vol. I*, Pl. 90) may have belonged to a bell-shrine, though its shape, with the two large suspension rings, is very disconcerting.
[3] W. Frazer, 'On St Patrick's Crosses – Stone, Bronze and Gold', *J.R.S.A.I.*, 1899, pp. 35 sqq.; *C.A.A.I.*, vol. II, p. 157, vol. I, Pls. 68, 69, 70. It was kept at Temple Cross, Ballynacarriga (Westmeath), in a leather satchel of indefinite date.

Kells and, as Máire mac Dermott says, the birds are similar to those found on the croziers of the British Museum and of Longford (St Mel).[1] On the other side there are two animals face to face, entangled in a scroll of foliage, which can be connected with some of the animals engraved on bronze pails.[2] The motif itself may be a more recent borrowing from an ivory or a textile, but the process of transformation belongs to the same series of experiments. These various features seem to date the object to the ninth or tenth century, and though the figure is very different from the Evangelist on the Soiscél Molaise, its ornamental treatment reduces it to a few angular ribbons, like the symbols on the same reliquary.

The crest of a shrine of nearly identical shape in the Dublin Museum seems to be of a similar date (Pl. 56).[3] It has a human head in relief in the middle of a vegetable pattern; it has bands of niello with wavy lines of silver running through them, and the three decorative panels on the arc were gold plated. The foliage pattern is a slightly more agitated version of that which we have seen on the British Museum crozier and the Clonmacnois plaque. The object was bought in Ballymena (Antrim) and is said to have been found in the Bann. Reeves published it in 1868 from the collection of Robert Day[4] and suggested very cautiously that it might have come from one of the monasteries near the banks of the Bann. It bears an inscription indicating that it had been commissioned by somebody called Maelbrigte. This is a very common name, but Reeves pointed out that the death of a Maelbrigte, abbot of the monastery of Ahoghill[5] near the Bann, is recorded in 954.[6] Since then, this

[1] Mac Dermott, *Crosiers of St Dympna and St Mel*, pp. 167 sqq.

[2] *Vol. I*, Fig. 25.   [3] *C.A.A.I.*, vol. II, p. 156, vol. I, Pl. 36, 4,a,b.

[4] W. Reeves, 'On an ancient Shrine-Arch', *J.R.S.A.I.*, 1868–9, pp. 353 sqq.; E. C. R. Armstrong, 'Note on an inscribed Shrine-Arch', *J.R.S.A.I.*, 1918, pp. 180 sqq.

[5] Ath-thoghill; see: Archdall, *Mon. Hib.*, p. 91 (Dezert-toghill). The misspelling – or misprint – Aboghill seems to have been introduced by H. S. Crawford ('A Descriptive List . . .', loc. cit., p. 163) and is repeated in *C.A.A.I.* I am indebted to Dr Raftery for drawing my attention to this error.

[6] *A.F.M.*, 954: 'Successor of Mac Neissi and Colman Eala.' That is (Reeves): bishop of Connor and abbot of the churches of Muckainore and Ahoghill. *A.U.*, 955 (*recte 956*): id. See also Macalister's reading of the nscription in Armstrong's paper quoted above and in: *Corpus*, II, pp. 111–12.

suggestion of Reeves, relating to what might be a fortuitous coincidence, has often been mentioned as if it were a demonstrated fact. The strange side of this story is that Reeves was reluctant to make much of the identification because he thought the object was later than the tenth century, though in the present state of our knowledge that date would be quite acceptable.

The jewellery of this period, brooches, pins, etc., is very disconcerting. A few penannular brooches are continuations, in a rougher form, of the ordinary eighth-century types. As an example we might take the beautiful little silver brooch from Donegal in the British Museum (Pl. 64),[1] which has on one side animals similar to those on the croziers. On others the large triangular terminals are decorated with a series of semi-spherical silver rivet-heads. The terminal itself may be almost plain, though it is more often divided into panels filled by little animals whose bodies are covered with hatchings (Pls. 62, 63), varying a good deal, from the beautifully drawn to the nearly dismembered.[2] These brooches have turned up in Ireland, in the north of England and in Norway. Reginald Smith described them as a 'Viking type' of Irish brooch.[3] Recently David Wilson suggested that they may have been made in England.[4] Three nearly identical brooches in openwork silver with bosses of silver filigree have been found: one in Ireland, another at Hatteberg in Norway, and the third in the Cuerdale Hoard in Cumberland with coins of the early tenth century.[5] Such a distribution gives the impression that the whole series may have belonged to the kingdoms of Dublin and York which were associated for a while and that the brooches may have been made, as suggested by Shetelig, some by Irish, others by Scandinavian artists. This would explain the different treatments of the animals, dismembered by the Scandinavians and drawn in the usual coherent fashion by the Irish.

[1] Smith, *Guide Anglo-Saxon A.*, Fig. 179, p. 135.
[2] Coffey, *Guide*, Pl. IV.
[3] R. Smith, 'Irish Brooches of Five Centuries', *Archaeologia*, 1914, pp. 223 sqq.
[4] D. Wilson, 'A Group of Penannular Brooches of the Viking Period', *Third Viking Congress, 1958*, pp. 95 sqq.
[5] H. Shetelig, 'The Norse Style of Ornamentation in the Viking Settlements', *Acta Archaeologica*, 1948, pp. 69 sqq.; see p. 71.

Beside this, there is a whole series of gigantic silver brooches : the 'thistle brooches', which have a murderous-looking pin and three large bristling balls, sometimes gilt (Pl. 61), and others whose spheres are either smooth or decorated with key-patterns or gold filigree. These also have a wide distribution :[1] Ireland, north of England, Scotland, Orkneys, Shetlands, Norway. They may well be a type of jewellery evolved to satisfy the invaders' taste for local colour and gaudy orna-ment. Some of them, however, were worn by the native population and they are represented on carved figures as if they were a normal part of the Irish attire of the time (Pls. 79, I, etc.).

There are also several types of pins which would deserve study,[2] but for the most part they are difficult to date. The only kind we shall examine in detail are the large pins ending in a hinged pendant which are usually called, because of the shape of the pendant, 'kyte brooches'. The pin is in most examples rather stout and the pendant is held at some distance in front of it by a double-hinged tab (Fig. 17).[3] They seem to have been made to hang over the edge of something very thick, perhaps a leather or fur garment. The pendant is always a richly decorated jewel. In most cases a plated metal chain hung from its lower extremity.[4]

Hencken was inclined to date a small example of this type of pin found in Crannog No. 1 of Ballinderry[5] at *circa* A.D. 1000. Some others may be earlier. A certain number of penannular brooches which have a knob opposite the head of the pin, in the middle of the joined terminals,[6] supply the transition to two pendant-pins : one found in County Kilkenny and the other probably also from the same neighbourhood.[7] Their shape recalls that of the penannular brooch. Their decoration consisted of insets which have now disappeared from the frames into which they once fitted. All the other pins of this group have a shape which more clearly justifies their name of kyte brooches. One of them

---

[1] Op. cit., p. 77.

[2] See : E. C. R. Armstrong, 'Irish Bronze Pins of the Christian Period', *Archaeo-logia*, 1921–2, pp. 71 sqq.

[3] See also : Coffey, *Guide*, Fig. 37, p. 32.   [4] *C.A.A.I.*, vol. II, p. 74.

[5] Hencken, *Ballinderry No. 1*, pp. 144–5, Fig. 14, B.

[6] Such as : *C.A.A.I.*, vol. I, Pl. 37,4, and more remotely, Pl. 62,2.

[7] *C.A.A.I.*, vol. I, Pls. 40,1 and 41,2.

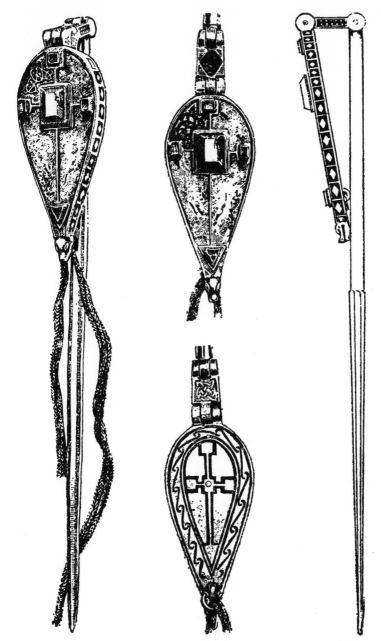

Fig. 17. Silver 'kyte-brooch' found in Clonmacnois, now lost (after R. Cochrane).

has only a few interlacings as decoration.[1] The two others are much more lavishly ornamented. The one found in Clonmacnois is now lost but is known by a very good engraving (Fig. 17).[2] The pin was 8 inches long, the silver pendant had a cross on each face, that in front being outlined on a background of interlace in what seems to have been fairly fine gold filigree. A metal chain hung from behind an animal head. The edges were decorated with that motif of lozenges which we have already noticed on other objects of the same period. Macalister remarked that the pendant, in its general shape, was similar to the Alfred jewel. This strange object with cloisonné bears an Anglo-Saxon inscription saying that it was made for King Alfred (end of the ninth century),[3] but as Brøndsted pointed out, the little gold filigree animal head in its lowest part is Irish in inspiration.[4] There seems to be a connection between the two objects, difficult to define exactly, but sufficient to justify the dating of the Clonmacnois pin to the late ninth or early tenth century. Another silver pendant pin, coming perhaps also from Clonmacnois, is of exactly the same shape and ends also in a little animal head, this time holding the chain in its jaws (Pl. 60).[5] Its surface is divided into panels each containing an animal outlined in gold filigree and covered with gold granulations. The lower panel has a full-face head with large round eyes also outlined in filigree. The threads are of the same coarsely beaded type as in the filigree work on the Soiscél Molaise. The ornament on this object is remarkable for its close kinship with ninth and tenth-century Scandinavian work. There are in fact some very similar animals on a box-brooch found at Grötlingbo (Sweden).[6] The full-face head is also common in this Scandinavian filigree style;[7] the great difference being that the Scandinavian ornament usually stands out in relief, with violently baroque effects of light and shadow. Here

---

[1] From Co. Kilkenny; *C.A.A.I.*, vol. I, Pl. 42,2 and 21,1.

[2] 'The Clonmacnoise Brooch' (in Miscellanea), *J.R.S.A.I.*, 1890–1, pp. 318 sqq.; Macalister, *Clonmacnois*, pp. 155–6; J. Romilly Allen, *Celtic Art in Pagan and Christian Times* (2d ed., London, 1912), pp. 219–20.

[3] J. Kirk, *The Alfred and Minster Lovel Jewels* (Oxford, 1948).

[4] Brøndsted, *Ornament*, p. 143. [5] *C.A.A.I.*, vol. I, Pl. 21,2.

[6] Holmqvist, *Germanic Art*, Fig. 121; also on a brooch found at Tingstäde; see: M. Stenberger, *Die Schatzfunde Gotlands der Wilkingerzeit* (Stockholm, 1958), vol. II, Fig. 141. [7] See: Stenberger, op. cit., vol. I, Figs. 68, 69.

on the contrary, everything remains on the same plane and the full-face head, with its large pointed ears, is clearly Irish. Everything considered, we seem to be faced here with one of the first imitations by an Irish artist of Scandinavian metalwork. If filigree work was studied in more detail, it might be possible to identify others. We have seen already that there is a hazy zone of mixed Hiberno–Scandinavian jewellery in which it would be difficult to establish distinctions of any subtlety. The silver brooches whose terminal spheres are inlaid with gold filigree are another example of these hybrids.[1] The pendant pins are however different, as the type of object is clearly Irish and the decoration is Scandinavian-inspired in one case only. It may be the only Irish object of that date to exhibit such imitation. From this point of view it appears as a forerunner of a fashion which will invade Irish art from the middle of the eleventh century and permeate all Irish Romanesque art.

One hardly dares to draw conclusions from the study of such a miscellaneous collection of fragments. However, a certain coarsening of the technique seems to be one of the features of this period of Irish metalwork. Filigree is thicker. Enamel becomes rare. On the other hand, niello, which already appears on the Steeple Bumpstead boss but was scarce in the eighth century is now much more common. The repertoire of ornament changes a certain amount: spirals are rarely found, interlacings become dry and monotonous, but foliage for the first time comes into its own. It is essential, however, to stress the fact that it has no relation with the foliage found in Scandinavian art, except perhaps a common ancestry in illuminations. On the contrary it is very close to the sharply drawn little scrolls so often found on Continental manuscripts of the ninth and tenth centuries, which around A.D. 1000 had been translated into stone work and appear for example on the capitals of St Martin du Canigou and on the lintel of St Genis-des-Fontaines in French Catalonia (Pyrenées Orientales). In Irish art they occur only occasionally and the most common ornament remains zoomorphic, whether it consists of isolated beasts or a weaving together of animal shapes as in the preceding period.

[1] Stenberger, op. cit., vol. I, Fig. 12.

The work of the metal smith, as earlier, was preceded by sketches and little trial-pieces engraved or carved on bones or on slate or schist plaques. The ruins of the 'school' at Nendrum have yielded a whole collection of these note-book pages which in this case carried scribal as well as drawing exercises, as various shapes of letters are found besides animals and ornaments (Belfast Museum).[1] A very similar plaque discovered in the excavations at Lissue (Antrim) is also in Belfast Museum (Pl. 57).[2] Lagore[3] and the lower level of Garryduff[4] have yielded others (Fig. 18). A quadrangular fragment of bone found in Dungarvan (Waterford) (Pls. 56, 57) shows combinations of animals treated in higher relief which may have been carved as a preparation for bronze casting. Their jaws are curled up like those of the beasts on the croziers. This object, however, may be fairly late, judging by the little 'fleur de lys' of Scandinavian type indicated between two of the animals. The sketches on a plaque from Killaloe (Clare) are less easily interpreted (Dublin Museum).

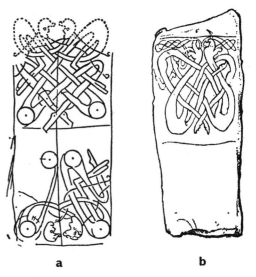

Fig. 18. Trial-pieces:
a, Garryduff; *b*, Lagore
(after O'Kelly and Hencken).

a   b

[1] Lawlor, *Nendrum*, pp. 144 sqq., Pl. XII.   [2] Bersu, *Lissue*, Fig. 11, Pl. I.
[3] Hencken, *Lagore*, p. 173, Fig. 89.   [4] O'Kelly, *Garryduff*, Fig. 15, pp. 78 sqq.

5. Carvings

A.D. 800-1020

In the eighth century, most of the large monasteries and even some less important ones had seen a sudden blossoming on their greens and in their courtyards, of stone crosses carved on all sides.[1] Facing the east and west they seem to have been thought of as protecting the monastery and they were probably used as gathering places for some of the offices and comunal prayers.

In the ninth and tenth centuries they were still one of the most striking features of the decoration of religious houses.[2] Their structure remained roughly the same: pyramidal base, rectangular shaft, large circle connecting the arms of the cross. But the clean and simple lines of the circle and opposing curve were complicated by the introduction of stone discs added either to the hollowed curves of the cross or to the opposing segment of circle. There was also a change in size. Admittedly there are still crosses ten, twelve, fifteen feet high, but many, when they were complete, were much higher. The highest of the eighth-century crosses (seventeen feet), that at Moone (Kildare), is largely exceeded by the West cross at Monasterboice (Pl. 86) and the cross at Arboe (Tyrone) (Pl. I), both more than twenty-two feet high. And it is not only a difference of a yard or two, it is a matter of a new formula for the monument which becomes much more massive and structural.

[1] See: *Vol. I*, pp. 177 sqq.

[2] For general reference on this subject, see: H. S. Crawford, *Handbook of Carved Ornament from Irish Monuments of the Christian Period* (Dublin, 1926); A. Kingsley Porter, *The Crosses and Culture of Ireland* (New Haven, 1931); F. Henry, *La Sculpture irlandaise pendant les douze premiers siècles de l'ère chrétienne* (Paris, 1932); E. H. L. Sexton, *A Descriptive and Bibliographical List of Irish Figure Sculpture in the Early Christian Period* (Portland, Maine, 1946); F. Henry, *Irish High Crosses* (Dublin, 1964); also: H. S. Crawford's invaluable repertories: 'A Descriptive List of Early Irish Crosses', *J.R.S.A.I.*, 1907, pp. 187 sqq., and its supplements in *J.R.S.A.I.*, 1908, pp. 181–2, and 1918, pp. 174 sqq.

133

Another difference is obvious: while ornament was the essential element in the early carvings, where even the coherent series of figured scenes on the Moone cross and the North cross at Ahenny were confined to outsize bases, figure sculpture becomes now predominent, whether it spreads over the whole surface of the cross or more often is distributed in a series of well-defined frames. Decorative patterns disappear almost completely or are confined to the narrow sides of the cross and the segment of the circle connecting its arms. In consequence the study of these crosses will deal chiefly with iconography and the plastic representation of human figures, and not so much with the fitting of patterns on the surface of the stone. Each panel in its rectangular frame becomes a carved picture which can be discussed separately as would an ivory plaque of which, in fact, it often happens to be an enlarged version.

Though it is necessary to define clearly the character of the monuments about to be described, one must always keep in mind the fact that there is no hard and fast line dividing the eighth-century crosses from those which come later. The transition between the two groups presents an infinity of shades, many of which are made more elusive by the fact that there are few chronological landmarks. There are obviously archaic and provincial schools, and on the other hand there are, working for some of the chief clergy and laity of the time, sculptors of genius, like the author of the South cross at Monasterboice, and these far transcend the style of their contemporaries.

There remain about thirty to thirty-five crosses or fragments of crosses with figured scenes scattered over about half the surface of Ireland, with the south and west remaining blank in the distribution map as in the preceding period (see map opposite). They are found in the largest monasteries, Armagh, Kells, Clonmacnois, Durrow, Clones; and also in their satellites, Monasterboice which belonged to Armagh, Drumcliff a monastery of the Columban order, consequently linked with Kells and Durrow, Galloon which probably depended on Clones.

Some groups have a strong local accent: the granite crosses west of the Wicklow Mountains are in many ways the continuation of the crosses of Moone and Old Kilcullen, carved in the same neighbourhood and out

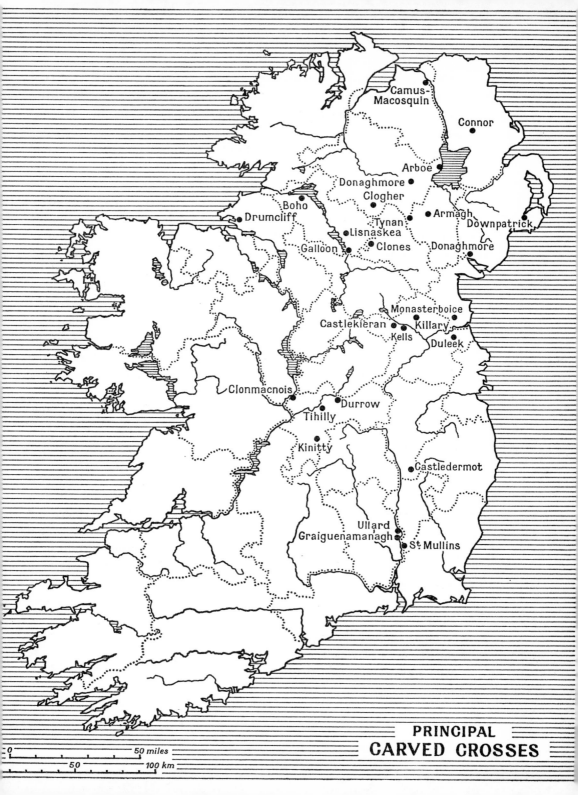

Camus-
Macosquin

Connor

Arboe

Donaghmore

Clogher

Boho
Drumcliff

Armagh

Downpatrick

Tynan

Lisnaskea

Galloon

Clones

Donaghmore

Monasterboice

Castlekieran

Killary

Kells

Duleek

Clonmacnois

Durrow

Tihilly

Kinitty

Castledermot

Ullard

Graiguenamanagh

St Mullins

0   50 miles

50   100 km

PRINCIPAL
CARVED CROSSES

of the same type of stone a very short time earlier. In the west, the crosses of Drumcliff and Boho favour a very individual style. The little granite cross at Donaghmore (Down) at the foot of the Mourne Mountains has a curiously uncouth appearance.

Most of the other crosses are cut out of a fine-grained sandstone and are much more closely akin to each other. It is nevertheless possible to distinguish two groups among them: one, which we shall call the Northern Group (Armagh, Clones, Galloon, Lisnaskea, Donaghmore (Tyrone), Arboe, Connor, Camus, Downpatrick) spreads out from the northern coast to Kells and its neighbourhood (Killary) and is characterized by the use of the same scenes arranged in very nearly the same order; the other, which we shall call the Monasterboice School, is under the sway of the powerful style of a great artist who shows a much greater eclectism in his choice of subjects and their arrangement. His masterpiece is the South cross at Monasterboice, generally called 'the cross of Muiredach'; the West cross at Monasterboice, the 'cross of the Scriptures' at Clonmacnois, the High cross at Durrow all belong to the same style, though they may be partly the work of pupils of the master of Monasterboice.

Besides these figured crosses there are others, belonging to the same time, which have no more than bosses in relief or lozenge-shaped panels filled with ornament. Curiously they generally occur in groups: three at Castlekieran, five at Tynan and Glenarb (now mostly moved to the grounds of Tynan Abbey and Caledon), two at Clogher. There was another at Armagh, a short distance from the cathedral, which is now reduced to a stump. Others, such as the East cross at Monasterboice and a cross at Duleek, have a Crucifixion on one side and several decorated discs on the other, and they are connected to the former group by a similar use of large smooth surfaces very slightly modulated. Both series seem to be contemporary with the figured crosses, as two of these, the West cross at Monasterboice and the cross at Donaghmore (Tyrone) have the same ornamented lozenges.

There were also, beside the large monumental crosses, much smaller ones of which few examples have survived because they were even more vulnerable than the high crosses. Their great number is attested however by the presence of small bases. A few more or less complete ones have survived. One was found at Monasterboice when a grave was being dug (Dublin Museum). Another (id.) probably comes from Moone. Drumcullin (Offaly) has a fragment.[1] This is enough to give some idea of their appearance and to show that they looked like slightly simplified reductions of the larger monuments.

One can hardly doubt that there existed also wooden crosses of which we know nothing and which may have been very different from the stone crosses.

There are very few data for the chronology of these crosses. The Annals are of little help, though the rare entries concerning crosses throw some light on their position and their function. The cross 'on the green' of the monastery of Slane has been mentioned already.[2] There are several entries featuring crosses at Clonmacnois: in one of them the cross described as 'high' or 'tall cross' (cross árd) is given as a landmark in fixing the limits of devastation in a plundering attack on the monastery;[3] in the other, a cross which may have marked a place of asylum is called the 'cross of the Scriptures' (cros na screaptra).[4] This last has always been identified, without absolute proof, with the cross in front of the cathedral. We have seen that several texts relating to Armagh mention crosses and that one of them can be identified with the figured cross whose fragments are now in the cathedral.

In a few cases the historical background may help to date a cross. For example in the case of the monasteries of Kells and Castledermot founded respectively in the first decade of the ninth century and in 812,[5] the crosses cannot be earlier than the foundation date and some of them may well have been erected a short time after it.

The inscriptions which can still be read on some of the crosses are not

---

[1] Henry, *Sc. irl.*, Pl. 97,3,8.   [2] *Vol. I*, p. 136.

[3] *A.F.M.*, 957; *A.U., Chr. Sc., A. Tig.*, 958; *A.C.*, 953.

[4] *Chr. Sc., A. Tig.*, 1058; *A.F.M., A.Clon, A.L.C.*, 1060. Another entry mentions crosses at Clonmacnois: *A.F.M.*, 1070 (Cross of Bishop Etchen, Cross of Congal); in addition, two entries (*A.U.*, 1020, *A.F.M.*, 1070) mention the 'Cairn of the three Crosses'.

[5] See p. 18 and 23.

quite as helpful as one might hope, but altogether they supply a mass of likely evidence which suggests a date early in the tenth century for the School of Monasterboice. Once this date is accepted it becomes comparatively easy to distribute in the ninth century and the beginning of the tenth the other figured crosses; and the inscription on the Tower cross at Kells confirms this hypothesis.

This cross (Pl. 75) is fairly small; even with its capstone, which is now lost, it could not have been much more than 8 feet high.[1] On the top edge of the east side of the base is an inscription deeply cut into the stone which has remained fairly clear and reads: 'PATRICII ET COLUMBE CR[UX] – the cross of Patrick and Columba.'[2] We have seen that Armagh owned vast stretches of land in the region which is immediately to the north of Kells, and that the 'gift' of Kells to St Columba mentioned in the Annals could well have been a gift from Armagh,[3] a possibility which the association of the two holy patrons in this inscription seems to confirm. This cross appears consequently as a monument erected a short time after the gift of Kells and recording it, thus dating from the first decade of the ninth century, a date which is contradicted neither by its iconography nor by its style.

The other inscriptions read by Macalister on the base of this cross and on that of the broken cross also at Kells seem scarcely convincing.[4] On the latter cross they would be in any case no more than graffiti of uncertain date and not an inscription cut by the sculptor himself.

The South cross at Monasterboice has a well-known inscription deeply but irregularly cut into the plinth at the foot of the west side of the shaft: 'OR DO MUIREDACH LAS NDERNAD I CHROSSA – pray for Muiredach who has caused this cross to be erected' (Pl. 79).[5] Two abbots of Monasterboice called Muiredach are recorded in the Annals. Of one nothing is known except that he died in 844. The other who probably became abbot in 887 and died in 923, was at the same time

---

[1] It is mentioned as being 'about 9 foot long and 3½ broad' in the Down Survey for East Meath. *An. Hib.*, 1938, pp. 426 sqq.

[2] Macalister, *Corpus*, II, pp. 36–7 (No. 587).

[3] See p. 20.

[4] Macalister, *Corpus*, II, pp. 36–7 (No. 587) and 34–6 (No. 586).

[5] Petrie, *Chr. Inscr.*, II, pp. 66 sqq.; Macalister, *Corpus*, II, pp. 31–2 (No. 580).

vice-abbot of Armagh and we have seen[1] that his obituary is full of significant features indicating that he was one of the important church-men of the 'Forty year Recess'. He would seem therefore more likely to have been the patron who commissioned this cross.

The Clonmacnois 'cross of the Scriptures' (Pls. 90, 93) had two inscriptions placed like that at Monasterboice on the plinth of the shaft, to the east and west.[2] They are both badly chipped. On the east side, only the letters: '... NDM ...' can be read now and the restitution proposed by Macalister and before him by Petrie: 'OR AR FLAIND MAC MAILESECHLAINN – pray for Flann, son of Maelsechlann' is no more than a guess. The other side however is not quite so badly worn so that part of the text is still legible, some rubbed letters re-appearing in certain lights. It is possible to make out: '... [C]OLMAN DORRO ... SSA AR[IN RIG]FLAIND – Colman caused this cross to be made for King Flann'. Of King Flann Sinna we know that a few years before his death in 915, he built a church in Clon-macnois,[3] probably close to the cross. So the inscription seems to give for this cross a date corresponding to that of the cross of Muiredach. As they are very close in style, this seems satisfactory.

On the high cross at Durrow (Pl. 98) there were also two inscriptions on the lower north and east parts of the shaft.[4] That on the north side is hopelessly worn except for the beginning where Margaret Stokes and Macalister both read: 'OR DO – pray for', which is still fairly legible. For the rest their readings differ completely and neither of them is convincing. The inscription on the west side is partly broken, but in the surviving fragment can be deciphered clearly the '... ODUBT' given by Margaret Stokes (and not the '... TDOT ...' of Mac-alister's reading). Margaret Stokes has suggested the restitution: 'OR DO DUBTACH' – pray for Dubtach', which is likely; but she identified this Dubtach with a steward of Durrow who died in 1010. It seems more likely that we have here a record of that Dubtach who, from 927 to

---

[1] See p. 12.

[2] Petrie, *Chr. Inscr.*, I, pp. 42 sqq.; Macalister, *Corpus*, II, pp. 70–1 (No. 849).

[3] See text p. 12, note 5.

[4] Petrie, *Chr. Inscr.*, II, p. 55; M. Stokes, *Castledermot and Durrow*, p. 11; Macalister, *Corpus*, II, pp. 39–40 (No. 591).

938, governed the monasteries of St Columba in Ireland and Scotland and amongst them Durrow, one of the first foundations of the saint.[1] Unless he was abbot of Durrow before emerging in the full light of history, which is in no way impossible, the cross, supposing that it dates from the time when he was head of the whole order, would be very slightly later than those of Clonmacnois and Monasterboice. As several of its panels are mere replicas of carvings on the cross of the Scriptures, this chronology does not seem unlikely.

The two other surviving inscriptions are on fragments of crosses at Galloon (Fermanagh) which were published in 1934 by Lady Dorothy Lowry-Corry.[2] Their position on the crosses is the same as those of all the other inscriptions, except that of the Tower cross at Kells. They are very faint. It remains nevertheless possible that they mention the one: 'DUBLITIR', the other 'MAELCHIARAIN', names of abbots of Clones who died in 879 and 915. The monastery of Clones, only 8 miles or so from Galloon, had, like Galloon, been founded by St Tigernach and both houses quite possibly may have been under the government of the same abbot. Máelchiarain was also, it seems, bishop of Armagh so that these crosses would thus be linked with St Patrick's monastery. The Galloon crosses are small, and even when their carvings were new they cannot have given any evidence of more than a very ordinary level of production. But when other things apart from their quality are taken into account they are undoubtedly connected with the carvings of several other crosses of the Northern Group.

Before coming to the description of the chief crosses, we shall have to examine the themes directing the organization of the picture sequences which cover them, as the scenes are not chosen in a haphazard way, but for the inner meaning of the episode represented. They have not been carved merely to depict an event, but to show it as forshadowing another event or as illustrating a theological idea. In this respect they fit perfectly into the representational pattern of paleo-Christian

[1] Reeves, *St Columba*, p. 393.
[2] Lady Dorothy Lowry-Corry, 'The Sculptured Crosses of Galloon', *J.R.S.A.I.*, 1934, pp. 165 sqq.; Macalister, *Corpus*, II, p. 122 (Nos. 956–7).

and Romanesque art. They are the pictorial form of a thought, before being a composition of figures in a frame. This does not necessarily mean that composition is considered as unimportant or negligible. Still it is essential to note from the start that the idea is the dominant factor and very often explains the composition or some of its features.

The symbolic themes which inform these scenes are as old as Christianity itself in their inspiration. Thus it has often been pointed out that the system of prefigurations, which sees in practically every episode of the Old Testament anticipations of events in the life of Christ was born when Christ said: 'As Moses lifted up the serpent in the desert, even so must the Son of man be lifted up.'[1] It was developed by the first Fathers of the Church. From St Ambrose and St Augustine it passed to Gregory the Great and Isidore. St Augustine sums it up in two striking formulas 'The Old Testament is nothing but the New covered by a veil and the New Testament is nothing but the Old unveiled', 'All that the Scriptures tell of Abraham really happened, but it was at the same time a prophetic image of things to come'.[2]

Ireland was acquainted with the system already in the seventh century and perhaps even earlier, through the writings of St Augustine and Gregory's *Moralia in Job* which were abridged in the middle of the seventh century by Laid-cend, a scholar from Clonard.[3] It is now also thought that the works of Isidore of Seville were introduced very early into Ireland[4] and his *Commentaries on the Old Testament* are a sort of encyclopedia of all the symbolical interpretations suggested from the time of Origen to that of St Gregory. Bede, a little later, gave only a slightly different treatment of the subject.

This system of prefigurations was very soon translated into pictures. It already directed the choice of subjects in the paintings brought back from Rome by Benedict Biscop at the end of the seventh century, and hung in his monastery of Wearmouth. Bede, who had often seen them in his childhood, and who gives us a glowing account of them,[5] mentions, among others, the parallelism between a picture of the Brazen Serpent

[1] St John, III, 14.   [2] *De Civ. Dei*, XVI, 26; *Sermo II*.   [3] *Vol. I*, p. 31.
[4] J. N. Hillgarth, 'Visigothic Spain and Early Christian Ireland', *P.R.I.A.*, 1962, pp. 167 sqq.   [5] Bede, *H. abb.*, 6.

and the Crucifixion and between Isaac carrying the wood of his sacrifice and Christ carrying his cross.

Though the parallelism is not stressed with the same rigour on the crosses, we shall see that the choice and disposition of the scenes on some of them are determined by the link established between some episodes of the Old Testament and the Crucifixion. The connection may be of a complex nature : Isaac about to be sacrificed by his father appears quite naturally as an image of the sacrifice of Christ. If his carrying the wood for the sacrifice is stressed, the general interpretation is thus enriched. In some cases the relationship may be one of those subtle and strange analogies so dear to Medieval minds. For example the Ark was looked upon as a symbol of the Crucifixion because it was made of wood like the cross and because its proportions were the same as those attributed to the human body (the length being six times the width).[1]

Another symbolic scheme, that of the Help of God, was studied long ago by Le Blant in connection with his work on the Arles sarcophagi where it was used extensively.[2] Later, Karl Michel developed this study.[3] Efforts to criticize their theory or minimise its importance have failed to upset the essential part of their conclusions.

The theme is based on a prayer to God for help, in the name of those who remained faithful under the Old Law and in the name of the miracles of Christ, which until recently formed part of the prayers for the dying (*Ordo commendationis animae*) 'Deliver, O Lord the soul of thy servant as thou didst deliver Noah in the flood . . . Isaac from the sacrificing hand of his father . . . Daniel from the lion's den . . . the three children from the fiery furnace' etc. This was originally a Jewish prayer which was early adapted to Christian use, and had numerous additions and changes in the course of the centuries. It seems to be the dominant scheme around which the various scenes represented on the fourth and fifth centuries sarcophagi and on contemporary ivories were planned. Admittedly several episodes quoted in the prayer are omitted,

[1] St Augustine, *De Civ. Dei*, XV, 26.
[2] E. Le Blant, *Etude sur les sarcophages chrétiens antiques de la Ville d'Arles* (Paris, 1878); Id., *Les Sarcophages chrétiens de la Gaule* (Paris, 1886).
[3] Karl Michel, *Gebeht und Bild*.

but it is rare to see an iconographical series literally following a liturgical text. Besides the prayer existed in so many different versions that it is hard to know exactly which may have been used as a guide to the artists. They obviously enlarged the series into an illustration of the theme of the Redemption, which led, logically enough, to the addition, at the beginning, of a representation of the Fall and, at the end, of a representation of Christ teaching amongst the Apostles or giving the New Law to St Peter and St Paul (*Traditio Legis*). Examples of this series of images dating from the following centuries on sarcophagi, ivories, metal jugs, belt buckles, etc., show that the theme was never abandoned. Its popularity revived in Carolingian times, when it appeared on numerous ivories. But at that time the Crucifixion generally took the place of the Teaching Christ in the earlier series.

We have, in the conclusion of the Martyrology of Óengus Céli Dé, written around 800,[1] proof that a version of the *Ordo* had reached Ireland before the end of the eighth century. Fragments of the original Latin text are included, but the main text, in Irish, is more florid and varied than its model:

'Hear thou, O Jesus,

  .   .   .   .

The soul of every son of Life
Through thou has been sanctified
Adam's seed that is highest
By thou has been freed.

Free me, O Jesus,
From every ill on earth
As thou savedst Noah
Son of Lamech from the Flood.

Free me, O Jesus,
Noble, wondrous king,
As thou savedst Jonas
From the belly *ceti magni* (of the great whale).

[1] Stokes, *Mart. Oengus.*

143

Free me, O Jesus,
Into thy many-graced heaven,
As thou savedst Isaac
From his father's hand.

Free me, O Jesus,
O Lord who are divinest,
As thou savedst Daniel
Of the den of lions.

Free me, O Jesus,
Who has wrought great marvels,
As thou freedst the Children
De camine ignis (from the fiery firnace).'[1]

This is not the only example of the adaptation of the prayer in Irish texts. Robin Flower has quoted several others.[2] The most striking is in the Stowe Missal, also written around 800, which has a background similar to that of the Martyrology: 'Thou who didst guide Noah over the waves of the Deluge, harken unto us; thou who didst call back Jonah by a word, deliver us; thou who didst hold out thy hand to Peter drowning, be aiding unto us, Christ, Son of God.'[3]

In both cases we are dealing with works connected with the reform movement directed by Maelruan, abbot of Tallaght, a movement which had a strong ascetic tone, but showed also a disposition to study liturgy in its symbolic aspect.[4] The quotation from the Stowe Missal shows that the text of the prayer had, by A.D. 800, become familiar enough to be incorporated into the Irish liturgy. This means that it was already known for some time and that any set of pictures illustrating it would be immediately intelligible, whether it came to Ireland as part of a book-binding, as a wooden icon, or on a metal object – the normal vehicles for the introduction of pictorial representations of the theme.

Apart from these two great schemes of organized scenes, each

---

[1] Id., pp. 283–4.
[2] Robin Flower, 'Irish High Crosses', *J.W.C.I.*, 1954, pp. 87 sqq.
[3] Warner, *Stowe Missal*, II, p. 13.   [4] *Vol. I*, p. 43.

episode represented may have a significance connecting it with other symbolical systems, or sometimes belonging especially to it. Let us for example examine again the Sacrifice of Isaac. In both texts quoted above it is considered as an example of God's help to the faithful, the emphasis being put on the fact that Isaac was saved from death. We have seen that Isaac carrying the wood of his sacrifice is a prefiguration of Christ carrying his cross. This is not all. The same episode may be taken as an example of a sacrifice agreeable to God. It is quoted, with this meaning, together with the sacrifices of Abel and Melchisedech, in the Canon of the Mass and, already in the sixth century, these three sacrifices, grouped together for the same reason, adorned the choir of the church of San Vitale at Ravenna.

On the other hand, from an early date, cycles and scenes grouped in their chronological order, especially scenes from the Childhood of Christ (Christmas cycle) and from the Passion (Easter cycle) developed in the East and from there slowly penetrated into the West. These series conditioned by liturgical considerations had an influence on the choice of scenes from the life of Christ, even when included in a symbolical scheme. In his study of thirteenth-century iconography, Emile Mâle[1] pointed out that in Gothic art there are very few representations of New Testament scenes and that one hardly ever finds in the thirteenth century the representations of the miracles of Christ which are so frequent in the catacomb paintings and on fourth and fifth-century sarcophagi. One could say the same thing of Romanesque art and it is remarkable that it is true already of the decoration of Irish crosses. Apart from the Multiplication of the Loaves and Fishes, the only scenes from the life of Christ which they bear are practically all connected with important feasts: Christmas (Holy Family, Appearance of the Angels to the Shepherds, Massacre of the Innocents); Epiphany, or feast of the Theophanies (Adoration of the Kings, Wedding at Cana, Baptism of Christ); Holy Week and Easter (Entry into Jerusalem, Passion scenes, Crucifixion, Women at the Tomb).

These iconographical schemes have all left their mark on the decoration of the crosses. They are sometimes combined, or there is a slightly

[1] Mâle, *Gothic Image*, pp. 176–7.

a

b

Fig. 19. Meeting of St Paul and St Anthony:
a, fresco at Der-Abu-Makar (Egypt);
b, Moone Abbey cross;
c, Armagh cross.

c

awkward transition from one to the other, and a consequent survival of rather meaningless characteristics. Occasionally a series is imitated without any understanding of the inner meaning directing the succession of scenes. It would be futile to assign any reason to the resulting incoherence other than the ineptitude of the sculptor or of his patron.

To grasp the development of this iconography of the crosses it is necessary to go back to an earlier date than the beginning of the ninth century. We have seen that already in the eighth century the carved panels of the cross at Moone (Kildare) were organized in a reasoned sequence: the Fall, followed by some examples of the Help of God drawn from the Old Testament – Sacrifice of Isaac, Daniel in the Lions' den, the Three Children in the Fiery Furnace – and by two examples from the New Testament – the Flight into Egypt and the Multiplication of the Loaves and Fishes –; then the Crucifixion accompanied by the twelve Apostles and, in conclusion, some examples of God's help taken from the lives of the saints: the Temptation of St Anthony and the bird from heaven bringing a loaf to St Paul and St Anthony (Fig. 19). Except for the fact that the representation of Christ teaching is replaced by the Crucifixion, this is a typical series of examples of the Help of God as found in paleo-Christian art. Even the presence of scenes taken from lives of saints is perfectly normal: in the prayer for the dying there is a mention of Peter and Paul freed from jail and episodes of the lives of St Martin, St Patrick and St Kevin are quoted in the Martyrology of Óengus. In itself there is nothing surprising in the choice of events from the lives of St Paul and St Anthony the Hermits as the ascetics of the Egyptian desert were the obvious patrons of the Irish monks striving to follow their example.

We are confronted with a certain number of similar scenes when we consider the carvings on the two crosses at Castledermot (Kildare)[1] (Pls. 65 to 72). These carvings were partly derived

[1] M. Stokes, *Castledermot and Durrow*: W. Hawkes, 'The High Crosses of Castledermot', *Repertorium Novum*, 1956, pp. 247 sqq.; Henry, *Sc. irl.*,

Fig. 20. South cross at Castledermot, Massacre of the Innocents.

from those on the Moone Cross of which they are close neighbours, but are slightly later in date as the monastery was founded in 812. But now, instead of being confined to a high pyramidal base as at Moone, the figured scenes cover the whole surface of the cross and this necessitated a reorganization of the general scheme. On the North cross the intersection of the arms of the cross becomes the centre of the whole composition, the focal point, where the Fall is shown on one side and the Redemption on the other. Around Adam and Eve are four subjects (Pl. 71): the Sacrifice of Isaac, Daniel in the Lions' den, David playing the Harp, and the Massacre of the Innocents which replaces the Flight into Egypt. Around the Crucifixion (Pl. 70) four groups of identical figures form a kind of halo of Apostles. However, there was still room available on the shaft of the cross and even on its base, and in this some scenes were arranged without much logic in the order of their presentation. The Temptation of St Anthony and his meeting with St Paul the Hermit were placed on each side of the shaft, while the base received a picture of the Multiplication (Pl. 72) less cryptic than the Moone panel where only the loaves and fishes were shown. Three figures in the lower panel of the west side of the shaft may be meant for the Three Children.

This rearranging of the scenes seems to retain some meaning but on the South cross confusion reigns. There the east side has only ornament (Pl. 67) for some unknown reason perhaps connected with the original position of the cross. The centre of the opposite side is occupied by the Crucifixion (Pls. 65, 66), surrounded by the Sacrifice of Isaac, the Three Children, David, and two unidentified scenes. On the shaft Adam and Eve are oddly placed between the two episodes from the life of St Anthony. The Apostles, grouped two by two, occupy one of the narrow sides of the shaft, whilst on the north side the Massacre of the Innocents and probably the Fight of Jacob and the Angel are depicted in several small panels. On the Barrow valley crosses (Graiguenamanagh, Ullard, St Mullins) the disorganization is even more complete and nothing remains but a sort of allusion to well-known subjects.

Pls. 46–8 (on Pl. 48, the texts of Figs. 2 and 3 have been interverted); Henry, *Irish High Crosses*, Pls. 19, 21–4; Sexton, *Fig. Sc.*, pp. 91 sqq.

a

b

c

Fig. 21. Multiplication of the Loaves and
Fishes: *a*, North cross, Castledermot;
b, fresco at Togale (Cappadocia);
c, Arboe cross.

The Tower cross at Kells (Pls. 74–5)[1] may be practically contemporary with one of the Castledermot crosses as the two monasteries were founded at nearly the same date, but it shows a completely different treatment of the sequence of subjects. One can feel there a considered judgment presiding over the rearrangement. The multiplicity of the symbolical meanings contained in each event has been kept in mind and there is obviously an effort to build them around a richer theme than the simple invocations of the *Ordo*. The subjects on the east side must be read upwards from the foot of the shaft and then turning clockwise. The Fall comes first but is accompanied by the murder of Abel, and Abel, innocent victim, has always been looked upon as a prefiguration of Christ. Then come first two scenes from the Book of Daniel: the Three Children and Daniel in the Lions' den. They are treated in a novel way: on both sides of the Children and of the protecting angel are two men piling wood on the fire with long forks. Their arrangement immediately suggests a parallel with the sponge and lance bearers on both sides of the representations of the Crucifixion. Daniel between the lions can be envisaged also as a prefiguration of the Crucifixion, so much so that on another Kells cross, at the corner of the Market Street, and on a fragment at Clones (Fig. 26), he is placed in the centre of the cross, his arms outstretched to stress the symbolism. On the south arm of the cross is represented the sacrifice of Abraham, with Isaac holding the wood for the sacrifice and the axe used in cutting it. At the top of the cross is shown a complex scene: two figures are seated in front of each other; the figure on the right holds round objects and the presence of two fishes crossed saltire fashion shows clearly that a picture of the Multiplication is intended. The crowd is shown in the background as on the South cross at Castledermot. But the strange thing is that the figure facing Christ on the left is playing the harp and is no doubt meant for David, introduced into the scene because of his rôle as a prophet. This presentation suggests, as a source of inspiration for a carved scene the illuminations of Greek or Oriental manuscripts such as the Rossano

[1] H. S. Crawford, 'The Early Crosses of East and West Meath', *J.R.S.A.I.*, 1926, pp. 72 sqq.; H. Roe, *The High Crosses of Kells* (Kells, 1959), pp. 10 sqq.; Henry, *Sc. irl.*, Pls. 57–8; Sexton, *Fig. Sc.*, pp. 182 sqq.; Henry, *Irish High Crosses*, Pls. 26–9.

Gospel-book or the Sinope Fragment,[1] where prophets holding scrolls accompany each Gospel scene. On the Sinope Fragment the representations of the two Multiplications of the Loaves have survived. On the scroll held in each case by the figure of David, one can read his prophecies: 'Praise the Lord . . . who giveth food to all flesh: for his mercy endureth for ever' (Ps. CXXXV), and: 'The eyes of all hope in thee, O Lord; and thou givest them meat in due season' (Ps. CXLIV). These quotations explain his presence in the carved scene also. On the north arm of the cross, St Paul and St Anthony are seated face to face, each holding a crook or crozier and receiving the round loaf brought by a bird plunging directly from heaven. Behind them a kind of griffin is probably an emblem of the desert where they are.

In this series of representations the stress is laid on the subtle links which connect each scene with the Crucifixion, and in the two last episodes with the Eucharist. The representation of the Crucifixion on this cross is however fairly low on the shaft, on the west side, as it was on the South cross at Clonmacnois and on the Moone cross. This is an archaic feature never found again, which seems to confirm the dating of the monument to the early ninth century. This cross is also, as we shall see, the only surviving Irish cross with a representation of the Apocalyptic Vision. These features give it a very special position. It was only to be expected in fact that all these symbolic subtleties would be found among the community of Iona–Kells whose scriptorium was probably busy at the same time with the decoration of the Book of Kells, full of similar preoccupations.

Three other crosses have survived in Kells. They are all partly broken, and one of them is unfinished[2] and yields much information as

---

[1] H. Omont, 'Peintures d'un manuscrit grec de l'évangile de St Matthieu copié en onciales d'or sur un parchemin pourpré et récemment acquis pour la Bibliothèque nationale', *Mon. Piot*, 1900, pp. 179 sqq., Pl. XVII; A. Muñoz, *Il codice purpureo di Rossano ed il frammente Sinopense* (Rome, 1907); A. Grabar, *Les peintures de l'Evangéliaire de Sinope (Bibliothèque nationale, suppl. gr. 1286)* (Paris, 1948), I, pp. 12–13, II, fols. 11 and 15; Cabrol-Leclercq, art: *Pain*.

[2] Crawford, *East and West Meath*; Roe, *Kells*, pp. 55 sqq.; J. Healy, 'The Unfinished Crosses of Kells', *J.R.S.A.I.*, 1890–1, pp. 450 sqq.; Henry, *Sc. irl.*, Pl. 82; Id., *Irish High Crosses*, Pl. 1.

to the way the sculptor went about his work (Pls. 7 and 101). Most of the block has only been roughed out and divided into panels, and only a carving of the Crucifixion has come near completion. The two other crosses are probably slightly later than the cross by the round tower and imitate some of its features. From another standpoint they are both connected with some other groups of crosses and have in consequence to be studied together with them.

As we have already seen, one of these groups belongs to the north of Ireland. It unfortunately consists mostly of very dilapidated fragments (Connor, Camus, Killary, Galloon, Clones, Armagh, Downpatrick).[1] Only two crosses are more or less complete, those at Donaghmore and Arboe[2] (Pl. I), both in County Tyrone, but they happen to be carved in a kind of sandstone which weathers easily, so that many of the figures are only shapeless masses. If it is difficult to estimate the quality of the carvings, it is still possible in most cases to identify the subjects and to be sure that they are divided into two groups, one on each of the main faces of the cross, with some complementary scenes on the narrow sides.

On one side there are events from the Old Testament: the Fall, the Sacrifice of Abraham, the Three Children, Daniel in the Lions' den. The other side is devoted to the New Testament. This series often starts with the Announcement to the Shepherds, followed sometimes by the Adoration of the Magi; then come the Baptism of Christ, the Wedding at Cana, the Multiplication of the Loaves and Fishes, the Entry into Jerusalem, a scene with three figures which might be either the Transfiguration or the Arrest of Christ; then, when the cross is complete, the Crucifixion, probably between two scenes of the Passion. Other subjects already familiar, such as the murder of Abel or the meeting of St Paul and St Anthony, are sometimes carved on the narrow sides, which however are more often occupied by ornament. Only once, at Donaghmore (Tyrone) is the murder of Abel given a panel on the main side of the cross, above the Fall.

[1] Henry, *Sc. irl.*, pp. 200 sqq.
[2] H. Roe, 'The High Crosses of the Archdiocese of Armagh; Co. Tyrone', *Seanchas Ardmacha*, 1956, pp. 79 sqq.; Henry, *Sc. irl.*, Pls. 69, and 67–8; Id., *Irish High Crosses*, Pl. 59; Sexton, *Fig. Sc.*, pp. 118–19 and 53 sqq.

The following table, which must be read from the bottom as the panels of the crosses, will give some idea of the arrangement of the scenes on the three most complete crosses of the series :

ARBOE		CLONES		DONAGHMORE	
	Transfiguration or Arrest				Transfiguration or Arrest
Three Children	Entry into Jerusalem	Daniel in the Lions' den	Multiplication of Loaves	Daniel in the Lions' den	Multiplication of Loaves
Daniel in the Lions' den	Mult. of Loaves or Last Supper		Wedding at Cana	Sacrifice of Abraham	Wedding at Cana
Sacrifice of Abraham	Wedding at Cana	Sacrifice of Abraham	Adoration of the Kings	Murder of Abel	Baptism of Christ
					Adoration of the Kings
Adam and Eve	Adoration of the Kings	Adam and Eve	Appearance of the Angel to the shepherds	Adam and Eve	Appearance of the Angel to the shepherds

The cross at Arboe, on the west shore of Lough Neagh, is probably still in its original position, a short distance from the ruin of a church, the remnant of a monastery which originally covered a very much larger stretch of ground than the narrow space of the graveyard surrounding the ruin. As in the case of Donaghmore, the monastery rarely appears in the Annals and the importance of both can only be evaluated by their proximity to Dungannon, the seat of one of the branches of the Northern Uí Néill. On the other hand, Clones[1] is known to have been

[1] W. F. Wakeman, 'On the Ecclesiastical Antiquities of Cluain-Eois, now Clones, County of Monaghan', *J.R.S.A.I.*, 1874–5, pp. 327 sqq.

an important monastic centre and a round tower, a large stone sarcophagus and the ruin of a church still mark the site of the monastery on
the slope of a hill. There remain, on the market place, fragments of two
crosses of different sizes now unfortunately combined into a single
monument. All memory of their original site among the monastic
buildings is now lost.

The position of the Armagh figured cross,[1] on the other hand, is
well documented. It is clearly shown at the entrance of the Rath on a
map drawn in the early seventeenth century by Richard Bartlett[2] so
that it can be identified with the 'cross at the gate of the Rath' mentioned
in an entry for 1166 in the Annals of Ulster. It seems to have been
knocked down towards the end of the seventeenth century, was raised
again in 1763 and placed in the centre of the Market place which is really
a piece of steeply sloping ground just below the old entrance to the Rath.
There is a lithograph done from a drawing dated 1812 which shows it as
it was at the time, with the head of the cross put on back to front, so that
the Crucifixion was above the Old Testament scenes. About that time
it was thrown down again in an outburst of street fighting. A drawing
made in 1852 shows a restoration of it done correctly. The three
battered fragments which have survived these vicissitudes are now
inside the cathedral. They are only partly decipherable, but with the
help of these various documents it is possible to reconstruct nearly the
whole series of scenes as : the Fall, the Ark (Pl. 97) and the Sacrifice of
Abraham on one side and on the other, the Appearance of the Angel to
the Shepherds, the Baptism of Christ and the Transfiguration or the
Arrest, below the Crucifixion. Looking at the Old Testament scenes and
the Crucifixion, one can guess at the original appearance of the carvings
and at the treatment which was perhaps slightly heavy but very
vigorous, similar probably in style to the carvings on the Broken cross
at Kells. This suggests that Armagh may have been the centre where

---

[1] J. Stuart, *Historical Memoirs of the City of Armagh* (Newry, 1819); W. Reeves,
The Ancient Churches of Armagh (Lusk, 1860); H. S. Crawford, *East and West
Meath*, appendix; H. Roe, 'The High Crosses of the Archdiocese of Armagh; Co.
Armagh', *Seachas Ardmacha*, 1955, pp. 107 sqq.; Henry, *Sc. irl.*, Pls. 62–4; Sexton,
Fig. Sc., pp. 61 sqq.; Henry, *Irish High Crosses*, pp. 19–20, 29–30, Pls. 36–8.

[2] Fig. 2. McCoy, *Ulster Maps*, map facing p. 6.

this northern type of cross was elaborated and from which it spread to some neighbouring monasteries and then as far as the north coast on one side and Killary, near Kells, on the other.

The Broken cross at Kells (Pls. 96, 97),[1] which is still with its base 11½ feet high, must have been about 20 feet high originally,[2] so that it was conceived on a completely different scale from the Tower cross. It was probably higher than the Armagh Cross, which cannot have been much more than 16 or 17 feet high, but it is still exceeded in height, amongst the crosses of the same Northern Group, by the Arboe cross which is some 23 feet high. Some of its panels are similar to those of the Armagh cross, the Ark especially (Pl. 96). For the rest it is very different. Several panels cannot be identified and it is not certain that the separation between Old and New Testament scenes was observed consistently as on the northern crosses. On the west side there is the Fall, the Ark, an unidentified scene, and the Brazen Serpent. On the other face the Baptism of Christ and the Wedding at Cana are followed by three obscure subjects and then by the lower part of the broken panel depicting the Entry into Jerusalem (Fig. 31).

Another cross at Kells, that on the Market place,[3] has traces of the same iconography, but strangely upset by the introduction of new scenes (Pls. 102, 104). On one side of the shaft there is a normal New Testament sequence: Adoration of the Magi, Wedding at Cana, Multiplication of the Loaves and Fishes; it may have started with the Appearance of the Angel to the Shepherds before the cutting of a seventeenth-century inscription on the lower part of the shaft. On the other side, there is a coherent block of scenes on the cross itself, following closely the arrangement on the Tower cross. Farther down, on the shaft, two scenes borrowed from a different iconographical system have

[1] Healy, *Unfinished Crosses*; Crawford, *East and West Meath*; Roe, *Kells*, pp. 44 sqq.; Henry, *Sc. irl.*, Pls. 70–1; Sexton, *Fig. Sc.*, pp. 188 sqq.; Henry, *Irish High Crosses*, Pls. 34–5.

[2] Though it is described in the Down Survey (presumably complete) as '15 foot long and 5 broad'; it is said also there to have been 'set up in remembrance of a queen of the O Neales that was buried there' (*An. Hib.*, 1938, pp. 426 sqq.)

[3] Crawford, *East and West Meath*; Roe, *Kells*; Henry, *Sc. irl.*, Pls. 72–3; Sexton, *Fig. Sc.*, pp. 176 sqq.; Henry, *Irish High Crosses*, Pls. 30–3.

been inserted : a group of warriors which may be an allusion to the Harrowing of Hell[1] and the Soldiers at the Tomb of Christ.

This apparent incoherence is probably brought about by the introduction of new subjects in the carvings of the crosses of the Monasterboice School. These crosses (two at Monasterboice, the cross of the Scriptures at Clonmacnois and the High cross of Durrow), are all in an excellent state of preservation. They are intact from base to finial and on some of the panels the modelling of the figures and the delicacy of engraved details can still be appreciated. As we have seen, they probably go back to the early part of the tenth century and they seem to have been carved under the patronage of a few outstanding churchmen who laboured, during the 'Forty year Recess', to give a new lustre to the war-scarred monasteries by rebuilding churches, protecting them with round towers, and decorating their forecourts with crosses carved by the best sculptors of the time.

These four crosses vary in size and structure. The blocks of stone are mostly 10 to 13 feet high. The differences are all in the way they are used and in the thickness of the slab. The material is a laminated sandstone which comes out mostly in fairly thin beds. In Monasterboice the sculptor worked on a grand scale. He has composed one of the crosses by the superposition of two blocks between the base and the separate capstone, so that the whole monument is 23 feet high. For the other, an unusually thick block, $10\frac{2}{3}$ feet high and about 7 feet wide has been used so as to yield the maximum surface for the carvings. The aim has been attained without loss of elegance by the addition of a very high capstone which allowed a shifting of all the proportions so that the shaft could reach the remarkable width of $2\frac{1}{2}$ feet. At Clonmacnois, on the other hand, the whole cross has been cut out of a relatively thin and narrow slab of sandstone and at Durrow the only addition to the main block is a low capstone. As a consequence these two crosses look more frail, homely and, as it were, within reach of the hand, than the two imposing Monasterboice monuments.

There are also variations in the position of the ornamental discs and in the shape of the connecting circle. For example the circle of the

[1] See pp. 174–5.

Clonmacnois cross has a superimposed look as if held in position by four relief discs. So there is nothing of monotonous or repetitive production in this group, but on the contrary we are faced with various experiments showing a very inventive spirit. The same can be said of the iconography which breaks sharply with the accepted sets of subjects and replaces them by a host of new images.

The best introduction to this novelty-laden world is a study of the cross of Muiredach[1] (Pls. 76–85 and 106–7). On the east side (Pl. 85) we find first two familiar subjects enclosed in the same frame : the death of Abel, beside Adam and Eve (Pl. 81). Then comes the Fight of David and Goliath so similar to a page of the Cotton Psalter (Pl. 41) but with the addition of the two figures of Saul and Jonathan, and next Moses striking the rock, with, on the panel immediately above, the Adoration of the Magi repeating the same composition. Widely spread on the arms of the cross is the most complete representation of the Last Judgment found on any Irish cross (Pls. 106–7).

On the other side the sculptor has given up the arrangement of crowded rectanguar frames and replaced it by three square panels each holding three commanding figures : first Christ between the two soldiers arresting him (Pl. 79), then Doubting Thomas and at the top, the *Traditio Legis* – Christ committing the keys to St Peter and the New Law to St Paul (Pl. 82). The centre of the cross is occupied by the Crucifixion accompanied, at the ends of the arms, by several other scenes of the Passion. At the very top, Moses between Aaron and Hur is at the same time a symbol of the power of prayer and a pre-figure of the Crucifixion.

This iconographical programme is almost entirely new though the fundamental theme remains, as before, the Redemption. There is a tendency to emphasize the establishment of the Church and its universal character. It is therefore probably not by chance that the *Traditio Legis* on one side of the shaft corresponds with the Adoration of the Magi on the other, which is itself paralleled by the scene of Moses striking the

[1] R. A. S. Macalister, *Muiredach, Abbot of Monasterboice, 890–923 A.D.* (Dublin, 1914); Id., *Monasterboice*; H. Roe, 'The High Crosses of the Archdiocese of Armagh; Co. Louth', *Seanchas Ardmacha*, 1954, pp. 101 sqq.; Henry, *Sc. irl.*, Pls. 75–7; Sexton, *Fig. Sc.*, pp. 223 sqq.; Henry, *Irish High Crosses*, Pls. 40–4.

Rock; Peter and Moses represent the Church of the Jews, Paul and the Magi the Church of the Gentiles. As for the scenes of the Passion, it may be that their inclusion in the carvings seems new to us only because most of the crosses of the Northern Group have lost their upper parts where these scenes may have been represented.

The Tall cross at Monasterboice (Pls. 86–9 and 111)[1] shows an extraordinary juxtaposition of subjects. David appears again, carrying Goliath's head and being anointed by Samuel, below a scene which may be the Adoration of the Golden Calf combined with Moses carrying the Tables of the Law. There are more usual subjects besides these, such as the Sacrifice of Abraham and the Three Children. As in the case of the Kells Market cross, one gets the feeling that new pictures have invaded the old series and upset its normal order. These intrusive subjects are mostly from the lives of David and Moses. They have their complement on one of the narrow sides of the Market cross at Kells, where Moses is shown receiving the Law under the shape of a book on which rests an enormous Hand of God; the panel below, which is partly broken, may have depicted Moses taking off his shoes in front of the Fiery Bush in which appears the figure of God. All this diverges from the set series of pictures, which was inspired no doubt by ivories or icons with the scenes already disposed in a coherent order; here, on the other hand, the variety of the borrowings gives the impression that they were derived from the illustrations of Bibles and Psalters where the sculptor chose a scene here, another there, without obeying a logical sequence. On the Tall cross at Monasterboice the scenes of the Passion are also displayed with a great wealth of detail and a singular vivacity of gesture and attitude (Pl. 87). Here, Carolingian ivories would supply points of comparison and are probably one of the sources of inspiration. This is true also of two panels at the foot of the shaft of the cross, showing the Soldiers watching over the Tomb of Christ and probably the Marys at the Sepulchre. The first scene we have noticed already on the Market cross at Kells. We shall meet it again at Clonmacnois and Durrow.

[1] Macalister, op. cit.; H. Roe, op. cit.; Henry, *Sc. irl.*, Pl. 74; Sexton, *Fig. Sc.*, pp. 221–2; Henry, *Irish High Crosses*, Pls. 56–8.

On the Clonmacnois cross,[1] the scenes of the Passion have completely invaded one side of the shaft, where the Arrest, probably the Flagellation, and the Soldiers at the Tomb are depicted (Pl. 112). These scenes are to be found almost identically on the cross at Durrow.[2]

After this general review of the chief crosses, it will be useful to take one by one some of the scenes represented in order to understand their significance and trace their affinities.

First of all, as they are of primary importance, let us examine the scenes which occupy the centres of the crosses. We have seen that occasionally these could be an event thought to provide a parallel with the Crucifixion: the Fall on the North cross of Castledermot and Daniel between the Lions on the Market cross of Kells and the Clones cross. However it is more usual to find the Crucifixion on one side and Christ in glory or Christ the Judge on the other.

It is possible to study the representations of the Crucifixion independently from those other scenes of the Passion from which it has long remained separate on the Irish crosses. When looking at Irish pictures of the Crucifixion, whether on the Duvillaun or Inishkea engraved slabs (late seventh or early eighth century) or on the ninth and tenth-century crosses, one is immediately struck by the invariable presence of Longinus the lance bearer and Stephaton the sponge bearer as two symmetrical attendants on each side of the cross;[3] there are sometimes angels in the upper part of the panel, but never the Virgin and St John

---

[1] T. J. Westropp, 'A description of the Ancient Buildings and Crosses at Clonmacnois, King' County', *J.R.S.A.I.*, 1907, pp. 290 sqq.; Macalister, *Clonmacnois*, p. 153. Henry, *Sc. irl.*, Pl. 78; Sexton, *Fig. Sc.*, pp. 105 sqq.; Henry, *Irish High Crosses*, Pls. 45–50.

[2] M. Stokes, *Casteldermot and Durrow*; S. de C. Williams, 'The Old Graveyards in Durrow Parish', *J.R.S.A.I.*, 1897, pp. 143 sqq.; Henry, *Sc. irl.*, Pls. 79–81; Sexton, *Fig. Sc.*, pp. 135 sqq.; Henry, *Irish High Crosses*, Pls. 51–5.

[3] Dom Louis Gougaud, O.S.B., 'The Earliest Irish Representations of the Crucifixion', *J.R.S.A.I.*, 1920, pp. 128 sqq.; M. Engels, *Die Kreuzigung Christi in den bildende Kunst* (Luxemburg, 1899); L. Bréhier, *Les origines du Crucifix dans l'art religieux* (Paris, 1904); J. Reil, *Die Frühkristliche Darstellungen der Kreuzigung Christi* (Leipzig, 1904); Id., *Christus am Kreuz in der Bildkunst der Karolingerzeit* (Leipzig, 1930); P. Thoby, *Histoire du Crucifix* (Nantes, 1959).

159

so commonly represented elsewhere. In fact the composition takes on, at an early date, a sort of abstract quality and its non-historical aspect is underlined by the combination of two actions, that of Stephaton before the death of Christ and that of Longinus immediately after.[1] This arbitrary symmetrical arrangement existed outside Ireland already in the fifth and sixth centuries and is found for example on the famous ivory plaque in the British Museum,[2] one of the oldest known representations of the Crucifixion, and a little later in the Gospel-book of Rabbula. It has obviously been borrowed at this stage of its evolution by the Irish artists, but in their works it appears more striking from the absence of other figures at the foot of the cross. As Emile Mâle pointed out,[3] Longinus, who is supposed to have had his blindness cured by the water and blood pouring from the side of Christ was perhaps taken as a figure of the Church, while Stephaton, bearer of the bitter sponge, represented the Synagogue. This would explain the popularity of this composition, as well as the position of Longinus, who is represented on the right of Christ on so many monuments.

Morey has however pointed out[4] that although at that time Longinus is generally represented on the right of Christ – in the Rabbula Gospels and on the cover of the relic-box in the Vatican, for example – still on the British Museum ivory, which seems to be of Western origin, the lance thrust is given to the left side of Christ. He adds the remark that this Western type passed into Irish art where it became the rule. The facts are really much more complex. Longinus is on the right of Christ on a number of Irish monuments: the Inishkea and Duvillaun slabs, Ms. A.II.17 of Durham, the Moone cross, the south cross of Castledermot, the south cross of Clonmacnois, the Arboe cross and some of the openwork metal plaques. These representations are spread over at

[1] See on this subject: Dom René-Jean Herbert, O.S.B., *Le problème de la transfixion du Christ* (Paris, 1940), though it seems hardly necessary to have recourse to an apochryphal text to explain this constant juxtaposition of Longinus and Stephaton, of a purely abstract nature.

[2] O. M. Dalton, *British Museum Guide to the Early Christian and Byzantine Antiquities* (2d ed., London, 1921), Pl. II.

[3] Mâle, *Gothic Image*, pp. 187–8 and 190.

[4] C. R. Morey, *Early Christian Art* (Princeton, 1953), p. 136.

least four centuries and are in accord with the commentary on the Mass in the Stowe Missal which dates from about A.D. 800.[1] The other school of thought is represented by the miniature of the Crucifixion in the St Gall Gospels and the Athlone plaque, both of the eighth century, and by most of the ninth and tenth centuries high crosses. So the link with the British Museum ivory becomes very questionable. On the cross of Muiredach at Monasterboice there is a strange contradiction which stresses the importance for that cross of new foreign inspiration : on the central panel of the west side (Pl. 76) Longinus is on the left of Christ, as on most of the crosses of that time, but farther down, in a scene never represented before in Ireland, and obviously copied without modification from some ivory, St Thomas puts his finger into a wound which is on the right side of Christ.

A careful examination of the Irish representations of the Crucifixion shows that Christ is never shown wearing the sleeveless tunic, the *colobium*, which is seen in the Rabbula illumination, the Vatican relic-box and the fresco of Santa Maria Antiqua.[2] He is often dressed in a long garment, but always with sleeves coming down to the wrists. Omitting various examples with twisted draperies, this dress is found on the Athlone openwork plaque, the Moone cross (eighth century), two late bronze plaques in the Dublin Museum (Pls. 8, 54) one of which was found in Clonmacnois, on the two Castledermot crosses (Pls. 66, 70), the Unfinished cross at Kells and the Armagh cross. Elsewhere, and even on the Inishkea and Duvillaun slabs, Christ is shown unclothed, occasionally with a slight indication of the *perizonium*. It seems quite impossible to define two separate or consecutive groups one of which would be characterized by the long dress and the wound on the right. All the different versions are hopelessly mixed, reflecting no doubt the diversity of the models imitated in Ireland at that time. From the start we are faced with the fact that the development of figurative art in Ireland does not depend on one current of influences only, but is

---

[1] 'The particle that is cut off from the bottom of the half which is on the (priest's) left hand is the figure of the wounding with the lance in the armpit of the right side' Warner, *Stowe Missal*, II, p. 41.

[2] Thoby, op. cit., Figs. 11 and 20.

conditioned by imports of varied origin which are imitated indiscrimin-
ately by the Irish artists.

Other features would deserve attention. One of them, which has been
studied by Dom Gougaud,[1] is the replacing of the sponge by a sort of
vase fixed at the end of a long pole. Another would be the representations of the sun and moon which are shown on both sides of the cross as
in many Continental versions.[2] They are often reduced to two human
heads or even to two bulbous protuberances. The sculptor of the cross
of Muiredach may have forgotten the significance of these shapeless
balls. While they are indicated on either sides of the legs of Christ, there
are also a full face bust on Christ's right and on his left a small kneeling
figure averting its face. These are probably due to the imitation of a
Carolingian ivory or illumination in which the two luminaries were
represented not by heads, but by busts or by little figures and where
Luna sometimes turns aside, weeping.

Finally one must emphasize the strangely hieroglyphic character of
the Crucifixion scene on most crosses. The tender gesture of the two
angels holding up the head of Christ on a few of the crosses is a rare
instance of unbending on the part of the sculptors. There is often in their
representation a dryness which is redeemed only by the offering gesture
of the two large, open hands, dryness which may result from endless
repetition, and which forms a striking contrast with the intensity of
expression found in some of the scenes of the Passion.

On the crosses which have come down to us there are different
representations of Christ in glory: either as he is described in the
Apocalypse, or presiding at the Last Judgment or – and this is very
rare – as a warrior chief surrounded by his army.

It may seem strange to find the Apocalyptic Vision on only one of
the Irish crosses, when one reflects that from the time of Constantine
to the thirteenth century it was one of the chief subjects which artists

[1] Gougaud, op. cit.

[2] L. Hautecoeur, 'Le soleil et la lune dans les crucifixions', *R.A.*, 1921;
L. H. Grondijs, 'Le soleil et la lune dans les scènes de la crucifixion, *Congrès int.
des Etudes byzantines* (Sofia, 1935); W. Deonna, 'Sol et Luna, Histoire d'un
thème iconographique', *Rev. Hist. des Religions*, 1947–8.

displayed on the apses of churches and that it appears so often in the twelfth century on the carved tympana of doorways.

From an early date Christ in majesty has been represented accompanied by the four winged symbols – Man, Lion, Ox, Eagle. This is a combination of the Vision of Ezechiel and of that of St John. Ezechiel saw a human figure above 'four living beings' which had each four faces, those of a man, of a lion, of an ox and of an eagle, and were associated with shining wheels.[1] St John describes[2] 'somebody'[3] sitting on a throne framed by a rainbow and surrounded by twenty-four Elders sitting on thrones. Around the throne, 'were four living creatures, full of eyes before and behind. And the first living creature was like a lion; and the second living creature like a calf; and the third living creature, having the face, as it were, of a man; and the fourth living creature was like an eagle flying'. And they were ceaselessly praising the one on the throne. The figure in glory has been always equated with Christ. The four living creatures were of old considered to be the symbols of the Evangelists and the two visions were summed up in a simplified formula where Christ, sitting on a throne and either blessing or holding a scroll, is surrounded by a halo of light from which emerge the busts of the four living creatures, each holding a book. Occasionally the vision is combined with the Ascension. Early in the fifth century it was carved in a slightly aberrant form on one of the panels of the door of Santa Sabina in Rome.[4] But on the mosaic of Hosios David in Salonika[5] and on a fresco of the Egyptian monastery of Bawit[6] the busts of the animals protrude from the mandorla surrounding Christ, according to a frequently used formula found also on the sarcophagus of Agilbertus in the crypt at Jouarre (seventh century).[7] Under one shape or another, Christ in glory surrounded by the four animals is found in a great number of Italian mosaics. On the vault of the archiepiscopal chapel in Ravenna,

---

[1] *Ezech.*, I, 5–21.   [2] *Apoc.*, IV, 6–9.

[3] 'And behold there was a throne set in heaven, and upon the throne one sitting' (*Apoc.* IV, 2).

[4] See a very clear photograph in Mâle, *Churches of Rome*, Fig. 35.

[5] Volbach, *Early Christian Art*, Pls. 133–5.

[6] Mâle, *XIIe siècle*, p. 35.

[7] Ivan Christ, *L'Abbaye de Jouarre et ses cryptes mérovingiennes* (Paris, 1955).

which dates from the late fifth or early sixth century, the motif has already acquired a formal appearance.[1] In typical Ravennate fashion, it is treated in an abstract way, the flaming monogram of Christ replacing his human figuration and the symbols floating in clouds around it.

A similar disposition, but with Christ figured in the middle of a round halo, is found on one of the pages of the Codex Amiatinus painted in the Northumbrian scriptorium of Jarrow–Wearmouth in the early eighth century.[2] This shows that the motif had penetrated to the extreme west of Europe by that time. In fact there may be other traces of it; considering that in the Ravenna chapel the monogram replaces the figure of Christ and that in the apsidial mosaic of Santa Pudentiana in Rome, the symbols are grouped around the cross instead of surrounding the figure of Christ, one may wonder if we have not also an allusion to the Vision in pages of manuscripts like that in the Book of Durrow, where the four symbols are placed in the four spandrels of a cross. It may be that the original intention was forgotten when in other manuscripts there is no more than a roughly cruciform combination of lines dividing the page into four compartments, each containing a symbol. This is found in the Lichfield Gospels and later in the Book of Kells, where, as we have seen, three pages are devoted to representations of the Evangelists' symbols (Pl. 23). It remains however very striking that the only explicit Irish representation of the Vision is at Kells on the Tower cross which may have been executed at the very time the Book was being illuminated in the scriptorium nearby.

There Christ is carved in the centre of the west side of the cross (Pl. 74) and he is given the same attitude as in the Irish carvings of the Last Judgment: he is standing squarely, feet wide apart holding the cross in one hand and in the other a sprouting bough, symbol of resurrection. The position of the staffs is strongly reminiscent of those held by Osiris–Judge in Egyptian funerary carvings and in the illustrations

[1] This composition, with the Lamb in the centre is found already in the vault of the chapel under the church of S. Pudentiana, in Rome, which dates from the second century (Wilpert, *R. Mosaiken*, IV, Pl. 235).
[2] *E.Q.C. Lindisfarnensis*, Pl. 24.

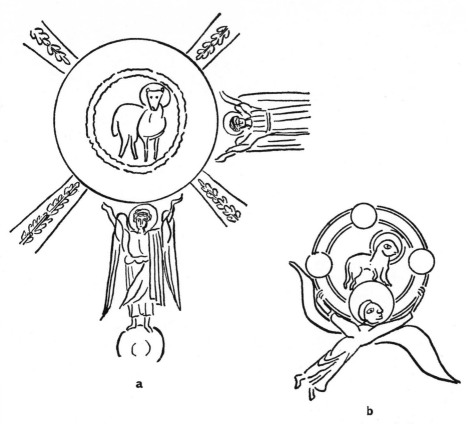

Fig. 22. Caryatid angels carrying the Lamb: *a*, mosaic in Church of S. Vitale, Ravenna; *b*, Amiens Psalter.

of the Egyptian *Books of the Dead*[1] which were executed mostly between 1400 and 1300 B.C. but continued to be produced until the Ptolemaic period (**Fig. 23**). Whatever the mode of transmission, there is already a picture of this type in the Lichfield Gospels;[2] another is found in the lower part of the Temptation miniature in the Book of Kells.[3] There are also some examples in English art of the ninth century.[4] It may be that

[1] E. Naville, *Das Egyptische Todtenbuch der XVIII bis zur XX Dynastie aus verschiedenen Urkunden* (Berlin, 1886), *passim*. G. Kolpaktchy, *Le Livre des morts des anciens Egyptiens* (Paris, 1955).

[2] *Vol. I*, Pl. F.   [3] *E.Q.C. Cennanensis*, II, fol. 202 v.

[4] R. Bruce-Mitford, 'Late Saxon Disc-Brooches', *Dark Age Britain*, pp. 171 sqq., Pl. XX (The Fuller Brooch); here, the figure holds two branches, and their stems

a   b

Fig. 23. a, Christ the Judge, Durrow High Cross; *b*, Osiris the Judge; Book of the Dead.

an ivory, a painting or a textile in the treasury of the monastery of Iona–Kells was the source of these representations. In any case it remains the characteristic representation of Christ in glory in Irish carvings.

The two winged quadrupeds, symbols of Mark and Luke, each holding his book, are carved on the arms of the cross on both sides of Christ. Above his head the human-shaped symbol of Matthew holds in its uplifted arms, like a caryatid, the circle-framed Lamb. This is the

---

do not cross. The other example is the enamelled figure on the Alfred Jewel (see p. 130). For various interpretations of the objects held by this figure, see: D. Talbot Rice, 'New Light on the Alfred Jewel', *Ant. Journ.*, 1956, pp. 214 sqq., and P. Lundström, 'The Man with the Captive Birds', *Acta Archaeologica*, 1960, pp. 190 sqq.; there is also a figure of this type on one of the crosses at Sandbach (Cheshire) (T. D. Kendrick, *Anglo-Saxon Art to 900* (London, 1938). p. 116, Pl. XCV.

complement of the Apocalyptic Vision, as the first apparition is joined immediately by that of the Lamb: 'And I saw: and behold in the midst of the throne and of the four living creatures, a Lamb standing as it were slain.'[1] If we try, however, to find the pictorial antecedents of this representation, it is probably again towards Ravenna that we have to look. On the ceiling of the archepiscopal chapel, between the symbols, are caryatid angels whose conjoined arms lift the sacred monogram to the centre of the vault. On the ceiling of the choir of San Vitale four angels hold on their uplifted arms a Lamb in a circular frame (Fig. 22). These two mosaics probably give us the closest parallels to the Kells carvings. Though there are three centuries between mosaics and carvings, portable objects of an intermediate date would no doubt explain the connection. Some surviving pictures, disregarding chronology, can give us an idea of what their appearance was like: an initial in the Amiens Psalter, for example, where an angel carries a disc bearing a Lamb (Fig. 22), or an ivory in the cathedral of Tournai dating probably from *circa* A.D. 900,[2] which has several of the features of the west side of the Tower cross at Kells: a Crucifixion below, then a large circular frame enclosing two angels carrying a Lamb-bearing disc, and above, Christ between the four symbols.

The Evangelists' symbols are seldom found on the other Irish crosses. The eagle and the ox are on the Duleek cross (Pl. 73, top) and the cap-stone, now missing, may have had the other two symbols. There may be also one on each side of the Crucifixion, on the Tall cross at Monasterboice, each held by a little human figure, perhaps an Evangelist (Pl. 87). We shall find the symbols of Matthew and John above the head of the Evangelist on the cross of the Scriptures at Clonmacnois (Pls. 91 and 95), but in that case, as we shall see, their presence has the value of a reference to a text.

Emile Mâle maintained,[3] probably rightly, that the Vision, which in the Apocalypse preludes the disappearance of the tangible world, was

---

[1] *Apoc.*, V, 6.

[2] A. Goldschmidt, *Die Elfenbeinskupturen aus der Zeit der Karolingischen Kaiser, VIII–IX Jahrhundert.* (Berlin, 1918), I, Pl. LXXI.

[3] Mâle, *Gothic Image*, pp. 356 sqq.

represented until late in the Middle Ages as a figure of the Last Judgment. This is a normal consequence of the reluctance, so manifest in Christian art up to the twelfth century, to depict the final reckoning in all its horror and splendour. This reluctance is all the more striking at a time when writers dealt freely with the subject. In this connection the fourth-century *Vision of Ephrem the Syrian* has often been quoted.[1] It supplies essential keys to the understanding of the later Byzantine representations of the Judgment. Much more relevant to our purpose are the three last books of St Augustine's *City of God* in which one finds an enumeration of the sacred texts concerned with the Judgment. The chief ones are of course Chapter XXIV of the Gospel of St Matthew, Chapter V of St John's Gospel, and the Apocalypse. Earlier books of the *City of God* insist however on the prophetic nature of the Psalter and give also a long quotation from that amazing apocryphal text giving a harrowing description of the Day of Doom, known as the 'Sibyl's Oracles'.[2] This is the first sketch of a theme which will be summed up in the 'teste David cum Sibylla' of the thirteenth-century *Dies irae*.

These various texts supply all the elements of the figured representations: the vision of the Judge, the sounding of trumpets, the scales in which the souls will be weighed according to their good or bad deeds, the dead issuing from their graves. Nevertheless the artists remain reluctant to be too explicit and resort to allusions and generalities. In Sant' Apollinare Nuovo in Ravenna, a small panel shows rather lamely the sorting out of the lambs and the goats.[3] Similar representations are found on sarcophagi.[4] The mosaics of the triumphal arch of St Paul outside the walls in Rome, given by Galla Placidia in the middle of the fifth century[5] show a wider but nearly as vague display of the twenty-four Elders acclaiming a bust of Christ while two angels blow their trumpets. The mosaic from San Michele in Affricisco in Ravenna (Berlin

---

[1] Diehl, *Manuel d'art byzantin*, p. 303.

[2] St Augustine, *De Civ. Dei*, XVII, 23. St Augustine attributed the Oracle to the Erythrean Sibyl.

[3] Volbach, *Early Christian Art*, Pl. 151.

[4] Wilpert, *Sarcofagi*, I, Pl. LXXXIII, 1; p. 69.

[5] L. Bruhns, *Die Kunst der Stadt Rom* (Vienna, 1951), Pl. 104.

Museum) was also lacking in definite details and simply showed trumpeter angels and a large figure of Christ holding his cross.[1] This is the theme which the painters of the St Gall Gospels[2] and the Turin manuscript (Pl. 40) adapted to the frame of a rectangular page. In the St Gall miniature, Christ in bust, holding the cross, is shown between two angels blowing trumpets and above the twelve apostles holding books. On the Turin leaf an immense crowd of small figures surrounds the Judge.

An ivory in the Victoria and Albert Museum[3] which was reworked on the reverse in the ninth century and may consequently date from the eighth century, gives a very curious representation of the Judgment (Pl. VIII): at the top is Christ the Judge between six angels blowing trumpets; below him, St Michael standing precariously on the moon's crescent is surrounded by the Dead emerging from their sarcophagi. The lower part is occupied by simplified representations of Heaven where the Elect are greeted by an angel, and of Hell where an enormous human head swallows up the Damned. This ivory has several features in common with the manuscripts of the Amiens neighbourhood and might be another manifestation of the iconographical wealth of this milieu. We shall see that it is linked with the carvings on the high crosses by a special feature.[4]

Meanwhile in the East more colourful and topical depictions were taking shape. Coptic artists probably adapted to a Christian use some of the illustrations of the *Books of the Dead*, especially the figure of Osiris-Judge which we have compared to the presentation of Christ in the Kells Apocalyptic Vision,[5] and the representations of the weighing of the souls where the tiny figure standing for the soul sits in one of the scales while Thoth, the animal-headed scribe of the gods, watches over the balance (Fig. 24). These new figurations then spread out of Egypt

[1] Galassi, *Roma o Bisanzio*, I, p. 109, Fig. 43, and p. 110, Fig. 44 (drawing of the mosaic before restoration).

[2] *Vol. I*, Pl. M.

[3] Goldschmidt, *Elfen.*, I, Pl. LXXXIII, No. 178; p. 85. G. Voss, *Das jüngste Gericht*, pp. 37–8. J. Beckwith, 'Some Anglo-Saxon Carvings in Ivory', *The Connoisseur*, 1960, pp. 241 sqq. The carving on the back may have been done in England.

[4] See p. 184.   [5] See p. 166.

adapted to celebrated texts,[1] that of the prophet Daniel: 'Thou art weighed in the balance and are found wanting,'[2] and that of Job: 'Let him weigh me in a just balance.'[3] Already in the fifth century, St Michael holding scales in his hands was carved on one of the jambs of the monastery-church at Alahan,[4] in Isauria. A fresco in the church of

Fig. 24. Weighing of the Souls, Book of the Dead.

Peristrema in Pisidia[5] and the pictures of the Weighing of the soul found in late Armenian manuscripts[6] are other landmarks in the evolution of the theme in Asia Minor and Armenia.

It was incorporated in the Byzantine representations of the Last Judgment based on the *Vision of Ephrem the Syrian*, which had already reached an extreme pitch of complication at the point where we first

---

[1] L. Kretzenbacher, *Die Seelenwaage* (Klagenfurt, 1958); P. Perry, 'On the Psychostasis in Christian Art', *Burl. Mag.*, 1912–13, pp. 94 sqq. and 208 sqq.

[2] *Daniel*, V, 27.

[3] *Job*, XXXI, 6; quoted by St Augustine, *Sermo de Temp. Barbarico*; see also St Augustine, *Sermo I In Pentec.*, VI and I *In Virgin.*

[4] Gough, *Early Christians*, Fig. 28.

[5] H. Rott, *Kleinasiatischen Denkmäler aus Pisidien* (Leipzig, 1908), p. 270.

[6] F. Macler, *Documents d'art arménien* (Paris, 1924), *passim.*

apprehend them – that is to say in the eleventh century. From that time we have several versions of the theme in various pages of Ms. Grec 74 of the Paris Bibliothèque nationale, others very similar on two icons of the monastery of St Catherine on Mount Sinai,[1] to which can be added the slightly later mosaic of Torcello and an ivory in the Victoria and Albert Museum. If, however, Ebersolt was right in thinking that a good deal in the illuminations of Ms. Grec 74 proceeded from pre-iconoclastic models,[2] we may be able to go back a little farther. In these representations we shall confine ourselves to some aspects which are directly related to the Irish ones: the Weighing of the souls with a large St Michael near the scales at which black and skinny devils are pulling in the same position as Thoth in the Book of the Dead pictures (Pls. VI, VII); the resurrection of the Dead; the trumpeter angels; and the devils which worry the Damned and push them towards Hell.

These features existed no doubt in some pre-iconoclastic Eastern representations from which they passed to psalters of the Carolingian period such as the Stuttgart and Utrecht Psalters.[3] In both manuscripts there are scales and devils harrying the Damned (Pl. VII). But they are absent from the other Western Continental representations of the Judgment until the twelfth century, being found neither in the pages of the Ottonian manuscripts, nor in the frescoes of Reichenau and Sant' Angelo in Formis.[4] On the other hand, they were adopted by the Irish sculptors.

This development of the pictorial theme of the Last Judgment in Irish art fits in with the considerable place given in Irish literature to the speculations concerning the Other World and Doomsday. Besides the vision of St Fursa, related in his *Life*[5] and in a chapter of Bede's *Historia Ecclesiastica*,[6] and the vision attributed to Adamnan, there is a whole collection of sermons,[7] some of which go back for their original

---

[1] Sotirou, *Icones du Sinaï*, Pls. 150, 151.   [2] Ebersolt, *Miniature byzantine*.
[3] Ps. IX,8 and LXVI.
[4] P. Jessen, *Die Darstellung des Weltgerichts bis auf Michelangelo* (Berlin, 1883).
[5] Colgan, *AA.SS.Hib.*, pp. 75 sqq.   [6] Bede, *H.E.*, III, 9.
[7] C. S. Boswell, *An Irish Precursor of Dante* (London, 1908); W. Stokes, *Fis Adamnáin* (Simla, 1870); J. Strachan, 'An Old-Irish Homily', *Eriu*, 1907, J. G. O'Keefe, 'A Poem on the Day of Judgment', *Eriu*, 1907, W. Stokes, 'The Evernew

171

redaction to the ninth or tenth centuries. One of them lists some of the textual sources concerning the Judgment, stressing especially, after a mention of St Matthew's Gospel, quotations from 'the royal prophet David'. We shall see what light can be thrown on contemporary carvings by such a text.

The Last Judgment is figured in great detail on two of the high crosses: the cross of Muiredach at Monasterboice (Pls. 106–7) and the cross of the Scriptures at Clonmacnois (Pl. 110). A more abbreviated version is found also on the High cross at Durrow (Pl. 109) and on those at Arboe and Termonfechin (Pl. 108). There is no essential discrepancy between them. In each a large figure of Christ, similar to that on the Tower cross at Kells, occupies the centre of the composition. There is no halo or mandorla; in Clonmacnois and Durrow Christ stands over a sort of worm or serpent; above him there is either the Lamb (Durrow) or the dove (Clonmacnois, Monasterboice). On the Monasterboice cross he is standing between two figures sitting in armchairs, one playing the harp, another a sort of reed-pipe. Behind the harpist is a trumpeter, then comes another figure holding a book. Behind them the Elect are arranged in three superposed rows, looking at Christ. The Damned are just as methodically disposed on the other side, but they are looking away and are dispatched energetically by emaciated little devils, one of them armed with a fork. Just below Christ's feet, St Michael is shown weighing the souls; a tiny figure standing in one of the scales clings to his left hand, while he is busy transfixing with a lance or Tau-crozier the head of a devil pulling at the scales.

This lively animated picture takes us very far from the simplified representation in the St Gall Gospel-book, but it has several curious features: first the abundance of books: one, open beside Christ, seems to float in the air; a small kneeling angel holds another; and to the figure on the right of Christ who seems to follow something in the leaf of a book, corresponds on the other side a devil, who has the same air of checking an account; this recalls that 'Book of the Devil' mentioned

Tongue', *Eriu*, 1905; W. Stokes, 'Tidings of Doomsday, an Early Middle Irish Homily', *Rev. Celtique*, 1879–80.

in some Irish texts,[1] and the book which will be consulted by the angels during the Last Judgment, according to a Judeo-Christian second-century text emanating probably from Egypt, the so-called 'Testament of Abraham'.[2] All this elaborate computing depicted on the cross is in fact wrecked by the dictatorial ways of St Michael. One may wonder who are the two figures sitting on thrones or armchairs; there can be little doubt that the harpist inspired by a bird is meant for David.[3] As for the figure playing on a reed-pipe, it may well be the Erythrean Sibyl in her capacity as a prophet of the Judgment already mentioned by St Augustine and amplified later in the Middle Ages.

The carvings on the cross of the Scriptures at Clonmacnois are closely parallel to those at Monasterboice. The main scene is compressed on a much smaller surface (Pl. 110) and has, in consequence, to be reduced to its essential elements : on the right of Christ a trumpeter angel, to his left a shifty devil; beyond, anonymous and vague crowds of Elect and Damned. The sculptor has however made an effort to complement these by the carvings in the side panels of the shaft. At the top are two of the Evangelists : on one side, Matthew holding a Tau staff and sitting below his winged symbol (Pl. 95); on the other John holding a crozier below a full-faced eagle (Pl. 91). Then comes David playing the harp (Pl. 91) whose analogy with an illumination in the Cotton Psalter (Pl. II) has already been noted; he is balanced on the opposite side of the shaft by the figure with the reed-pipe accompanied by a sort of acrobatic monster. On the lower panel of the same side, a seated figure transfixing with a lance a little prostrate being probably stands for St Michael fighting with the devil (Pl. 95). So that the Clonmacnois Judgment, at first sight more abbreviated, is in fact nearly as elaborate as that of

---

[1] *Eriu*, XIX, pp. 6, 20, 24. The Devil holds a book in the Last Judgment page of the Liber Vitae from the New Minister at Winchester (A.D. 1016–1020) and argues violently with an angel who also holds a book. St Peter settles the argument in as arbitrary a fashion as the Monasterboice St Michael, by bringing his keys down on the head of the Devil (D. Talbot Rice, *English Art, 871–1100* (Oxford, 1952, Pl. 84).

[2] M. R. James, *The Testament of Abraham* (Cambridge, 1893).

[3] David is often shown with an inspiring bird; cf. a representation on the Breac Moedhog, *C.A.A.I.*, vol. I, Pl. 62.

Monasterboice; Matthew and John, authors of the chief relevant texts, being included as well as David and probably the Sibyl. Only the balance is missing and all those books which are so much in evidence at Monasterboice.

The carvings at Durrow are much more simplified (Pl. 109). A large and imposing figure of Christ occupies the centre of the cross. To his right the angel blows a trumpet and a human head below him probably represents the whole human race; on the other side, a supplicating angel is half kneeling. David plays the harp on one of the arms of the cross, but one may wonder whether he is there as a prophet of the Judgment, or to balance another episode of his life, his fight with the lion, represented on the other arm. On the Termonfechin cross there are only two human heads on each side of the Judge. It is difficult to decipher the very worn carvings at Arboe; they seem to include scales surrounded by flames, but without representations of St Michael or the soul.

There is a third representation of Christ in glory which is much more surprising. It is found in the centre of the east side of the Tall cross at Monasterboice (Pl. 111), where a group of ten warriors carrying shields and swords surround a larger figure armed in the same way, but exactly similar in its attitude to the figures of Christ the Judge. In his left hand he holds a shield and a sword and in the right a staff ending in an animal head, the exact equivalent of David's shepherd's crook in the Psalters of the Cotton Collection and of St John's College, Cambridge (Pls. 41, N); an angel is flying on his left. Macalister had already suggested that this was a representation of Christ as a victorious warrior surrounded by the Apostles.[1] Helen Roe, when studying a similar panel on the Market cross at Kells,[2] pointed out a remarkable connection with the Utrecht Psalter where the verse from Psalm XXIII: 'Lift up your gates, O ye princes, and be ye lifted up, O eternal gates: and the King of Glory shall enter in. Who is the King of Glory? the Lord of hosts, he is the King of Glory,' is illustrated by a figure of Christ with a cruciform halo, dressed as a warrior and carrying a cross-ended spear, walking towards the fortified gate of a city, followed by twelve warriors armed with spears and shields, while above appears

[1] Macalister, *Monasterboice*, p. 47.   [2] Roe, *Kells*, p. 30.

the Hand of God surrounded by a flight of angels.[1] It may be that there is a further interpretation of this scene. The passage from Psalm XXIII quoted above has sometimes been applied to the Ascension, but it figures also in the description of the Descent into Limbo or Harrowing of Hell in the Gospel of Nicodemus,[2] an apocryphal text which was known in Ireland in the ninth century. 'Be ye lifted up, eternal gates' is there addressed to the gates of Hell which collapse before the risen Christ. So perhaps the carvings on this cross were meant to represent either the Ascension, or the Descent into Limbo, a subject which occupies such an important place in Byzantine iconography, but depicted there in a very literal way.

After examining the important themes which determine the iconography of the crosses, it remains to point out some peculiarities of their figured decoration.

Some of the representations of Old Testament scenes do not call for much comment. Adam and Eve are always figured standing on each side of the Tree, in perfect symmetry (Fig 39, Pls. 81, 100) as on the fourth and fifth-century sarcophagi,[3] and the serpent is often shown as if speaking in Eve's ear – Eve who, from her place in this series of scenes seems ready to utter the lamentations which an Irish poem puts in her mouth :

'. . . 'Tis I that outraged Jesus of old;
   'Tis I that robbed my children of Heaven;
   By rights 'tis I that should have gone upon the Cross.
. . . There would be no Hell, there would be no sorrow,
   There would be no fear if it were not for me.'[4]

The representations of the Three Children in the Fiery Furnace are more unexpected. They depart from the type found on the sarcophagi which survived very late in some Greek manuscripts,[5] where the furnace is shown in detail with three oven-like hearths filled with piles of burning

[1] Wald, *Utrecht Psalter*, Ps. XXIII.   [2] Mâle, *Gothic Image*, pp. 224 sqq.
[3] Wilpert, *Sarcofagi*, II, pp. 225 sqq.   [4] Meyer, *E. Irish Poetry*, p. 34.
[5] M. V. Alpatoff, 'A Byzantine Illuminated Manuscript of the Paleologue Epoch in Moscow', *Art Bull.*, 1930, pp. 207 sqq., Fig. 7 (the miniatures, on pages originally left blank, are of the fourteenth century).

175

logs.[1] They do not follow either the Egyptian version which is found for example on an icon of the monastery of St Catherine on Mount Sinai,[2] on a fresco in the Soudanese church of Faras and on the silver casket from S. Nazzaro Maggiore in Milan[3] – a version where the 'fourth' seen by the king beside the Children, whom Honorius Augustodunensis later identified with Christ, is shown amongst them, holding sideways a long staff ending in a cross. The Irish figuration (Fig. 27) is much nearer, as Kingsley Porter pointed out,[4] to that found in Byzantine Psalters,[5] where an angel spreads his protecting wings over the Children. Sometimes, as we have seen, the executioners are shown piling wood on the furnace. On the Tall cross at Monasterboice, they also blow on the fire through long horns (Pl. 86).

Daniel in the Lions' den is represented in various ways. On the Moone cross he is surrounded by the seven lions mentioned in the Book of Daniel.[6] On the Tower cross at Kells (Fig. 26, Pl. 75) he stands high above two small lions, rather in the same way as on sarcophagi carvings. In several cases his arms are outstretched cross-wise (Fig. 26, Pl. 102) an attitude which is also found occasionally on sarcophagi and on ivories, for example on the Brescia casket.[7]

Fig. 25. Cross at Camus – Macosquin, the Ark.

The scenes from the life of David[8] appear fairly late. David and Goliath are figured on the cross of Muiredach (Pl. 85) and in the Cotton

[1] Wilpert, *Sarcofagi*, II, pp. 259 sqq., Pls. CCVI, CCXIII, etc.
[2] Sotirou, *Icones du Sinaï*.
[3] Volbach, *Early Christian Art*, Pl. 114 (fourth century).
[4] Porter, *Crosses and Culture*, p. 114.
[5] For example Br. M. Add. Ms. 11836.   [6] Daniel, XIV, 31.
[7] Morey, *E.C. Art*, Fig. 146 (fifth century).
[8] H. Roe, 'The "David Cycle" in Early Irish Art', *J.R.S.A.I.*, 1949, pp. 39 sqq.

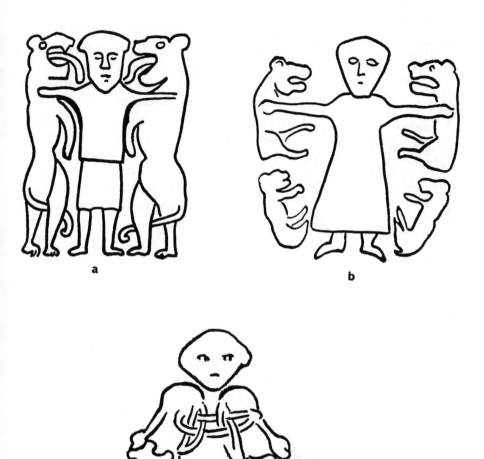

Fig. 26. Daniel in the Lions' den: *a*, Arboe cross; *b*, Clones cross (upper part); *c*, cross of the Tower, Kells.

Fig. 27. Arboe cross, the Three Children in the Fiery Furnace.

and Cambridge Psalters (Pls. 41, N); Goliath challenging the Israelites, David bringing back the head of Goliath and David anointed by Samuel are figured on the tall cross at Monasterboice (Pl. 88). There is a curious similarity of attitude between David carrying sling and shepherd's crook in the Cotton Psalter and on sarcophagi carvings at Rheims (Fig. 33) and at Vienne in the Dauphiné,[1] David carrying his crook on his shoulder as represented on the cross of Muiredach has an equivalent on another sarcophagus from Vienne.[2] Still it is likely to be through psalter illustrations inspired by paleo-Christian carvings that these representations were known in Ireland. There are in Greek manuscripts representations of David anointed by Samuel which exactly parallel that on the Tall cross at Monasterboice.[3]

The New Testament scenes offer the same variety of inspiration. For the Appearance of the Angel to the Shepherds, a scene seldom found, and in any case with a different presentation, in paleo-Christian art, the nearest parallels are in Carolingian ivories where the angel and the shepherds often balance each other on both sides of a row of superposed sheep (Fig. 29),[4] exactly as they do on the Irish crosses. This is different from the Greek iconography of the scene, which makes it part of the Nativity, the angel usually leaning above the rocks or the clouds surrounding the main group, to address the shepherds scattered below him.

[1] Wilpert, *Sarcofagi*, I, p. 18, II, pp. 264 sqq. Pl. CLXXXXIV, 2.

[2] Id. II, Pl. CLXXXXIV, 1.

[3] Beside the famous Paris Psalter (Paris, Bibl. nat., Grec 139), one might quote : the Homilies of Greg. Naz. (Paris, Bibl. nat., Gr. 510 fol. 174v; Ebersolt, *Miniature byzantine*, Pl. XV, 2); the Bible of Leo the Patrician (Vat. Libr. Regina, Gr. 1, fol. 263; Rice, *Byzantium*, Pl. 127), the Psalter of Basil II (Venice, Marcian Libr., Cod. Gr. 17, fol. 2; Rice, *Byzantium*, Pl. 127).

[4] Goldschmidt, *Elfen.*, I, Pl. VIII, No. 14 (Victoria and Albert Museum).

Fig. 28. Donaghmore (Tyrone) cross, the Appearance of the Angel to the shepherds.

Fig. 29. Carolingian ivory in the Cathedral treasury, Aachen, the Appearance of the Angel to the shepherds.

In the representations of the Holy Family and the Adoration of the Magi there is a great variety of attitudes, the Virgin sometimes facing us (Fig. 30), elsewhere being shown in profile. On the cross of Muiredach (Pl. 83) the bearded figure is probably St Joseph preparing to take the Child in his arms to show him to the three Magi, all identical and clasping to their breast shapeless objects, no doubt their presents.

The Flight into Egypt is figured only twice: on the Moone cross St Joseph leads the donkey carrying the Virgin and the Child. On the High cross at Durrow (Pl. 99) the Holy Family is on foot, as on a Carolingian ivory box in the Louvre.[1] The Baptism of Christ is never shown according to the iconography of the sarcophagi of Gaul and Italy where the Jordan appears as a sort of waterfall, and St John the Baptist generally holds a crook in his hand. Here the connection is with Oriental representations, such as that on the lid of the relic-box in the Vatican which was brought from the Holy Land,[2] or on the Monza ampullae[3] of similar origin. St John the Baptist and a group of Israelites or angels are on both sides of the composition, while Christ stands between them in the river (Pl. 97). The Jordan itself in the Irish

[1] Id., I, Pl. XLI. [2] Morey, *E.C. Art*, Fig. 129
[3] Grabar, *Ampoules de Terre Sainte*.

179

carvings is represented by several ribbons placed horizontally which sometimes form an interlacing with the legs of Christ; these ribbons come out of two discs representing the two springs attributed to the Jordan, as to most illustrious rivers, in the geography of the time. This tradition is mentioned by Adamnan in his *Treatise on the Holy Places* written at the end of the seventh century.[1] In Greek manuscripts the two springs, Jor and Dan, are often personified by figures holding urns, and the Stuttgart Psalter follows this tradition.

The Irish carvings of the Wedding at Cana do not follow the standard representations of the sarcophagi where Christ is shown touching with a wand the urns at his feet. In a few cases there is no more than figures holding jars, but the scene may be more detailed, as on the Kells crosses (Broken cross and Market cross) (Pl. 104) where the steward kneels at the feet of Christ. As always in the early Middle Ages there is no fixed number of urns, so that they are obviously not given the symbolic meaning, which Walafried Strabo in the ninth century gave to the six urns representing the six ages of the world.[2]

Fig. 30. Clones cross (shaft), Adoration of the Magi.

In the case of the Multiplication of Loaves and Fishes, there is the same break with the paleo-Christian pictures where Christ blesses with arms outstretched to the right and left the loaves and fishes presented to him by the disciples. On the Moone cross it is figured in an elusive way only by the objects of the miracle. On the North cross at Castledermot (Pl. 72) Christ seen in profile seems to throw them into space with a gesture curiously similar to that found on a fresco at Toqale in Cappadocia[3] (Fig. 21). On the South cross an effort has also been made to figure the multitude by a row of small figures. At

[1] Adamnan, *De Locis Sanctis*, ed. D. Meehan (Dublin, 1958).
[2] Mâle, *Gothic Image*, p. 195.
[3] G. de Jerphanion, *Les églises rupestres de Cappadoce*, I (Paris, 1925).

Fig. 31. Kells, Broken cross, Entry into Jerusalem.

Fig. 32. Arboe cross, Entry into Jerusalem.

Kells on the Tower cross and the Market cross (Pls. 75, 104) a sort of stylization, perhaps symbolical, is used, as the fishes are crossed in the shape of the Greek letter Chi, the first element of the monogram of Christ (Chi–Rho). On other crosses, for example at Arboe and at Donaghmore (Tyrone) (Fig. 21), one may wonder whether it is the Multiplication that is intended, or the Last Supper, or even the Meeting at Emmaus as the large dish with fish and bread is found also in Carolingian representations of these scenes.

The crosses of the Monasterboice School offer a particularly good opportunity for studying the scenes of the Passion. The Arrest is placed in a conspicuous position on the shafts of the cross of Muiredach and of the crosses of Clonmacnois and Durrow. The Monasterboice carving is the best preserved. The scene there has an infinitely more realistic appearance than in the Book of Kells, though the composition is similar. Christ holds a staff in his right hand – the staff or wand with which he is represented in most of the miracle scenes in the sarcophagi, but which finds itself there suddenly transferred to St Peter who holds it in

181

the carvings representing his own arrest, while Christ, in the corresponding scene of the Arrest, is empty handed.[1] If Christ is shown with a staff in Passion scenes, it is generally at the Crowning of thorns, where it is a mock sceptre. Still in one of the small scenes painted in the Gospelbook of St Augustine of Canterbury certainly meant for the Arrest, Christ seems to hold a staff or a roll in his left hand (Fig. 33, b).[2] This representation may well have been transmitted from this manuscript, which was probably in Canterbury from the seventh century on, to other parts of England and then to Ireland.

Some other carved panels on the Durrow and Clonmacnois crosses are too worn to allow identification of the subject. However the end of the south arm of the cross of Muiredach is occupied by a panel showing Pilate washing his hands (Pl. 105) not very different from the sarcophagi treatment of the same subject[3] except perhaps by the crafty expression given to Pilate. As A. T. Lucas has shown,[4] there is a representation of the Crowning with thorns on the Tall cross at Monasterboice (Pl. 87). Carvings on the three other arms of the same cross may show various episodes of the Arrest: below, the soldiers arriving with torches, then the taking of Christ on the right and at the top Peter putting his sword back into its sheath.

As in all Early Christian art, the actual moment of the Resurrection is never explicitly shown. On Continental ivories, the two scenes of the Soldiers at the Tomb and the Marys arriving and greeted by the angel are shown instead. In Ireland, except on the Tall cross at Monasterboice where they occupy two superposed panels, these two events are usually combined: two soldiers face to face and holding lances occupy part of the composition (Pl. 112); the cross sometimes appears behind them, and the Marys arrive on the right behind the angel. The Tomb is

---

[1] Wilpert, *Sarcofagi*, I, Pls. CXXVI, 2; CXXVII, 1.

[2] F. Wormald, *The Miniatures in the Gospels of St Augustine, Corpus Christi College, MS. 286* (Cambridge, 1954), Pls. I, III, V.

[3] This scene is also found at an early date on the Brescia casket (fifth century) (Volbach, *Early Christian Art*, Pl. 89, and on the door of Santa Sabina in Rome (Morey, *E.C. Art*, Fig. 149).

[4] A. T. Lucas, 'The West Cross at Monasterboice: a Note and a Suggestion', *Louth J.*, 1951, pp. 123 sqq.

a   b   c

Fig. 33. a, Milan sarcophagus, Doubting Thomas; *b*, Arrest of Christ, Gospels of St Augustine of Canterbury; *c*, David with sling and shepherd's crook, sarcophagus from Rheims (now destroyed).

never figured by a little building more or less reminiscent of the Holy Sepulchre rotunda as in so many ivories. Instead the soldiers seem to be seated on the lid of a sarcophagus, which is open in the foreground to reveal either a naked body (market cross at Kells) or, in most cases, a mummy all wrapped up whose face only is uncovered. On the Clonmacnois and Durrow panels, a bird is shown introducing its beak into the mouth of Christ. This strange feature of a bird entering the mouth of a corpse to signify its resurrection is found also in the Last Judgment ivory of the Victoria and Albert Museum (Pl. VIII). There birds are shown flying towards the Dead in their sarcophagi and in one case at least the bird is in the action of entering the mouth of a corpse.

Fig. 34. The Soldiers at the Tomb, ivory buckle, Arles.

183

So the coming of the bird signifies the moment when the body becomes alive again and the introduction of the bird in the scene of the Soldiers at the Tomb is tantamount to showing the exact moment of the Resurrection, though by very different means from those used by Medieval artists which culminate in the dissimilar evocations of Piero della Francesca ans Grünewald. One may wonder about the ultimate origin of this singular identification of the soul with a bird.[1] It has obvious similarities with the representation of the soul of a dead person as a bird in Egyptian carvings and illuminations,[2] though a parallel is supplied also by some fifth century sarcophagi which bear a cross, on which perch two birds, standing between two symmetrical soldiers very similar to those on the Irish crosses. Here the birds may be images of the soul of Christ or of that of the dead person buried in the sarcophagus.

It remains to examine a few scenes belonging to the period between the Resurrection and the Ascension and one scene connected with the Acts of the Apostles. There is little to say about the Incredulity of St Thomas. But on both the cross of the Scriptures and the cross of Muiredach appears the *Traditio Legis* – the committing of the keys to St Peter and of the New Law to St Paul.[3] The giving of the keys is often represented on sarcophagi with St Paul standing on the other side of

---

[1] See p. 169. Cf. Kingsley Porter's remarks on the subject of the soul under the aspect of a bird, *Crosses and Culture*, pp. 44–5. He quotes an eighth-century Irish poem on the death of a king :

> 'Aed is in the clay
> The king is in the cemetery
> The dear pure little white bird (his soul)
> Is with Ciarán at Clonmacnois.'

Under a different aspect, there are other examples of this theme in the Early Middle Ages, especially in some of the Spanish illustrations of Beatus's *Commentary on the Apocalypse*. It is found also in the panel of the late fourteenth-century Apocalypse Tapestry in the Castle of Angers which shows the resurrection of the Two Witnesses. The cartoons of the tapestry were inspired by various earlier manuscripts, which may explain the transmission (R. Planchenault, *Les Tapisseries d'Angers*, No. 33).

[2] See : A. Champdor, *Le Livre des Morts* (Paris, 1963), pp. 114, and 156–7.

[3] See a study of the iconography of this subject : J. Hunt, 'The Cross of Muiredach, Monasterboice', *J.R.S.A.I.*, 1951, pp. 1 sqq.

Christ, usually making a gesture of applause,[1] an anachronism similar
to the introduction of St Paul in representations of the Ascension. In
other carvings the two saints each receive a roll figuring the Law. This
is found for example on the sarcophagus of Junius Bassus in St Peter's.[2]
In this case, as in several carvings of the same subject, a small human
bust has been placed under the feet of Christ. It has been interpreted as a
representation either of Heaven or of the mountain where the scene is
taking place.[3] The version of the scene in which St Paul receives a book
or roll and St Peter the keys seems to be of later date than this and
occurs on several late Carolingian ivories. It must have been known
earlier, however, as it is described in one of the inscriptions composed
by Cellach, late seventh-century abbot of Péronne to accompany
paintings in one of the chapels of his monastery:

'Justus apostolicos aequat Salvator amicos:
Clavibus hic Petrum, hic Paulum legibus ornat.

The just Saviour shows an equal friendship to the two Apostles:
To Peter giving the keys, to Paul the Law.'[4]

The link with the sarcophagi carvings is clearly indicated at Monasterboice by the presence of a little animal head between the feet of Christ –
obviously derived from the human bust in the same position on the
Junius Bassus sarcophagus (Pl. 82). Now that the crosses have been
cleaned the keys held by St Peter can be seen clearly. On the cross of
Muiredach the surface of the book given to St Paul has obvious traces
of decoration as have all the books figured on the same side of the cross.
Although Macalister thought he read there the letters SOISC, abbrevia-
tion for *Soiscél* (Gospel),[5] it seems that there is only the decoration of
the binding, now very worn.

[1] Wilpert, *Sarcofagi*, I, pp. 172 sqq.; Le Blant, *Sarcophages de la Gaule*, Pl. XII,
1, Pl. XLVII, 3. In these last examples, St Peter holds keys or a key, as he does in
one of the apses of Santa Costanza in Rome and on the Parenzo mosaic (above the
arch) (Morey, *E.C. Art*, Fig. 186). Elsewhere he often holds a roll of parchment.
[2] A. de Waal, *Der Sarcophag von Junius Bassus* (Rome, 1900).
[3] Wilpert, *Sarcofagi*, I, p. 32.   [4] P Grosjean, *An. Boll.*, 1960, p. 369.
[5] Macalister, *Monasterboice*, p. 39 and note 19.

185

Fig. 35. The Fall of Simon Magus; *a*, capital in Autun cathedral; *b*, Monasterboice, Tall cross; *c*, Monreale (Sicily).

The scene of St Peter walking on the water is carved on the Tall cross at Monasterboice, just above the Lord of Hosts (Pl. 111), in its usual presentation. It is found for example on some sarcophagi[1] and on one of the ampullae from Bobbio.[2] This is its only surviving representation in Irish art.

On the other hand the Fall of Simon Magus is figured several times, notably on the Tall cross at Monasterboice and on the Market cross at Kells (Pls. 86, 104). In both cases St Peter and St Paul are shown holding croziers with which they hasten the head-downwards fall of the flying magician. Macalister had doubts about the interpretation of the scene because St Peter alone is mentioned in the relevant text of the Acts. But there seem to have been different sets of representations.[3] In frescoes in St Paul's outside the Walls and in the old St Peter's, the text of the Acts was faithfully adhered to. But at an early date an apocryphal tradition grew up in Rome, associating in this event the two Apostles martyred on the same day. In the sixth century, Gregory of Tours mentions the stones which were supposed to have kept traces of their knees when they were praying against Simon. This tradition, originating in Rome, had obviously found credit in the East and it is embodied in the late Byzantine mosaics of Palermo and Monreale where St Paul, figured beside St Peter, also watches the falling magician[4] (Fig. 35). This Oriental type of representation was the inspiration of the Irish sculptor probably through a manuscript illumination. The confuting of Simon had a very special significance in Ireland where the tonsure of St Peter is sometimes contrasted with 'that of Simon Magus' worn by the Columban monks until the time of their acceptance of the Roman computation of Easter. This attitude is clearly defined by a sentence of one of the Annalistic fragments copied by Mac Firbis: 'The tonsure of Peter the Apostle was taken by the family of Ia (Iona),

[1] Wilpert, *Sarcofagi*, pp. 161–2; also, Id., *La cripta dei papi e la capella di Santa Cecilia nel cimitero di Callisto* (Rome, 1910), Pl. VI, 1.

[2] Grabar, *Ampoules de Terre Sainte*, Pl. XLIII.

[3] Macalister, *Monasterboice*, p. 48. See: Cabrol-Leclercq, *Simon le Magicien*, A. Vacant, E. Mangenot, E. Amann, *Dictionnaire de théologie catholique*, XIV, 2 (Paris, 1941), col. 2130–40.

[4] O. Demus, *The Mosaics of Norman Sicily* (London, 1949), pp. 294 sqq.

for it was the tonsure of Simon Magus they had till then, as had Colum Cille himself.'[1]

If there is profit to be found in studying the subjects represented on the crosses, it may be equally interesting to list those which are conspicuous by their absence. The most outstanding example is the Nativity with the connected scenes of the Annunciation and the Visitation. This is an aspect of that curious archaism already noted in Irish iconography. Other scenes represented in Irish manuscripts, like the Ascension, are not found in the carvings. There is no example on the crosses of Ireland of a representation of the Virgin and Child surrounded by angels, which is not a historical representation like the Nativity or the Adoration of the shepherds and the Magi, but an image to be venerated, deriving probably from an icon. But it is found in a page of the Book of Kells and on the Iona crosses (Pl. 105), which suggests that these last representations were inspired by a painting owned by the monastery of Iona where the decoration of the Book of Kells was begun.

The absence of some other scenes from the repertoire of the crosses has the value of a chronological datum. The Deposition from the cross, for example, is not represented before the tenth century and becomes popular only in the eleventh. The fact that it does not appear on the crosses confirms the dates which the inscriptions seem to give.

These carvings on the high crosses played in the decoration of an Irish monastery of the ninth or tenth century the part which the carved portals and capitals were to play in the Continental monasteries of the eleventh and twelfth centuries. In most cases they displayed all the ornamental and didactic art seen by the visitor before he entered the churches.

A few indications, however, suggest that sometimes the church portals were also decorated. Several carved lintels of rectangular doors have survived, often not in their original position. One of them belonged to a doorway in the monastery of Dunshaughlin (Meath)[2] – the fort of Sechlann – built on the shore of the lake in which was the crannog of Lagore, seat for a long time of the Southern Uí Néill. Secundinus or

---

[1] *Fragm*, pp. 20–1; see also pp. 112–13..   [2] Hencken, *Lagore*, p. 16.

Sechlann was one of the companions of St Patrick and the foundation probably goes back to the fifth century. Its importance is attested by the great number of kings of the Southern Uí Néill called Máel-Sechlainn (servant of Sechlann). The lintel (Pl. 6) obviously comes from a rectangular door, of the type of those of Fore and Clonamery,[1] where the cross above the door was replaced by a Crucifixion. Such a lintel could conceivably belong to the eighth century, but it is so similar to carvings on the crosses that it is more likely to belong to the ninth century; one feels tempted in fact to ascribe it to the moment when the crannog of Lagore was re-built shortly after 848, following a total destruction which may well have extended to the monastery itself.[2]

Another more elaborate lintel has survived in two separate fragments inserted in the walls of the cathedral of Raphoe (Donegal).[3] The ends of the uprights of the door are plainly visible, so that there can be no doubt that the carvings come from a door and not from a broken cross. There was in the centre a Crucifixion, now in a sad state, and to the left a scene with several figures which seems to be the Arrest of Christ. The treatment is remarkably close to that of the ninth–tenth-century crosses such as those at Armagh and Monasterboice. As Mac Durnan was in the late ninth and early tenth-century abbot of Raphoe as well as Armagh,[4] one may well think that the portal belonged to the time of his abbacy, which would explain these similarities.

There is also a lintel perhaps still in its original position, above the west door of the ruined church at Clonca (Donegal).[5] Its carvings are very rubbed but seem to represent the Last Supper. The portal of the church at Maghera (Derry),[6] possibly of later date (eleventh century?) shows a similar type of decoration applied to a rectangular doorway surrounded by a raised frame of the type of those found at Aghowle (Wicklow) (Pls. 5–6) and Banagher (Derry).[7]

[1] *Vol. I*, Pls. 22–3. [2] *Vol. I*, p. 77.
[3] Porter, *Crosses and Culture*, Fig. 31, Henry, *Sc. irl.*, Fig. 145; Id., *Irish Art* (London, 1940), Pl. 79. [4] See p. 103.
[5] W. J. Doherty, 'Some ancient Crosses and other Antiquities of Inishowen, County Donegal', *P.R.I.A.*, 1891–3, pp. 100–16.
[6] A more detailed study of this portal will be found in Vol. III of this series.
[7] Henry, *Sc. irl.*, Pl. 111,3.

Fig. 36. Panel of the Market cross
at Kells.

So far the carvings on crosses and doorways have been studied chiefly from the point of view of iconography. The formal treatment also calls for some consideration. All the figure panels have one characteristic in common : the frame is crammed to breaking point, the figures touching it with their heads and feet, filling it with their substance and leaving a minimum of unoccupied space. This is reminiscent of the late Roman sculptor who presses his tightly packed reliefs into the available space. This method passed from the sarcophagi through some ivory carvings to the Irish sculptor who was dazzled by such virtuosity, especially as he was already, from his ancestral training inclined to entirely cover the surface of the stone. This impression is confirmed by the squat proportions of the figures which, like those of the sarcophagi, are only four or five heads high. Nevertheless the habit of seeing everything as ornament, which had prevailed for so long in the Irish workshops, does not remain without its effects on this new type of carving. Most compositions are built on strong rhythms. Only occasionally however does the ornament rule them completely and the interlaced strands of the Jordan, the woven figures on the Market cross at Kells (Fig. 36) are exceptions. But a few master-lines are stressed in each composition and this can give it, from a distance, the deceptive appearance of an ornament. The most striking example of this is supplied by the symmetrical groups of the Elect and the Damned on the arms of the Monasterboice Cross (Pls. 106–7) : from afar they look like those patterns of swollen spirals which were so common at that time, the heads of the small figures playing the part of the semi-spheres of the spirals.

The figures in themselves offer an amazing variety of treatment, ranging from the cut-out puppets of the crosses in the Barrow valley, reduced to a surface plane connected to the background by nearly per-pendicular sides, to the very subtle modelling amounting almost to high relief, of the Monasterboice School, including also the semi-flat low-reliefs, delicately modulated, of the Kells crosses.

Comparisons between several versions of the same scene show these

190

contrasts clearly: the Fall, for example on the Castledermot crosses (Pls. 65, 71) and on the Broken cross at Kells (Pl. 96), with the figures not much more than flat silhouettes, and its description on the cross of Muiredach where Adam and Eve display all the magnificence of their thick-set, luxuriant bodies (Pl. 81), or the more spiritual treatment of the subject on the Durrow cross (Pl. 100).

Occasionally the sculptor ventures into the domain of realism, for example when, in the Arrest scene (Pl. 79), he contrasts the sorrowful and serene dignity of Christ with the coarse appearance and bestial faces of the two soldiers. In scenes involving contemporary personalities he strives no doubt towards a local colour whose accuracy is difficult to evaluate. On one of the panels of the cross of the Scriptures (Pl. 92), the figure on the left is obviously a churchman who carries on his back his book-satchel, while the other is a warrior in a short tunic. They seem to combine their efforts to press into the earth a post ending in a human head which may be the church foundation-post planted by Abbot Colman and King Flann, unless it stands for a simplified figuration of the cross itself which they donate by presenting it in their joined hands. The two jocund creatures with plaited beards, armed with long swords, on the next panel (Pl. 92) may be neighbouring chieftains and are shown also offering an unidentified object which they hold at both ends.

Behind all these variations of the sculptor's work there remains a very strange fact: the fairly sudden transformation of an essentially ornamental and abstract art into a figurative art bent on being intelligible. Ornament does not disappear, but it is now carefully relegated to a few compartments within the ambit of well-defined frames which isolate it from the agitation of figures in movement and turn it into a minor element in the carvings of the crosses.

Another type of monument remains to be studied. Irish carvings of that time were not all in low relief and there are a few surviving examples of statues, varying from about 20 to 40 inches in height. One of them was found with ninth-century funerary slabs near the cathedral of Lismore (Waterford), to a wall of which it has since been affixed

(Pl. 13).[1] The others have been found on White Island in Lough Erne (Fermanagh)[2] (Pls. 12, 14, I). There was a small monastery on the island whose circular enclosure can still be traced. At one time a workshop there was producing stone figures. Some are no more than blocked in, others are completely finished. A small church with a Romanesque doorway was built on the island in the twelfth century and the carvings were used as building material in its walls, a fact which shows that at that time they were old enough to have lost all prestige, so that they are likely to date back to the ninth or tenth century. Six finished statues, an unfinished one and a block with only a carved head have been extracted from the walls. The statues are all of different sizes. They were originally used as caryatids and have definite cuts in the upper parts of the blocks probably intended to support beams. The lower parts, crudely cut, seem to have been made to be sunk in the ground. In consequence they cannot have been corbels supporting a roof, a function for which they would in any case be too large. If they were all part of the same monument, their various sizes could only fit them to be the supports of the steps of an ambo or preaching chair. But they may also be the remains of a stonecutter's workshop whose work was intended for several churches in the neighbourhood. Their iconography is most disconcerting. One figure holds a shield and a sword like the companions of the Lord of Hosts on the Tall cross at Monasterboice (Pl. I). He also wears a large penannular brooch of the same type as fastens the mantle of Christ in the scene of the Arrest at Monasterboice (Pl. 79). Another holds by the

[1] F. Henry, 'Figure in Lismore cathedral', *J.R.S.A.I.*, 1937, pp. 306–7; R. A. S. Macalister, Corpus, II, p. 109 (No. 938) and Id., 'The Lismore corbel', *J.R.S.A.I.*, 1938, p. 299; Macalister thought that he could read, inscribed on the open book a quotation, which, unfortunately, he could not identify. After careful examination I am convinced that no coherent text can be read and that what appears as letters may well be only irregularities of the stone. The statue was a caryatid.

[2] G. V. du Noyer, 'Remarks on Ancient Effigies sculptured on the walls of the Ancient Church on White Island, Lough Erne, Parish of Magheraculmoney, County of Fermanagh', *J.R.S.A.I.*, 1860–1, pp. 62 sqq.; W. F. Wakeman, 'The Church on White Island, Lough Erne, Parish of Magheraculmoney, County of Fermanagh', *J.R.S.A.I.*, 1879–82, pp. 276 sqq.; Lady Dorothy Lowry-Corry, 'A Newly Discovered Statue at the Church on White Island, County Fermanagh', *U.J.A.*, 1959, pp. 59 sqq.; D. M. Waterman, 'Note on a Recent Excavation', *U.J.A.*, pp. 65 sqq.

neck two winged griffins as do the two figures on one of the carpet-pages of the Turin Gospel-book (Pl. 39). A figure holding a crozier and a bell helps to date the whole series to the ninth or tenth century, because of the shape of the crozier (Pl. 14; cf. Pl. 52). A figure of similar iconography, though carved in very low relief on one of the sides of a pillar is found at Killadeas (Fermanagh)[1] also on the shore of Lough Erne (Pl. 9). There the alertly walking figure is in profile, with a nut-cracker face which gives the impression of a vivid portrait. It is striking to find on the side of this pillar a very simple wide interlacing which has an exact parallel on the side of one of the White Island figures. In spite of the very different styles, the two sculptures have thus a close kinship. Other comparisons come to mind as pagan statues had been carved centuries before on some of the islands of Lough Erne, amongst them the double statue from Boa Island. Something of this age-old tradition had probably lingered in the neighbourhood, and some features of the prehistoric figures survive in their distant successors of Christian times.[2]

Besides these stone carvings there were also, no doubt, others cut in wood, of which some may have belonged to the decoration of wooden churches, while others were part of the wooden partitions and furniture of stone churches. The only example of Irish wooden carving which has come down to us is the yew-wood gaming-board found in Crannog No. 1 of Ballinderry (Westmeath) (Pl. 15),[3] which probably dates of the end of the tenth century. It is decorated with interlacings similar to those found in stone carvings of the same time and has also a pattern of chains of rings, which was compared, at the time of the discovery, to ornaments on the stone crosses of the Isle of Man. But it is found as well on some Irish metalwork objects, for examples on the corner motifs

[1] Lady Dorothy Lowry-Corry, 'The sculptured Stones at Killadeas', *J.R.S.A.I.*, 1935, pp. 23 sqq.

[2] A figure of much cruder style than the White Island and Lismore ones, found in a field near the castle of Downdaniel (Cork), belongs probably to the same series. It seems to have stood for a long time over or beside a holy well. See *J.C.H.A.S.*, XIII, pp. 61 sqq.

[3] Hencken, *Ballinderry No. 1*.

of the Soiscél Molaise or on a fragment of crozier preserved in the Belfast Museum.[1] The question arises here of the possible relations of these Irish wood carvings with Scandinavian objects in wood and also with the decoration of the Norwegian churches carved in a milieu where contacts with Ireland were numerous. There seems to be a very strong influence of Irish models in the ornament of the Oseberg chariot[2] and also in the eleventh-century carvings of the Church at Urnes.[3]

Fig. 37. Two details from the cross at Duleek.

[1] Catal. L. 50–33, no loc.; it is found also on St Conall's Bell (*C.A.A.I.*, II Pl. 124), which comes from Inishkeel (Donegal).
[2] *Osebergfundet*, III, pp. 26 sqq.   [3] Id., III, p. 324.

6. Conclusions

WHEN TRYING to encompass at a glance this art of the ninth and tenth centuries, one is immediately faced with a series of contradictions and paradoxes. The stupendous complexities of the Book of Kells are contrasted with the massive simplifications of volumes in the stone figures; endless meanders of ornament appear beside smooth modelling. One is tempted to sum it up as transitional art. Transition there certainly is, from ornament still half steeped in a prehistoric past to the foreshadowings of Medieval art in the carvings of the crosses. Still such a view may well be lacking in insight. In actual fact the figure carvings are more in the nature of an interlude, as meanders and abstract complexities, far from disappearing, find renewed favour in the eleventh and twelfth centuries, thus revealing themselves as a fundamental element of Irish art and not one on the road to decay. If they have outlived the great stage of creative invention in the seventh and eighth centuries, they are still vigorous enough to constitute one of the essential characteristics of Irish Romanesque art, while figured carvings, after the brilliant ninth–tenth-century episode, are relegated to a secondary place and change completely in appearance where they are still tolerated.

The principles which govern the structure of Irish abstract decoration and their pre-Christian background have been studied in the first volume of this series,[1] and there is no need to dwell further on this subject in connection with the decoration of the ninth–tenth-century manuscripts which would only supply us with fresh examples – admittedly of extraordinary significance in the Book of Kells – without adding anything really new to what we have already learned.

All that need be said here about ornament concerns the very varied aspects which it takes in the different techniques. While in the eighth

---

[1] *Vol. I,* pp. 203 sqq.

century there was little difference between the repertoire of interlacings, key-patterns and spirals used by the metalsmiths, the manuscript painters and the sculptors, and the only noticeable difference between them was the almost complete absence of animal-interlacing in one group of crosses, things are very different from the ninth century on. Now, each group of craftsmen, whether working on books, metal or crosses, goes its own way, giving its own version of the old patterns. In the ninth and tenth centuries the painter persists in using traditional ornament, bringing it to a pitch of subtlety and complication in the Book of Kells. In the other manuscripts the only outstanding facts are the near disappearance of the spiral and the growing importance of animal patterns, the only ones which seem to interest the artist and stimulate his imagination. But in metalwork there are many novelties. There also, spirals become scarce and animals often take on a new appearance. It is on metal objects that contacts between Scandinavian and Irish art occur with the greatest ease and there are already in the ninth and tenth centuries some advanced signs of the Scandinavian-Irish art which flourished in the eleventh and twelfth centuries.

Carvings, on the contrary, do not show any signs of contact with Viking art. There, the decoration remains, absolutely, obstinately traditional, with still almost the same balance between the various patterns. Spirals are still prominent, but now they either look like coils of rope as on the Barrow valley crosses, or swell up into half-spheres. In both cases they are carved to stand out clearly in the light instead of being reduced to an engraving on the surface of the stone. This tendency to model the ornament in relief disappeared in the eleventh century, but it is so characteristic of the aesthetic of the tenth-century sculptor that it affects also the animal or human interlacings where the heads often stand out in bold relief. One of the most striking examples is found in a composition of four stylized and woven human figures carved in almost the same way on the cross of Muiredach (Pl. 78) and on the cross of the Scriptures at Clonmacnois.

The great novelty of the crosses is, however, the amount of space given to figured scenes. There was already in the eighth century a definite consciousness of the sharp difference between ornament and a picture which was meant to *say* something, which was intended to transmit an idea. Although they were stylized up to a point, the figures on the Moone cross or the Banagher pillar and those on the base of the North cross at Ahenny were clearly meant to tell a story and as a consequence their appearance remained easily intelligible and their gestures were made as expressive as possible. Their importance as vehicles of thought vastly outdistanced any attempt at turning them into decorative motifs.

It may be that this dual aspect went back to pagan times, as there were in pagan Irish art clearly defined statues as well as blocks of stone covered with ornament. It is found also in Gaulish art and in other arts, such as Scandinavian, where ornament is predominant.[1] But in the ninth century the balance between representation and ornament was upset and soon 'picture' carvings covered most of the surface of the cross. A strong impulse given by the imitation of Carolingian ivories was perhaps partly responsible for this, but it may have been sustained also by a trend of thought which developed at that time. The Tallaght reform which showed a distinct taste for symbolical speculations may well have fostered such a figurative art. Even if this interest in iconography was thus awakened before the appearance of the Vikings, it could only have been strengthened by the presence of the invaders and by the desire on the part of the Christian Irish to proclaim their faith, to expound it in all its orthodoxy as a protest against the sacrileges of the pagans. Indeed some of the crosses, with the many illustrations of the help given by God to the faithful, with all the examples of miraculous rescues from death and oppression, appear as cries of hope raised in the distress of threatening raids, and the old prayer 'Save us as thou didst save the Three Children from the Fiery Furnace, Daniel from the Lions' den, Jonah from the whale', must have been taken sometimes in its most literal meaning.

Such incentives brought about the blossoming of figured carvings which are, with those of some English crosses (especially at Ruthwell, Bewcastle and Easby) the most important prelude to Romanesque

[1] See for example the contrast between the Oseberg tapestry and the carvings found in the same tomb.

sculpture, with the exception of Ottonian art. Kingsley Porter in the study of pre-Romanesque sculpture, which constitutes the introduction to his book on Spanish Romanesque sculpture[1] considers it as an intermediary between late antique carvings and medieval art and also between the East and the West. Henri Focillon[2] saw in Irish art chiefly the method which informs it and in consequence he gave perhaps more attention to the decoration of the manuscripts than to that of the crosses. This point of view will have to be discussed in the third book of this series. For him, Irish art constituted a 'preliminary experiment' for Romanesque art. This is surely more perspicacious than to make of it simply a landmark in these five centuries nearly devoid of carvings in western Europe. The statement needs however to be re-examined in the light of our present knowledge. Preliminary experiment. Preparation for Romanesque art. Yes, certainly. But the value of this art for its own sake must not be overlooked. Since the Irish crosses have been cleaned from the moss and lichen which marred their appearance, the quality of these sculptures has become manifest. It cannot be denied that the carvings of the Monasterboice School constitute a remarkable and original phase of Christian art, and a phase in many ways different from Romanesque sculpture. It is a curious paradox that their figures are less dominated by geometrical methods of construction than those of Romanesque art. There was a sort of exchange in which Ireland probably lent to Romanesque art, through the manuscripts, tendencies to abstraction, while, on the other hand, she received from the Carolingian ivories a heavy semi-realistic style of very different inspiration.

All this chiefly concerns the plastic treatment of this art. Its iconography raises much more complicated problems. Ernst Kitzinger, having shown what can be learned from the study of the Book of Kells Madonna about Byzantine iconography, remarked: 'This gives it a significance which goes far beyond the orbit of insular art of the Dark Ages.'[3] This observation is relevant to many panels of the crosses. They

[1] A. Kingsley Porter, *Spanish Romanesque Sculpture* (Florence, 1928), Introduction.
[2] H. Focillon, *L'Art des sculpteurs romans* (Paris, 1931), pp. 97 sqq.
[3] E. Kitzinger, 'The Coffin-Reliquary', *Relics of St. Cuthbert*, p. 258.

appear as witnesses, and most revealing ones, of a stage in the development of Early Christian art which is badly represented in the other surviving Western monuments. Occasionally they even supply a certain amount of information about some vanished aspects of Oriental art. They constitute invaluable documents for the systematic study of the iconography of the Early Middle Ages, this most arduous of all tasks.

A detailed study would reveal first of all the extreme complexity of the inspiration of that art. If one tried to visualize the miscellaneous objects which must have managed to reach Ireland, one would conjure up icons from Italy or the East whose obvious influence we have traced several times, perhaps some ampullae containing oil from the lamps of the Holy Land shrines – a few of them were found in Bobbio, an Irish foundation – relic-boxes also brought back by some pilgrim from the Holy Land, similar to the example preserved in the Vatican, books of the most varied origins, Byzantine, Coptic, Italian, Carolingian, whose bindings carried plaques of ivory or metalwork, whose pages were illuminated. Every detail of all this was susceptible of imitation, and when studying the discrepancies in the Irish representations of the Crucifixion, we have been able to gauge this multiplicity of influences, the inconsequences bred from indiscriminate admiration of various models. The very incoherence of the precious odds and ends which no doubt managed to reach the extreme West, tends to show the vanity of too easy simplifications about Rome or the East, Rome or Byzantium. At this date, everything is mixed, churned up by the naïve eclecticism which presided at the acquisition of objects often treasured mostly for their contents or associations, and then imitated for the same reason.

The study of the Irish version of the Last Judgment shows clearly how much of these artificial antitheses are due to our ignorance of the lost links between the surviving objects. When opposing the Byzantine type to the Occidental one, we should remember that the Byzantine version is not known to us before the eleventh century. The stereotyped version which has reached us was no doubt preceded by other, and different, Greek representations. And it is these archaic versions, going back to the seventh and eighth centuries and to the pre-iconoclastic period, which have inspired the Irish as well as the Medieval

199

representations of the Judgment. But one would look in vain for their special features in the other Western Judgments of the tenth and eleventh centuries, whether at Reichenau, or Sant' Angelo in Formis or in the Gospel-book of Henry II in Munich.

In the same way, we have seen how much the theme of the Virgin and Child as found in Ireland can tell us about vanished models. In this special case a few examples of a previously unknown type have turned up recently, providing a new background to the startling representation of the Child in profile in the Irish manuscript. One may hope that some

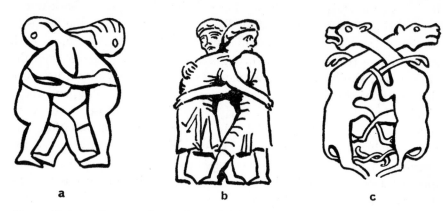

Fig. 38. Fighting figures and animals: a, Jacob and the Angel, Market cross at Kells; b, Jacob and the Angel, N. D.-la-Grande, Poitiers; c, animals, Tower cross, Kells.

day a fortunate chance will recover for us some features of the lost pictures of the Last Judgment. Until then one can only presume their existence, but with a maximum of likelihood.

When examined carefully the Irish representations of the Last Judgment show quite surprising connections. They certainly have their original features, among them the unique representation of the Christ–Judge in the Osirian attitude and the presence of the reference figures symbolizing the authors of the chief texts depicting the Judgment. But this apart, such a widely spread scene, with the Weighing of the souls below the Judge, Hell on one side, Paradise on the other, is not the Romanesque figuration of the Judgment. There is here no parallel to

a

b

c

Fig. 39. The Fall: a, cross at
Donaghmore (Tyrone);
b, High Cross, Durrow;
c, Vézelay, capital.

the Conques tympanum[1] where the Weighing of the souls is almost
hidden away in a corner above a pediment, nor to the Autun carvings[2]
where it is given a large place on the left of the Judge. This sym-

[1] G. Gaillard, M.-M. S. Gauthier, L. Balsan, Dom Angelico Surchamp, O.S.B.,
Rouergue Roman (Zodiaque, 1963), Pl. 3; A. M. Cocagnac, O.P., *Le Jugement
dernier dans l'art* (Paris, 1955), p. 32.

[2] D. Grivot, G. Zarnecki, *Gislebertus Sculpteur d'Autun* (Paris, 1960), Pls. B
and J.

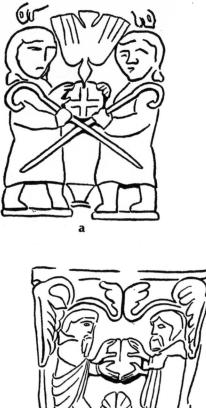

a

b

c

Fig. 40. a, Monasterboire, cross
of Muiredach; *b*, Clermont-Ferrand,
Notre-Dame-du-Port, fight
of virtues and vices;
c, Vézelay, St Paul and St Anthony.

metrical and perfectly balanced composition has much more in common
with the thirteenth-century tympana of the cathedrals of Bourges[1] or
Amiens, or even with the fifteenth-century altarpiece of Van der
Weyden in the Beaune Hospital.[2] And the gamboling of the devils

[1] R. Gauchery, C. Gauchery-Grodecki, *Saint-Etienne de Bourges* (Paris, 1959),
Pls. 48, 52; Cocagnac, op. cit., pp. 50 sqq.
[2] J. Lassaigne, *Flemish Painting, The Century of Van Eyck* (Skira, 1957), Pl. p. 88.

hustling the Damned with their forks are already depicted at Monaster-boice in the cynical spirit which will gradually expand in the course of the Middle Ages.

Other similarities may start us wondering : that between the way the Fall of Simon Magus is represented at Autun and at Monasterboice (Fig. 35); the presence on the Irish crosses of the two scenes – Adam and Eve and the Fight of Jacob and the Angel – which are the beginning and the end of a series of carved scenes on the west front of Notre-Dame-la-Grande in Poitiers (Fig. 38), the parallelism of the presenta-tion of St Paul and St Anthony sharing the bread from Heaven on a capital of Vézelay and on the Cross of Muiredach (Fig. 40). There are also purely formal analogies such as that of the two croziers on this last panel and the lances crossed in the same way on a capital of Notre-Dame-du-Port at Clemont-Ferrand (Fig. 40). These are only a few examples taken at random. It would be rash to try and give a precise explanation of such phenomena. To outline them suffices to stress the problems they raise. The traditional explanation which tries to trace back each of the parallel pictures to their common ancestor in some illumination may be the only wise one. Attempts at establishing a direct link between them would be thwarted by insuperable chronological difficulties. If the dates we have assigned to the Irish crosses are correct – and the cumulative evidence of inscriptions, of figure style and of the treatment of ornament hardly leaves room for doubt on the subject – those with figured scenes were carved in Ireland up to about the middle of the tenth century. How then can we bridge the gap of more than a century which divides them from the first great works of Romanesque carving? How anyway could one precisely imagine the link? Through travelling sculptors? In itself this is not an absurd hypothesis and we have already seen Irish painters spreading the fashion for their abstract decoration by their wanderings. But it is opportune to remember what has been pointed out earlier about the composition of the Irish carvings where geometry plays a small part and abstract schemes are of much less importance than for the capitals and even more the tympana of Romanesque churches.[1] Besides, Irish Romanesque art itself has few

[1] J. Baltrusaitis, *La stylistique romane* (Paris, 1929).

figurative carvings to show. From whatever angle one examines it, and though at first it seems tempting, the hypothesis of a direct filiation, between the art of the crosses and Continental Romanesque carvings has little to recommend it.

'Preliminary experiment' seems thus, when all has been considered, the only exact definition, the Irish crosses showing the first manifestation in stone of themes which will be the standard ones of Romanesque art. Still it is essential to remember the remark made above about the value of this art as such, and not only in its relation to Romanesque art.

In fact, if one pursues this aspect carefully strange facts will be revealed there also, and it will appear that the approach to the textual sources of Romanesque art has been too simplified. The later writers have invented very little. Honorius Augustodunensis has been no more in fact than a clear-thinking compiler. And Abbot Suger has usually only deepened the meaning and the plastic possibilities of all sorts of themes which for centuries had haunted the thoughts of commentators on sacred texts. For example his systematic arrangement on the enamelled cross of St Denis[1] of parallel scenes, disposed two by two, illustrating the age-old theme of the prefigurations, is nothing novel, and artists had thought of the device before him. Bede quotes examples of it in the seventh century. It had been used in the time of Charlemagne for the now lost frescoes of the palace of Ingelheim. Though the artists who carved the Irish crosses do not use rigid series of parallels, their choice of subjects is clearly inspired by the theme itself and helps to trace its continuity through the history of Christian art until it blossoms out in the twelfth century.

In the same way, the association of the four great prophets with the four Evangelists can be traced back to an early period through Irish documents. Finally in the tenth century at San Sebastianello in Rome[2] and in the thirteenth at Chartres and Bamberg[3] it gives us those amazing representations of the prophets carrying the Evangelists or

---

[1] E. Panofsky, *Abbot Suger on the Abbey Church of St Denis and its Art Treasures* (Princeton, 1948), pp. 56 sqq. Mâle, *XIIe siècle*, pp. 152 sqq.

[2] Mâle, *Churches of Rome*, pp. 108 sqq.

[3] E. Mâle, *The Gothic Image*, pp. 9–10.

the Apostles on their shoulders. But it is found already in the eighth-century plan in the Book of Mulling where each of the four crosses named after the great prophets is accompanied by a cross named after an Evangelist,[1] and it reappears in the early ninth century in a series of manuscripts of the School of Tours whose links with Ireland through Alcuin are well known. There the prophets and the Evangelists or their symbols surround Christ blessing or the Lamb accompanied by a chalice. In pictorial form it is the equivalent of the arrangement in the plan in the Book of Mulling.

These few examples show the wealth of information which Irish art can supply on the background of Romanesque and Gothic iconography. This is a province which has so far been completely neglected and which deserves to take its place in the history of Medieval thought as applied to art.

Fig. 41. Book of Kells, detail.

---

[1] Margaret Stokes already pointed out the connection between the Mulling plan and the Chartres window (*Castledermot and Durrow*, p. XII). She compares with the plan the famous prayer of Colgu Ua Duineachta: 'I beseech with thee, O Jesus holy, thy four Evangelists who wrote thy Gospel divine, to wit, Matthew, Mark, Luke, John. I beseech with thee, thy four chief prophets who foretold thy incarnation, Daniel, Jeremiah, Isaiah and Ezekiel.' To establish a clear link with the miniatures of the School of Tours one would be tempted to accept that Colgu, the master of Alcuin was in fact Colgu the author of the prayer (see p. 28).

Bibliographical Abbreviations

AA. SS. Boll. – *Acta Sanctorum*, edited by the Bollandists.

A. Clon. – *Annals of Clonmacnoise, being Annals of Ireland from the earliest period to A.D. 1408. Translated into English A.D. 1627 by Conell Mageoghagan*, ed. D. Murphy, Dublin (*J.R.S.A.I.*), 1896.

A.F.M. – *Annals of the Kingdom of Ireland by the Four Masters, from the earliest period to the year 1616*, ed. John O'Donovan, Dublin, 1851.

A.I. – *The Annals of Inisfallen* (*Ms. Rawlinson B. 503*), ed. Seán Mac Airt, Dublin, 1951.

A.L.C. – *The Annals of Loch Cé*, ed. William M. Hennessy, London (R.S.), 1871.

An. Boll. – *Analecta Bollandiana*.

Anglo-Saxon Chr. – Dorothy Whitelock, with D. C. Douglas and S. I. Tucker, *The Anglo-Saxon Chronicle*, London, 1961.

An. Hib. – *Analecta Hibernica*.

Archdall, *Mon. Hib.* – M. Archdall, *Monasticon Hibernicum*.

Arch. Journ. – *The Archaeological Journal*.

A. Tig. – *Annals of Tigernach*, ed. Whitley Stokes, *R.C.*, 1895, pp. 174 sqq., 1896, pp. 6 sqq., 118 sqq., 336 sqq.

A.U. – *Annals of Ulster, otherwise Annals of Senat, A Chronicle of Irish Affairs from A.D. 431 to A.D. 1540* – ed. William M. Hennessy, Dublin, 1887.

Bede, *H. abb.* – *Historia abbatum auctore Baeda* (see Plummer).

Bede, *H.E.* – *Baedae Historia Ecclesiastica Gentis Anglorum* (see Plummer).

Bersu, *Lissue* – G. Bersu, 'The Rath in Townland Lissue, Co. Antrim', *U.J.A.*, 1947, pp. 30 sqq.

Bieler, *Ireland* – Ludwig Bieler, *Ireland, Harbinger of the Middle Ages*, London, New York, Toronto, 1963.

C.A.A.I. – *Christian Art in Ancient Ireland*, Dublin, vol. I, ed. by Adolf Mahr, 1932, vol. II, ed. by Joseph Raftery, 1941.

Cabrol-Leclercq – Rme Dom Fernand Cabrol – R.P. Dom H. Leclercq, *Dictionnaire d'Archéologie chrétienne et de Liturgie*, Paris, 1907 sqq.

Chr. Sc. – *Chronicum Scottorum, A Chronicle of Irish Affairs from the earliest times to A.D. 1135, with a supplement containing the events from 1141 to 1150*, ed. William M. Hennessy, London (R.S.), 1866.

Coffey, *Guide* – George Coffey, *Guide to the Celtic Antiquities of the Christian Period preserved in the National Museum, Dublin*, Dublin, 1909 (the 2nd edition (1910) is here quoted).

Colgan, *AA. SS. Hib.* – J. Colgan, O.F.M., *Acta Sanctorum veteris et majoris Scotiae, seu Hiberniae sanctorum Insulae*, Louvain, 1645 (only vol. I published). See: *The Acta Sanctorum Hiberniae* (Irish Manuscripts Commission), Dublin, 1947.

Crawford, *East and West Meath* – H. S. Crawford, 'The Early Crosses of East and West Meath', *J.R.S.A.I.*, 1926, pp. 72 sqq.

Dark Age Britain – *Dark Age Britain, Studies presented to E. T. Leeds*, ed. by D. B. Harden, London, 1956.

Diehl, *Manuel d'Art byzantin*, Charles Diehl, *Manuel d'Art byzantin*, Paris, 1910.

Ebersolt, *Miniature byzantine*, J. Ebersolt, *La Miniature byzantine*, Paris, 1926.

E.Q.C. Cenannensis – *Evangeliorum Quattuor Codex Cenannensis*, Berne, 1950–1, vol. I and II : facsimile, vol. III : text by E. H. Alton, P. Meyer, G. O. Simms.

E.Q.C. Durmachensis – *Evangeliorum Quattuor Codex Durmachensis*, Olten-Lausanne-Fribourg, 1960, vol. I : facsimile, vol. II : text by A. A. Luce, G. O. Simms, P. Meyer, L. Bieler.

E.Q.C. Lindisfarnensis – *Evangeliorum Quattuor Codex Lindisfarnensis*, Olten-Lausanne-Fribourg, vol. I, 1956 : facsimile, vol. II, 1960 : text by T. D. Kendrick, T. J. Brown, R. L. S. Bruce-Mitford, H. Rosen-Runge, A. S. C. Ross, E. G. Stanley, A. E. A. Werner.

Flower, *The Two Eyes of Ireland* – Robin Flower, 'The Two Eyes of Ireland, Religion and Literature in Ireland in the eighth and ninth centuries', *Report of the Church of Ireland Conference held in Dublin, 11th–14th October, 1932*, Dublin, 1932, pp. 66 sqq.

Fragm. – *Three Fragments copied from Ancient Sources by Dubhaltach Mac Firbisigh*, ed. John O'Donovan, Dublin, 1860.

Friend, *Canon Tables* – A. M. Friend Jr., 'The Canon Tables of the Book of Kells', *Medieval Studies in Memory of Kingsley Porter*, Cambridge, Mass., 1939, pp. 611 sqq.

F.-S. M. Néill – *Féil sgríbhinn Eóin Mhic Néill, Essays and Studies presented to Professor Eoin Mac Neill*, ed. by J. Ryan, S.J., Dublin, 1940.

Galassi, *Roma o Bisanzio* – G. Galassi, *Roma o Bisanzio*, Rome, 1953.

Goldschmidt, *Elfen.* – A. Goldschmidt, *Die Elfenbeinskulpturen aus der Zeit der Karolingischen Kaiser*, VIII–XI. Jahrhundert, Berlin, 1918.

Gough, *Early Christians* – M. Gough, *The Early Christians*, London, 1963.

Grabar, *Ampoules de Terre Sainte* – A. Grabar, *Les Ampoules de Terre Sainte*, Paris, 1958.

Grabar-Nordenfalk – A. Grabar-C. Nordenfalk, *Early Medieval Painting* (Skira, 1957).

Gwynn, *Lib. Ardm.* – J. Gwynn, *Liber Ardmachanus, The Book of Armagh*, Dublin, 1913.

Healy, *Unfinished Crosses* – J. Healy, 'The Unfinished Crosses of Kells', *J.R.S.A.I.*, 1890–1, pp. 450 sqq.

H.B.S. – Henry Bradshaw Society.

Hencken, *Ballinderry No. 1* – H. O'Neill-Hencken, 'Ballinderry Crannog No. 1', *P.R.I.A.*, 1936 (C), pp. 103 sqq.

Hencken, *Lagore* – Hugh Hencken, 'Lagore Crannog, an Irish Royal Residence of the 7th to the 10th centuries A.D.', *P.R.I.A.*, 1950 (C), pp. 1 sqq., including (pp. 18–34): Liam Price, 'The History of Lagore from Annals and other Sources'.

Henry, *An Irish Manuscript* – F. Henry, 'An Irish Manuscript in the British Museum', *J.R.S.A.I.*, 1957, pp. 147 sqq.

Henry, *Irish High Crosses* – F. Henry, *Irish High Crosses*, Dublin, 1964.

Henry, *Sc. irl.*, F. Henry, *La sculpture irlandaise pendant les douze premiers siècles de l'ère chrétienne*, Paris, 1932.

Henry, *Three Psalters* – F. Henry, 'Remarks on the Decoration of Three Irish Psalters', *P.R.I.A.*, 1960 (C), pp. 23 sqq.

Henry – Marsh-Micheli, *Illumination* – F. Henry – G. L. Marsh-Micheli, 'A Century of Irish Illumination (1070–1170)', *P.R.I.A.*, 1962 (C), pp. 101 sqq.

Holmqvist, *Germanic Art* – W. Holmqvist, *Germanic Art during the First Millenium A.D.*, Stockholm, 1955.

I.H.S. – Irish Historical Studies.

Irish Min. of St Gall – The Irish Miniatures in the Cathedral Library of St Gall, Berne-Olten-Lausanne, 1954, text by J. Duft and P. Meyer.

J.C.H.A.S. – Journal of the Cork Historical and Archaeological Society.

J.W.C.I. – Journal of the Warburg and Courtauld Institutes.

Kendrick, *Vikings* – T. D. Kendrick, *A History of the Vikings*, London, 1930.

Kenney, *Sources*, J. Kenny, *The Sources for the Early History of Ireland, An Introduction and Guide*, vol. I : *Ecclesiastical* (the only volume published), New York, 1929.

Koehler, *Karol. Min.* – W. Koehler, *Die Karolingische Miniaturen*, Berlin, I, 1930, II sqq., 1958.

Lawlor, *Nendrum* – H. C. Lawlor, *The Monastery of St Mochaoi of Nendrum*, Belfast, 1925.

Leask, *Ir. Churches* – Harold G. Leask, *Irish Churches and Monastic Buildings*, I : *The First Phases and the Romanesque Period*, Dundalk, 1955.

Leroquais, *Psautiers* – V. Leroquais, *Les Psautiers des bibliothèques publiques de France*, Mâcon, 1940–1.

Little, *Dublin* – G. Little, *Dublin before the Vikings*, Dublin, 1957.

Louth J. – Journal of the County Louth Archaeological Society.

Lowe, *C.L.A.* – Elias Avery Lowe, *Codices Latini Antiquiores*, I, *Vatican City*, Oxford, 1935; II, *Great Britain and Ireland*, 1935; III, *Italy (Ancona-Novara)*, 1938; IV, *Italy (Perugia-Verona)*, 1947; V, *France (Paris)*, 1950; VI, *France (Abbeville-Valenciennes)*, 1953; VII, *Switzerland*, 1956; VIII, *Germany (Altenburg-Leipzig)*, 1959; IX, *Germany (Maria Laach-Würzburg)*, 1959.

Macalister, *Clonmacnois* – R. A. S. Macalister, *The Memorial Slabs of Clonmacnois, King's County*, Dublin (*J.R.S.A.I.*), 1909.

Macalister, *Corpus* – R. A. S. Macalister, *Corpus Inscriptionum Insularum Celticarum*, 2 vols., Dublin, 1945, 1949.

Macalister, *Monasterboice* – R. A. S. Macalister, *Monasterboice, Co. Louth*, Dundalk, 1946.

McCoy, *Ulster Maps* – G. A. Hayes McCoy, *Ulster and other Irish Maps*, Dublin, 1964.

Mac Dermott, *Crosiers of St Dympna and St Mel* – Máire Mac Dermott, 'The Crosiers of St Dympna and St Mel and Tenth century Irish Metalwork', *P.R.I.A.*, 1957 (C), pp. 157 sqq.

Mac Dermott, *Kells Crosier* – M. Mac Dermott, 'The Kells Crosier', *Archaeologia*, 1955, pp. 59 sqq.

McGurk – Patrick McGurk, *Latin Gospel-books from A.D. 400 to A.D. 800*, Paris, etc., 1961.

McGurk, *Pocket-books* – P. McGurk, 'The Irish Pocket Gospel-Books', *Sacris Erudiri*, 1956, pp. 249 sqq.

Mac Neill, *Phases* – Eoin Mac Neill, *Phases of Irish History*, Dublin, 1920.

Mahr – See : *C.A.A.I.*

Mâle, *Churches of Rome* – Emile Mâle, *The Early Churches of Rome*, (trans., with notes by David Buxton from : *Rome et ses vieilles églises*) Rome, 1960.

Mâle, *XIIe siècle* – E. Mâle, *L'art religieux de XIIe siècle en France*, Paris, 1922.

Mâle, *Gothic Image* – E. Mâle, *The Gothic Image* (trans. by Dora Mussey from the 3rd edition (1913) of: *L'art religieux au XIIIe siècle en France*) London–Glasgow, 1961.

Manitius, *Lat. Lit.* – Max Manitius, *Geschichte der lateinischen Literatur des Mittelalters*, Munich, 1911–23.

Meyer, *E. Irish Poetry* – Kuno Meyer, *Selections from Early Irish Poetry*, London, 1911.

Micheli, *Enluminure* – G. L. Micheli, *L'enluminure du Haut Moyen Age et les influences irlandaises*, Brussels, 1939.

Micheli – See : Marsh-Micheli.

Mon. Alcuiniana – W. Wattenbach-X. Duemmler, *Monumenta Alcuiniana*, Berlin, 1873.

Mon. Piot – *Monuments Piot.*

Morey, *E.C. Art* – C. R. Morey, *Early Christian Art*, Princeton (New Jersey), 1953.

Nordenfalk – See : Grabar-Nordenfalk.

O'Meara, *Giraldus Cambrensis* – John O'Meara, 'Giraldus Cambrensis In Topographia Hibernie', *P.R.I.A.*, 1949 (C), pp. 113 sqq.

Osebergfundet – A. W. Brögger, Hj. Falk, Haakon Shetelig, *Osebergfundet*, Christiania, 1917.

Petrie, *Chr. Inscr.* – George Petrie, *Christian Inscriptions in the Irish Language* (ed. by Margaret Stokes), 2 vols., Dublin, 1872, 1878.

Petrie, *Round Towers* – G. Petrie, *The Ecclesiastical Architecture of Ireland anterior to the Anglo-Norman Invasion, comprising an Essay on the Origin and Uses of the Round Towers of Ireland*, Dublin, 1845.

Plummer – C. Plummer, *Venerabilis Baedae Opera Historica*, Oxford, 1896 : *Historia Ecclesiastica Gentis Anglorum*, vol. I, pp. 1 sqq.; *Historia abbatum auctore Baeda*, vol. I, pp. 364 sqq.; *Historia abbatum auctore anonymo*, vol. I, pp. 388 sqq.

Porter, Crosses and Culture – Arthur Kingsley Porter, *The Crosses and Culture of Ireland*, New Haven, 1951.

P.R.I.A. – *Proceedings of the Royal Irish Academy.*

P.S.A.Sc. – *Proceedings of the Society of Antiquaries of Scotland.*

R.A. – *Revue Archéologique.*

Raftery – See : *C.A.A.I.*

R.C. – *Revue celtique.*

Reeves, *St Columba* – William Reeves, *The Life of St Columba, Founder of Hy, written by Adamnan*, Dublin, 1857.

Relics of St Cuthbert – *The Relics of St Cuthbert, Studies by various authors*, ed. by C. F. Battiscombe, Oxford, 1956.

Rice, *Byzantium* – David Talbot Rice, *The Art of Byzantium*, London, 1959.

Roe, *Kells* – Helen Roe, *The High Crosses of Kells*, Kells, 1959.

R.S. – *Rolls Series.*

Sexton, *Fig. Sc.* – E. H. L. Sexton, *Irish Figure Sculpture of the Early Christian Period*, Portland (Maine), 1946.

Smith, *Guide Anglo-Saxon A.* – Reginald Smith, *British Museum Guide to Anglo-Saxon Antiquities*, London, 1923.

Sotirou, *Icones du Sinai* – G.-M. Sotirou, *Les Icones du Mont Sinai*, Athens, 1956.

M. Stokes, *Castledermot and Durrow* – Margaret Stokes, *The High Crosses of Castledermot and Durrow*, Dublin, 1898.

M. Stokes, *Early Christian Arch.* – M. Stokes, *Early Christian Architecture in Ireland*, London, 1878.

Stokes, *Martyr. Oengus* – Whitley Stokes, *The Martyrology of Oengus the Culdee*, London (*H.B.S.*), 1905.

Thesaur. Palaeohib. – Whitley Stokes – John Strachan, *Thesaurus Palaeohibernicus, A Collection of Old Irish Glosses, Scholia, Prose and Verse*, 2 vols., Cambridge, 1901, 1903.

Traube, *Perrona Scottorum* – L. Traube, 'Perrona Scottorum, ein Beitrag zur Ueberlieferungsgeschichte und zur Paleographie des Mittelalters', *Sitzungsberichte der philos., philol., und der hist. Klasse der königlig. bayerische Akademie d. Wissenschaft*, 1900, pp. 469–538.

Tr.R.I.A. – *Transactions of the Royal Irish Academy.*

U.J.A. – *Ulster Journal of Archaeology.*

V. Ant. – *Viking Antiquities in Great Britain and Ireland*, Oslo, 1940, vol. I, H. Shetelig, *An Introduction to the Viking History of Western Europe.* III, J. Bøe, *Norse Antiquities in Ireland*; V, J. Petersen, *British Antiquities of the Viking Period found in Norway*; VI, A. Curle, M. Olsen, H. Shetelig, *Civilisation of the Viking Settlers in relation to their old and new countries.*

Vita Malachiae – *Vita S. Malachiae Episcopi, a Beato Bernardo edita,* trans. H. J. Lawlor, *St Bernard of Clairvaux's Life of St Malachy of Armagh*, London–New York, 1920.

Vol. I – First volume of *Irish Art* (London, 1965).

Volbach, *Early Christian Art* – W. F. Volbach, *Early Christian Art*, London, 1961.

Wakeman, *Inismurray* – W. F. Wakeman, *A Survey of the Antiquarian Remains on the Island of Inismurray*, London–Edinburgh, 1867.

Wald, *Stuttgart Psalter* – E. T. de Wald, *The Stuttgart Psalter*, Princeton, 1930.

Wald, *Utrecht Psalter* – E. T. de Wald, *The Utrecht Psalter.*

War – *Cogadh Gaedhel re Gallaibh, The War of the Gaedhil with the*

Gaill, or the Invasions of Ireland by the Danes and other Norsemen, ed. J. H. Todd, London (R.S.), 1867.

Warner, *Stowe Missal* – G. F. Warner, *The Stowe Missal,* 2 vols., London (H.B.S.), 1906, 1915.

Westwood, *Paleographia Sacra Pictoria* – John Obadiah Westwood, *Palaeographia Sacra Pictoria,* London, 1843–5.

Wilpert, *R. Mosaiken* – J. Wilpert, *Die Römischen Mosaiken und Malereien der kirchlischen Bauten vom IV bis XIII Jahrhundert,* Freiburg-am-Brisgau, 1916.

Wilpert, Sarcofagi – G. Wilpert, *I sarcofagi cristiani antichi,* Rome, 1929–36.

Zimmermann – E. Heinrich Zimmermann, *Vorkarolingische Miniaturen,* (1 vol. text, 4 vols. plates), Berlin, 1916.

General Index

Figures in brackets refer to footnotes (pages).
Figures in square brackets refer to relevant pages where the word is not mentioned.
Figures in italics refer to line illustrations (pages).

Q

List of Monochrome Plates

All monochrome photographs without indication of origin are by Belzeaux-Zodiaque. The others are from the Photographic Archives of the Department of Archaeology, University College, Dublin, and for these the origin of each negative has been indicated.

1. Glendalough (Wicklow), gate of the monastery
2. Monasterboice (Louth), round tower (*Ph. F. Henry*)
3. Cashel (Tipperary), round tower
4. Inis Cealtra (Clare), round tower and Church of St Caimin
5. Aghowle (Wicklow), church
6. Dunshaughlin (Meath), lintel of doorway (*Ph. F. Henry*), Aghowle (Wicklow), doorway of church
7. Kells (Meath), round tower and Unfinished cross
8. Gilt-bronze Crucifixion plaque (N.M.D.)
9. Killadeas (Fermanagh), carved pillar (*Ph. F. Henry*)
10. Glendalough (Wicklow), Reefert Church, interior
11. Glendalough (Wicklow), Trinity Church, apse
12. White Island (Fermanagh), caryatid (*Ph. F. Henry*)
13. Lismore (Waterford), caryatid (*Ph. F. Henry*)
14. White Island (Fermanagh), caryatid (*Ph. F. Henry*)
15. Ballinderry (Westmeath), Crannog No. 1, yew-wood gaming-board (N.M.D.) (*Ph. N.M.D.*)
16. Clonmacnois (Offaly), funerary slab
17. Book of Kells (T.C.D.), Virgin and Child
18. Book of Armagh (T.C.D.), symbol of St John
19. Book of Kells (T.C.D.), symbol of St John
20. Book of Kells (T.C.D.), Chi–Rho
21. Book of Kells (T.C.D.), horseman (*Ph. F. Henry*); Melchisedech (*Ph. F. Henry*)

46. British Mus., Ms. Cotton Vitellius F.XI, beginning of chapter (*Ph. F. Henry*); Psalter of Ricemarcus (T.C.D.), beginning of chapter
47. Psalter of Ricemarcus (T.C.D.), beginning of chapter
48. Southampton Psalter (Cambridge, St John's College), page of text; Double Psalter of St Ouen (Rouen, Ms. 24), initial (*Ph. Institut pour l'Histoire des textes*)
49. British Museum crozier, lower knop
50. Bell from Lough Lene (N.M.D.) (*Ph. N.M.D.*)
51. Gilt-bronze book-binding ornament, from the Phoenix Park, Dublin (N.M.D.); detail from bell found at Bangor (Down) (Bangor Town Hall) (*Ph. Bel. M.*)
52. Crozier found at Toome (Antrim) (Bel. M.) (*Ph. Bel. M.*); British Museum crozier
53. Openwork bronze Crucifixion plaque (N.M.D.) (*Ph. N.M.D.*)
54. Bronze Crucifixion plaque (N.M.D.) (*Ph. N.M.D.*)
55. Corp naomh, upper part (N.M.D.); fragment of bronze cross, back and front (Br. M.)
56. Upper part of a bell-shrine, possibly from Ahoghill (Antrim) (N.M.D.) (*Ph. N.M.D.*); carved bone from Dungarvan (Waterford) (N.M.D.), detail
57. Stone trial-piece from the rath of Lissue (Antrim) (Bel. M.) (*Ph. Bel. M.*); carved bone from Dungarvan (Waterford) (N.M.D.), detail
58. Soiscél Molaise (N.M.D.), detail
59. Soiscél Molaise (N.M.D.), detail
60. Kyte-brooch, possibly found at Clonmacnois (Offaly) (N.M.D.), detail
61. Thistle-brooch found in Ireland (Cambridge, Arch. Mus.)
62–3. Silver brooches found in Ireland (Br. M.)
64. Silver brooch found in Donegal (Br. M.), front and back
65. Castledermot (Kildare), South cross, west side
66. Castledermot (Kildare), South cross, detail
67. Castledermot (Kildare), South cross, detail of east side
68. Castledermot (Kildare), North cross, detail of the base

69. Castledermot (Kildare), North cross, detail of the base
70. Castledermot (Kildare), North cross, Crucifixion
71. Castledermot (Kildare), North cross, west side
72. Castledermot (Kildare), North cross, detail of the base: Multiplication of the Loaves and Fishes
73. Duleek (Meath), detail of cross
74. Kells (Meath), Tower cross, detail: Apocalyptic Vision
75. Kells (Meath), Tower cross, east side
76. Monasterboice (Louth), cross of Muiredach, west side
77. Monasterboice (Louth), cross of Muiredach, detail
78. Monasterboice (Louth), cross of Muiredach, ornamental panels on south side
79. Monasterboice (Louth), cross of Muiredach, Arrest of Christ
80. Monasterboice (Louth), cross of Muiredach, *Dextra Dei*
81. Monasterboice (Louth), cross of Muiredach; Adam and Eve, Murder of Abel
82. Monasterboice (Louth), cross of Muiredach: *Traditio Legis*
83. Monasterboice (Louth), cross of Muiredach, east side
84. Monasterboice (Louth), cross of Muiredach, Crucifixion
85. Monasterboice (Louth), cross of Muiredach, detail of east side: Adam and Eve, Murder of Abel; David and Goliath; Moses striking the Rock; Adoration of the Kings
86. Monasterboice (Louth), West cross, east side
87. Monasterboice (Louth), West cross; Crucifixion and scenes from the Passion
88. Monasterboice (Louth), West cross; scenes from the Life of David
89. Monasterboice (Louth), West cross: Sacrifice of Abraham, Moses holding the Tables of the Law
90. Clonmacnois (Offaly), cross of the Scriptures, east side
91. Clonmacnois (Offaly), cross of the Scriptures, detail
92. Clonmacnois (Offaly), cross of the Scriptures: Foundation of the cross (?)
93. Clonmacnois (Offaly), cross of the Scriptures (west side) and cathedral

94. Clonmacnois (Offaly), cross of the Scriptures: *Ecce Homo* (?)
95. Clonmacnois (Offaly), cross of the Scriptures, north side: St Matthew, St Michael
96. Kells (Meath), Broken cross: the Fall, the Ark (*Ph. F. Henry*)
97. Armagh, cross at the Gate: the Ark (*Ph. F. Henry*); Kells (Meath), Broken cross: Baptism of Christ (*Ph. F. Henry*)
98. Cross at Durrow (Offaly), east side (*Ph. F. Henry*)
99. Durrow (Offaly), High cross, Flight into Egypt (*Ph. F. Henry*); Id., Fight of Jacob with the Angel
100. Durrow (Offaly), High cross, the Fall
101. Kells (Meath), Unfinished cross, Crucifixion
102. Kells (Meath), Market cross
103. Cross at Duleek (Meath)
104. Kells (Meath), Market cross
105. Iona (Scotland), St Martin's cross (*Ph. L. de Paor*); Monasterboice (Louth), Pilate washing his hands (*Ph. F. Henry*)
106–7. Monasterboice (Louth), cross of Muiredach, Last Judgment
108. Cross at Termonfechin (Louth)
109. Durrow (Offaly), High cross; Last Judgment (*Ph. F. Henry*)
110. Clonmacnois (Offaly), cross of the Scriptures: Last Judgment
111. Monasterboice (Louth), West cross: The Lord of the Hosts and various scenes
112. Clonmacnois (Offaly), cross of the Scriptures: the Resurrection

List of Documentary Plates

2

4

9

aequila.

ƔENERATIO

res

ae

ob

ac

rachan

rae

nachon

scruc

ragai

filiţ

eber

sala

cana

guiscredatuo

les nonpuntas

emo sert

minis sert

Guterum

tul, oterince

Aorebant

erant uu

Cuit illis ue

uos coram hon

eoroqueftra c

22

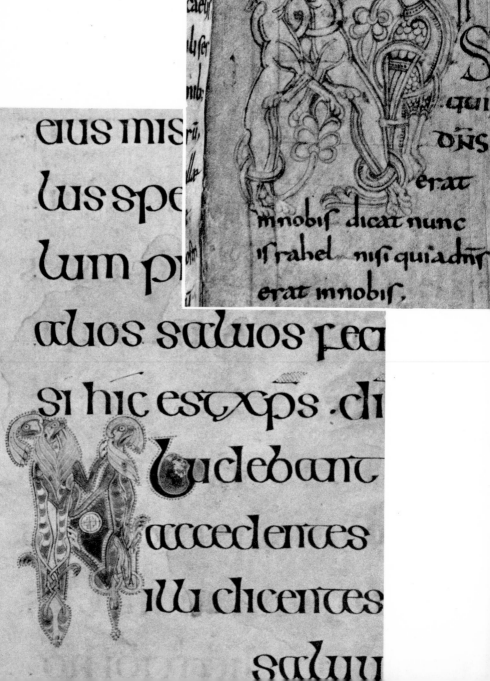

eus misri,

lus spe

lum pr

alios saluos fea

si hic est xps . di

uidebant

accedentes

illi dicentes

salut

quid
dns
erat
mnobif dicat nunc
israhel nisi quiadns
erat mnobif.

27

28

M
qui
dem

multi cona
ti sunt ordi
nare narr
ationem sicut
nobis conple
ti sunt rerum
sicut tradide
runt nobis qui
ab initio ipsi uide
runt et ministri
fuerunt sermonis
uisum est et mihi ad

29

... habens plura uobis scribere
nolui per chartam et atramentum
spero enim me futurum apud uos et os ad
os loqui ut gaudium uestrum plenum
sit. Salutant te filii
sororis tuae electae.

Incipit argumentum.

Senior Gaio carissimo quem ego
diligo in ueritate. Carissime
de omnibus oportet te bene
agere et ualere sicut omnibus
orationem facio prospere in-
gredi et ualere sicut prospere agit
anima tua gauisus sum ualde
de uenientibus fratribus et testimo-
nium perhibentibus ueritati tuae sicut
tu in ueritate ambulas maiorem
horum non habeo gratiam quam
ut audiam filios meos in ueri-

noster
refug
am &un
tuf adiutor min
balationib; quæin

unice ascende s

gloria coram

ic omnis qui

bitur etquis

cebat auter

rat. Cump

atenam noli uo

fratres tuos ne

uicinos diuites

inuitent etta

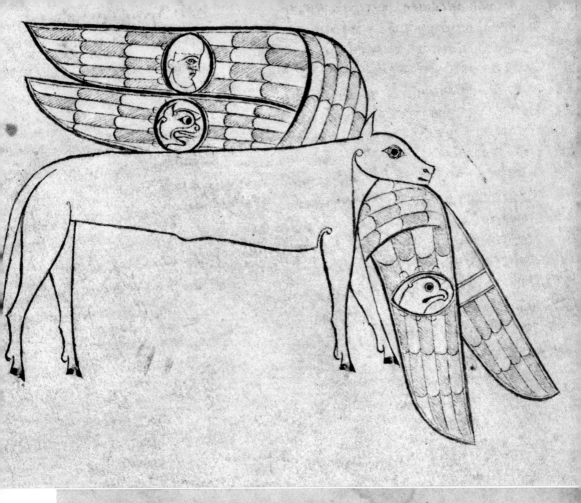

d ossanna in excel

ngerusolima uteem

rcum specas omnib:

sis :.

Ṁṗ

AU̇ TẼ ĊENERATIO

SIC ERAT CUM ESSET DIS

PON̈SṪA MA TER EIŬ

MARIA IOSEṗ ANTE

QUAM CONUE NIRENT

INUENTA ES

INUTERO ḃ

DE SṗŪ SĊO

IOSEṗ AU TM CIR

CUM ESSET IO MO IUS

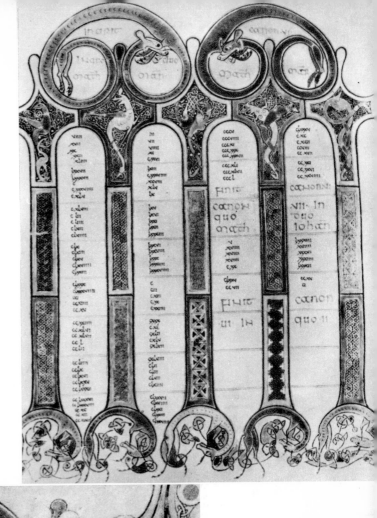

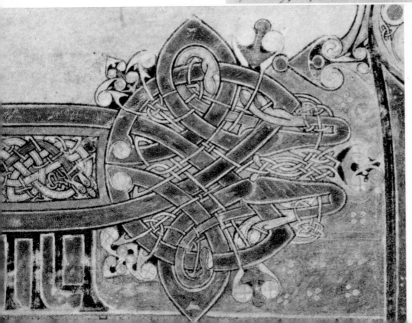

35

Initium
euangelii
dñi nñi ihū
xpi filii di
sicut scrip
tu̅ In esaia p
pheta Ecce
mitto angue
lum meum
ante faciem tuam qui prepa
rabit uiam tuam ante te · et re
Uox clamantis in deserto para
te uiam dñi rectas facite semitas e
Fuit Iohannis in deserto babti
zans et predicans babtismum
poenitentiae & inremissionem pec
catorum & egrediebatur ad illum om̅
iudeae regio & hierusolime uni
uersi & babtizabantur abillo in iorda
ne flumine confitentes peccata sua
et erat Iohannis uestitus pilis cameli
& zona pellicia circa lumbos suos

45

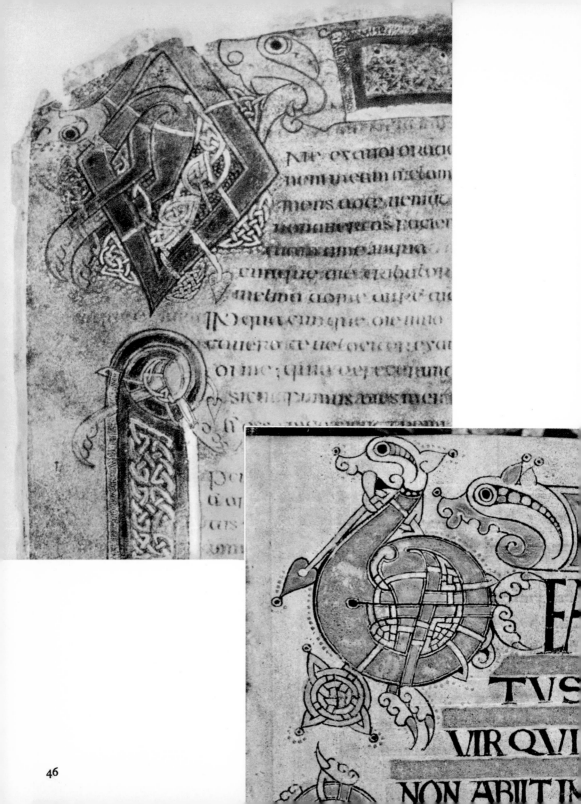

VID
GLORIARIS
INMALITIA ·
POTENSMI
SERICORDIA
DI TOTA DIE ·
INSIDIAS COGITAVIT
LINGUA TUA ·S· NOX
ACUA FACIEIS DOLU

47

Tanq̇ ꝑmictor l̄ debabilone ꝺ ſꝑo habeant· ꝓlo peſaſoꝝ ꝛ̄ꞇ·
uſcamꝑ iñ hoꝛeꝛc emꞇ h· ſnꝺ pꝺoe ꝛ̄ꝺe ꝛ̄eⁱ· ꝛ̄c̄ꝝ c̄uuꝺmꝺo
⸄illi· ꞇ꜡e ꜩaon· puⱳ ꜩeuꝯ̄ q̄ h· ꝺꝺoꝛ ꝯꝺuⱳ moꝺꞇoꝝ
ꜩꝙe a cꜩeꝭ ꞇꝺpaꝛꞇ· aꞇ uoꝛ apoꝛꞇoloꝛ̄ ⱳⱳꝼⱳ:

ᵖſalm̄ incōpeſſiōⁿ

Vbilate ꝺō omⁱⁱⱳ ꞇꝛꝛⱳ·
Serᵘite ꝺⁿō iⁱ leꞇⱳ·
Inꝗꝛoⱳe i꜡ꝭpecꞇu · ꞇ mexulꞇaoⁿe·
Scⱳꞇe qⁱ ꝺⁿꝭ ipſe eſꞇ ꝺⁿꝭ·
ipſe ꝼeciꞇ noꝭ ꞇꞇ non ipſi noꝭ·

Populuꝭ eⁱuꝭ ꞇꞇouⁱeꝭ paſcue eⁱuꝭ·
Iⁱꝗꝛoⱳe poꝛꞇaꝭ eⁱuꝭ incōpeſſiōⁿe·
aꞇꝗⁱa ꞇⁱꝛmⁱⁱꝭ cōꝓꞇemⁱⁱⁱ illⁱ·
cⁱuꝺaⱳe nomeⁿ ꞇ qⁱ ſⁱauⁱⱳꝭ eſꞇ ꝺⁿꝭ·
iⁱeꞇeꝛnⁱum miſſeꝛicoꝛꝺⁱa eⁱuꝭ·
ꞇ uſꝗⁱ iⁱⁱenerⱳaoⁿ· ꞇ ⱳeⁱⁱeⁱ n̄aⱳeⱭ·

ᵖſalm̄ ipꝛi ꝺ̄ꝺ

Miſſeꝛicoꝛꝺⁱam ꞇⁱuꝺⁱcⁱū canꞇⱳboⱳ ꝺⁿe·
pſallⱳ ꞇ iⁱꞇellⁱⱳam iⁱuⁱa
imⁱmⱳculⱳⱳa qⁿo uenieꝭ aꝺ me·
Pambulⱳbⱳ iⁱ iⁱⁱnocenⱳⱳ coꝛꝺⁱꝭ mei·
iⁱⁱmeꝺio ꝺomⱳ mee·

Nⱳ ꝓponⱳebⱳ̄ aⁿ oculoꝭ meoꝭ ꝛem iⁱuſꞇⱳ̄·
faciⱳenⱳeꝭ ꝓuⱳricⱳcⁱoneꝭ oꝺⁱuⁱ·
Non aꝺheſⁱꞇ coꝛ ꝓauⁱum·
ꝺeclⁱnⱳnⱳeꝭ ⱳme malⁱⱳnⱳ̄ n̄coꝭnoſceⱳⱳⱭ·
Deꞇꝛⱳheⱳnⱳem ſecꝛeⱳo ꝓ̄rⁱmo ſuo·
hunc perſⱳequeⱳⱳⱳ·
Supeꝛbo oculo ꞇ iⁱſⱳⱳⱳbile coꝛꝺe·
cum hoc non aeꝺebⱳⱳ· +
Oculi mei aꝺꝼⁱꝺeleꝭ ⱳeꝛꝛe·
uꞇ ſeꝺeꝛenⱳ mecum·
Ambulⱳⱳⁱꝭ iⁱuⁱa imⱳⱳculⱳⱳⱳ·
hⁱc mⁱhi mⁱⁱnⁱſquⱳbⱳⱳ·
Nⱳ habiⱳⱳⱳ iⁱⁱmeꝺio ꝺomⱳ meⱳ·
qⁱ paciꞇ ſupeꝛbⁱam·

49

51

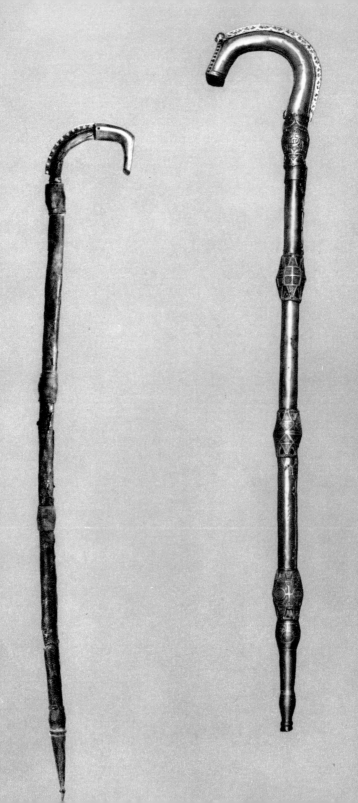

52

53

54

56

60

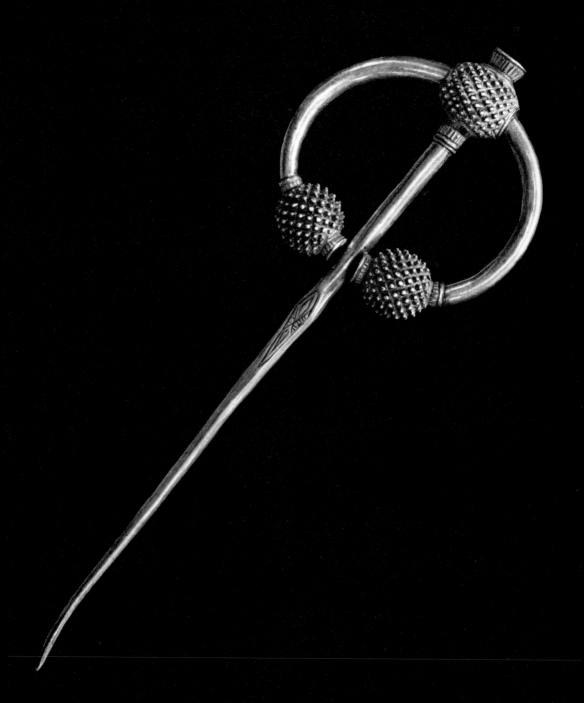

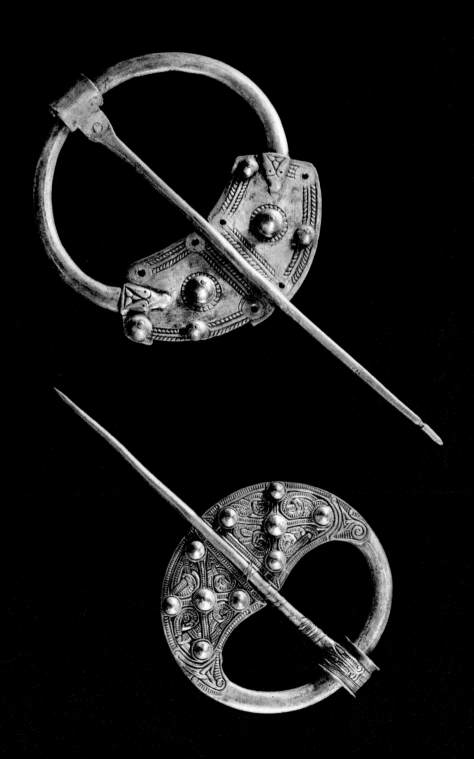

73

74

80

81

84

87

89

93

94

97

98

99

112

LIBER GENERATIONIS
ihuxpi filidauid filii
abraham;

ABRAHAM genuit ISAAC
ISAAC AUT IACOB IACOB AUT

GENUIT IUDAM

AUTEM GENUIT
ET THAMAR ph

ESROM ESROM

ARAM AUTEM

AMINADAB AU

NAASON AU

SALMON AUTE

BOOS GENUIT

OBET AUTEM G

IESSE AUTEM GENUIT DAUID REGE

DAUID AUT REX GENUIT SALOMONE

EX EA QUE FUIT URIAE

SALOMON AUTEM GENUIT ROBO

ROBOAM AUT

GENUIT ABIA

ABIA AUT GENUIT

ASA AUT GENUIT

IOSAPHAT IOSAPHAT AUTEM

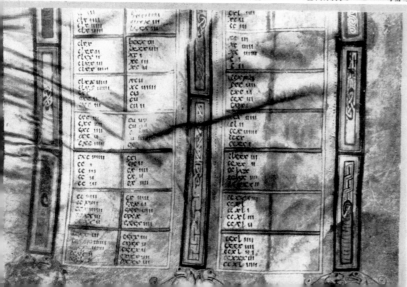

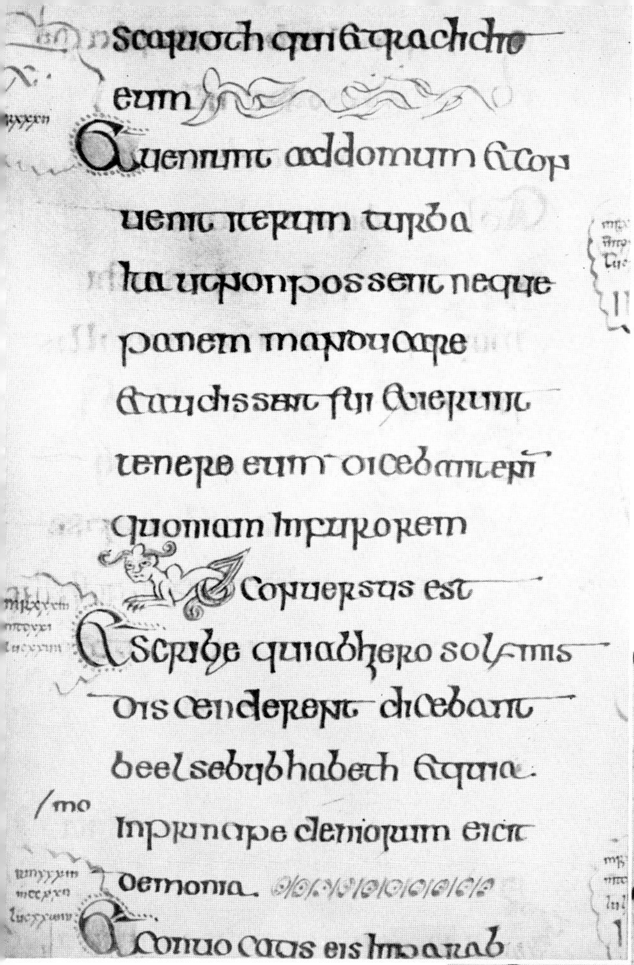

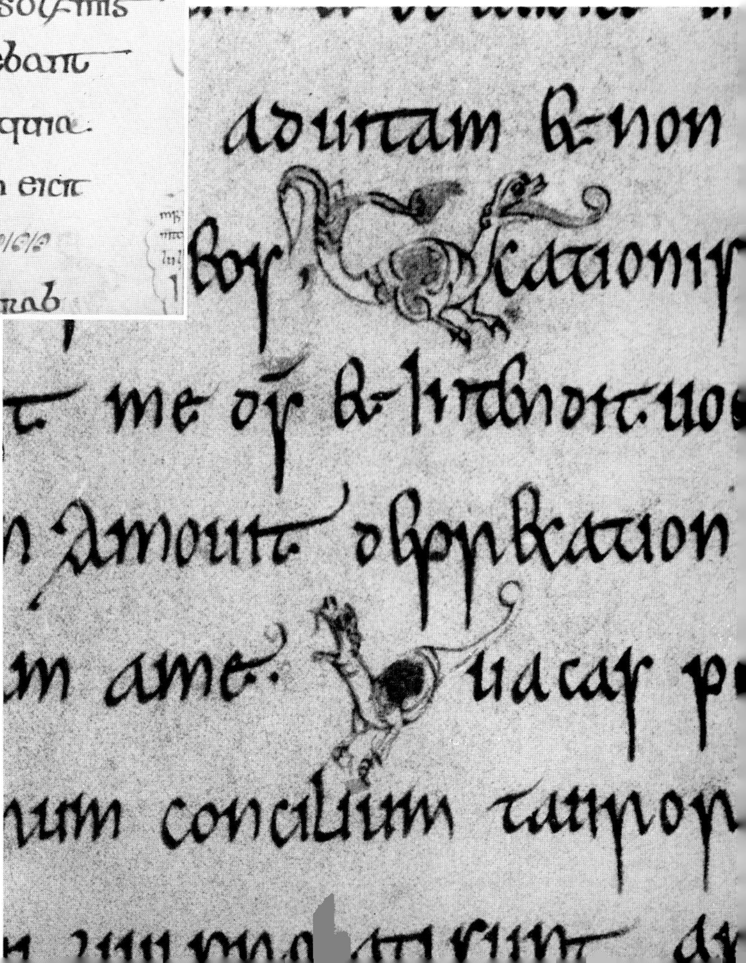

scarioth qui & tradidit
eum

Ueniunt addomum & con
ueniunt iterum turba
ita utnonpossent neque
panem manducare
& cumaudissent sui exierunt
tenere eum dicebant eim
quoniam infurorem
Conuersus est
Ascribae quiabhiero sol mis
dis cenderent dicebant
beelsebub habeth & quia.
inprincipe demoniorum eicit
demonia.
conuocatis eis inparab

adurtam & non
bor. catioinis
t me or & liichnott uos
n amouit oboblicationi
m ame. uacat p
um concilium tattion

ut custodiant te inomnibus uiis tuis:

Nmanibus portabunt te
ne forte offendas adlapidē pedem tuum